Beatles 101: The Need-to-Know-Guide

Richard Buskin

Beatles 101
The Need-to-Know Guide

Richard Buskin

Original Artwork by
Eric Cash

Parading Press
Chicago, Illinois

Also published by Parading Press

Solo in the 70s: John, Paul, George, Ringo 1970 - 1980
by Robert Rodriguez

Changin' Times: 101 Days that Shaped a Generation
by Al Sussman

For Melanie

CONTENTS

A word from Eric Cash about his Beatles artwork and the book's front-cover image *Top of the World*

"A Beatles fan all my life, I initially wanted to stay away from painting those guys. All the images of them leads to intense scrutiny, and even the most novice fan can spot when a depiction of John, Paul, George, or Ringo looks okay but something is off. I didn't want to fall into that trap. Yet, artistic passion being what it is, I eventually felt compelled to do this work.

"Over the years, developing an eye for what other like-minded Beatle People might want to see, I've created original images by Frankensteining photos and screen grabs of the group members: incorporating elements from one or more sources and then changing things around, such as the angle of an arm, the position of a head, or some of the background details. As a result, you may recognize certain aspects of a particular painting, but not the overall oil-on-canvas image.

*"*Top of the World *depicts the guys' first Ed Sullivan Show appearance and it's a favorite of mine. I saw a small concert picture of them taken from that overhead angle and I thought it was interesting, but The Beatles were partly obscured by their own guitars, amps, and cables. So, I then wondered what other stage I could put them on, and the one that immediately came to mind was the set specifically designed for*

that February 9, 1964 broadcast. We always see straight-on images taken from the same angle as we saw them on TV, but what if we saw them from above?

"My starting point was the middle arrow from the stage set that points straight at Ringo's bass drum. Overlaying each of the other arrows on tracing paper, I moved them around to get the right composition—they and the turquoise backdrop created a striking, really dynamic visual, and what I ended up with was not so much a portrait as a Beatles landscape; working within their natural habitat."

INTRODUCTION

What are the necessary ingredients for superstar status? Unique talent or plenty of charm? Likeability or sheer magnetism? The ability to influence and inspire, or perhaps just a knack for capturing people's attention?

The truth is, in today's Warholian famous-for-15-minutes world any one of these attributes can suffice (while certain lucky devils get by with none at all). No one has the complete package of superstar goodies, but when complementary forces come together, great things can happen... and one of the greatest was a supergroup by the name of The Beatles. Four seemingly ordinary guys from an industrial city in northwest England, John, Paul, George, and Ringo basically had it all: unique talent, incredible charm, charismatic personalities, and an ability to influence, inspire, and entertain that resonates to this day.

There has never been anyone or anything quite like The Beatles. So many great songs, so much teen adulation, such widespread acclaim. But how did it all happen? What inspired the Fab Four in the first place and brought them together? What did they have to do in order to become the most successful act in the history of popular entertainment? And what is it about their music, their lives, their every word that, more than four decades after the band's demise, continues to attract new generations of fans, not to mention collectors, critics, and news hungry media hounds? This book answers all of the questions, telling it how it was...and how it is.

As a four-year-old, I was swept up in the first tidal wave of Beatlemania when it flooded Britain back in 1963, and I've been trying to clear my eyes, ears, and nostrils ever since. Nothing works. Once you've been bitten by the Beatle bug it's impossible to shake off, so why bother? Better to listen to those records, watch those movies and TV appearances, and indulge in Beatle small-talk with like-minded victims. You see, there is a lot to talk about. Aside from the group's history, its vast catalogue of work, and that of its individual members, there are also the fan clubs, the inner circle of family, friends, and helpers, and, of course, all of those rumors that need confirming or denying. It can get really interesting... and pretty complicated.

This is where *Beatles 101* comes in. I'll supply all of the vital stories and statistics, while negotiating the minefield of facts and fiction so that even those of you who are complete novices will soon be able to consider yourselves Beatle-know-it-alls.

What You'll Learn in Beatles 101

This book is divided into six parts that tell you all you need to know about The Beatles. You'll learn how the group really struggled for its success, how talent and luck combined to achieve it, and how the world reacted in the wake of Beatlemania.

Part 1, "All Together Now," discusses the social and cultural conditions that aided The Beatles in their rise to prominence, their social impact, their record-breaking achievements, and the reasons for the group's lasting popularity. We'll take a look at the people who have been most clearly influenced by the Fab Four, as well as the personal and professional qualities of John, Paul, George, and Ringo. Lastly, I'll provide you with details of the trends that they set and just about everything you need to know about the people in their "inner circle."

Part 2, "Crying, Waiting, Hoping—Years of Struggle," tells you about The Beatles' birthplaces and families, as well as their major influences on radio and on record during their formative years. You'll then read about their adventures as students, their earliest musical performances, and their initial successes in Germany and in Liverpool. I'll also tell you about the Pre-Fab Three's search for a name as well as for a drummer, their musical collaborators, and their life in Hamburg—on the streets, in the clubs, and in the recording studio.

Part 3, "A Taste of Honey—The Rise of The Beatles," starts off with a look at the group's manager, Brian Epstein, including his efforts to clean up its stage appearance and acquire a recording contract. After recounting Ringo's replacement of Pete Best on drums, I describe the contribution of producer George Martin, as well as that of his sound engineer colleagues, before illustrating how The Beatles began playing in front of more prestigious audiences.

Part 4, "To the Toppermost of the Poppermost," tells you how The Beatles presented themselves on radio and television, as well as to the press. I then provide the main events of the Beatlemania years and a breakdown of the group's big screen efforts, before you'll learn about their final concerts, individual activities, and the era in which they reigned.

Part 5, "Upsetting the Apple Cart," looks at the reasons for some of the more negative publicity attracted by the group, Brian Epstein's tragic death, and the subsequent rift between his charges. You'll then read about the solo careers of John, Paul, George, and Ringo before delving into the *Beatles Anthology* project and subsequent Fab Four-related activities.

Part 6, "The Beatles' Studio Crew Interviews," features Sir George Martin, Norman Smith, Geoff Emerick, Eddie Kramer, Ken Scott, Glyn Johns, John Kurlander, and Alan Parsons offering their observations on working with the group and how the magic was created.

To round out this comprehensive guide, there's a chronology of events in Appendix A, chart positions in Appendix B, a list of films, videos, documentaries, and biopics in Appendix C, and a list of the Beatles-related books used to research *Beatles 101* in Appendix D.

PART 1

ALL TOGETHER NOW

When The Beatles performed live on the rooftop of their Apple office building in London toward the end of the Let It Be movie, it was really nice of that old guy in the street down below to assert in Cockney tones, "The Beatles are classic, y'know. You can't beat 'em." But when he went on to say, "They've got a style of their own," and "They can sing well," he was only telling part of the story.

Obviously talent played a large part in the group's massive success, but then so did a slew of other factors. So, if you're ready to take a whirlwind ride through The Beatles' career, let's cue the music—one-two-three-faw!

Chapter 1

Twilight of the Gods—The Fab Four Phenomenon

When, in 1970, John Lennon described The Beatles as "just a band who made it very, very big," he was making one of the great understatements of our time. Basically, The Beatles' success and influence were such that, for half a century, they have managed to transcend changing tastes and trends. Today their music, their statements, their personalities, and—in the case of the two surviving members—their every movement continue to excite, amuse, and inspire.

Still, it took more than the talents of John, Paul, George, Ringo, and those around them to achieve success on the scale that they did. In this chapter we'll explore the factors that were beyond their control—the state of the music business and events going on in the world around them—during the biggest pop culture explosion of the 20th century. This resulted in record-breaking achievements that were not even a pipe dream when our heroes were singing for someone else's supper during the late 1950s and early 1960s.

Britain: Post-War Blues

Post-war, pre-Beatle Britain was a pretty drab place to be, especially if you were a teenager. The nation may have been one of the chief victors in the fight against Hitler, but you could have been forgiven for not knowing it, especially if you compared the general standard of living with that in the United States.

Food rationing continued in Britain for several years after the war, and the sight of bombed out craters and prefabricated housing lasted a lot longer. The 1953 coronation of Queen Elizabeth II may have helped to lift the gloom (and sell tens of thousands of TV sets), but unfortunately the Monarch and her family also appeared to lead the nation's fashion sense. Still, things could only get better…and they soon did. The arrival of rock 'n' roll during the mid-fifties certainly helped wake up the kids and wind up their parents. While America blazed the trail, the Brits responded with cover versions of U.S. hits and a few dozen Elvis clones, complete with moody expressions, curled upper lips, and an ability to sing, "I lurv ya, baybeh," in an accent that would put true Americans to shame. This was just the beginning.

By the early 1960s, the first generation of Brit rockers—names such as Billy Fury and Marty Wilde—were about to be overtaken by "respectable" teen crooners who had the parents' stamp of approval. (Much the same was happening in the United States.) Young musicians such as Mick Jagger and Keith Richards, for instance, were beginning to adapt the material from across the Atlantic and perform it in their own style. Others, such as Lennon and McCartney, were even writing their own songs. Enter The Beatles. Having been used to American domination of the film and music scenes for years, Britain's teens (1963 model) were ecstatic that they finally had worthy idols of their very own to scream about. What's more, while their parents rolled their eyes and snickered among themselves, it was pretty obvious that they were won over by The Beatles as well. After all, these four "youngsters with the scraggy hairdos" all appeared to be nice, clean-cut boys-next-door: cheeky, charming, and not at all impressed by the fame and fortune.

Instead of trying to escape for a while by taking bland trips to Elvis' *Blue Hawaii*, people in the U.K. could now sit back and watch some homegrown talent live out their own fantasies on foreign shores. Meanwhile, the good old British press was more than willing to promote some innocent fun after all of the sleaze and scandal surrounding the resignation of Government Defense Minister John Profumo. (This was following Profumo's confession that he'd shared a mistress with a Russian spy.) Money, music, and fun were on the fall '63 agenda, and London and the rest of Britain were ready to swing.

Stateside—The Right People at the Right Time

America was still the unrivaled leader in Western pop music at the end of 1963, and most of its entertainers and entrepreneurs would have been very happy if things had stayed that way. However, certain events that had already taken place were about to drastically and irreversibly alter the status quo.

American rock 'n' roll had suffered some serious blows: the deaths of stars such as Buddy Holly and Eddie Cochran; the U.S. Army's transformation of Elvis Presley into Perry Como; Little Richard's conversion to a life of religion; Chuck Berry's imprisonment for statutory rape; and the furor over Jerry Lee Lewis' marriage to his 13 year-old cousin. These events had virtually stopped the rock 'n' roll revolution in its tracks. In its place came a succession of insipid, approved-by-parents smoothies with names like Fabian and Troy Shondell. Nice boys with smiles more dazzling than their talent. Thankfully, they were soon countered by the groundbreaking recordings from Berry Gordy Jr.'s Motown label, the 'Wall of Sound' created by producer Phil Spector, and the California surf 'n' hot rod bands led by The Beach Boys.

During this period of transition, American records no longer dominated the British pop charts. The new wave of Liverpool acts, led by The Beatles and backed up by Gerry and the Pacemakers, The Searchers, Billy J. Kramer with the Dakotas, Cilla Black, The Swinging Blue Jeans, The Fourmost, and The Merseybeats, scored hit after hit while creating a new and exciting sound of their own. Still, would this trend ever cross over the Great Pond to America? Few thought so—no British pop acts had yet made a lasting impression on America's youth.

Then, on November 22, 1963, just hours before The Beatles stepped onto the stage of the Globe Cinema in Stockton-on-Tees, Durham, England, President John F. Kennedy was assassinated in Dallas, Texas. Although Britons were still getting over the shock and titillation of the Profumo scandal, this was small-fry compared to the mass American depression that followed the slaying of its youngest and perhaps most charismatic president. Clearly something, or someone, was needed to help revive the spirits of the people, and the Brits just happened to have a Merseybeat tonic up their sleeves.

Eleven weeks to the day after JFK's death, The Beatles arrived at New York's newly re-christened Kennedy Airport. Their timing couldn't have been better.

That Was Then—Their Social Impact

During the early years of their success, The Beatles charmed virtually everyone while also representing the voice of youth. Then, later on, they led the way in redefining their own generation. As a result, they managed to wreak havoc on society across two broad fronts…

Those Adorable Moptops

Never mind the effect that The Beatles' music had on the public consciousness during their early years of megastardom. Just about everything else to do with the group seemed to be of incredible importance as well.

First off, aside from the "yeah, yeah, yeah" refrain in "She Loves You," which the press immediately glommed onto, there was the unmistakable hairstyle that helped launch a million wigs. That's right, the moptop, so called because of the shaggy way it was combed from the top of the head to create bangs just above (or below) the eyebrows.

According to the press, parents, and even heads of state, to have a moptop was to have long hair. Never mind that it was way shorter than the pompadour style preferred by Elvis, Tony Curtis, and millions of their followers (including the pre-fame Beatles).

During those early years, John, Paul, George, and Ringo could basically do no wrong in most people's eyes and even royalty joined in the adulation. In 1965, Queen Elizabeth II awarded each of The Beatles an MBE (the Membership of the Most Excellent Order of the British Empire) on the recommendation of Prime Minister Harold Wilson, a "fellow Liverpudlian" with a sharp eye for self-promotion. While fans were proud of their heroes' accomplishment, many soldiers and bona fide war heroes had their noses put out of joint: imagine Elvis Presley being rewarded with the Congressional Medal of Honor. (In 1970, he'd receive a special narcotics agent's badge from Richard Nixon, but that wasn't quite the same thing.)

The strength of The Beatles' impact in America was that they not only paved the way for other British pop acts, but they also opened the doors to their fellow Brits in other fields. These included Cockney film star Michael Caine; Sean Connery as James Bond; stick-thin supermodel Twiggy; fashion designer Mary Quant; and celebrity photographer David Bailey...

British was best, London was supposedly swinging, and even the Union Jack became a fashion symbol, adorning clothes, bags, and wristwatches. Suddenly, it was cool in America to have a British accent and, thanks to The Beatles' global impact, there was a boom in the domestic fashion industry along with a sharp rise in the number of tourists from overseas. That is why John, Paul, George, and Ringo officially received their MBEs for "services to British export."

The Generation Game

Initially steeped in hope and superficial innocence, the 1960s rapidly developed into an age when anything seemed possible and a lot of it actually happened; from student protests and large-scale music festivals to frozen TV dinners and landing a man on the moon. Consequently, the kids and adolescents who grew up during that time were likely to take even the most ridiculous things for granted.

The phantasmagorical, psychedelic, peace 'n' love, flower-power era had arrived, and leading it were The Beatles. By 1967, their concert tours had come to an end and the teen screaming had stopped, to be supplanted by more way-out clothes and less happy-go-lucky attitudes. Indeed, the glossy Fab Four image was shed in favor of the band members' true personalities as they became more outspoken in terms of their socio-political beliefs, and this resulted in them assuming their rightful position at the forefront of the burgeoning counter-culture movement. No longer did they keep quiet about the war in Vietnam, apartheid in South Africa, or the hallucinogenic drugs in their bloodstream. Instead, having achieved all of the fame and fortune that they needed, they now felt entitled—in the words of the Buck Owens song covered by Ringo—to *act naturally*.

In the July 24, 1967 edition of *The Times*, John, Paul, George, Ringo, and Brian Epstein all lent their names to a petition calling for the legalization of marijuana. Of course, this immediately set them apart from many of the moms and pops who, until then, had considered them "adorable." Yet, it also helped reaffirm their credibility with many people of their own generation.

As the clean-cut teen sensibilities of the first half of the decade became increasingly out of step with what was now going on in the world, The Beatles could have easily turned into overnight has-beens. It's therefore a testament to their talent, astuteness, and strength of character that they actually continued to set the trends, sing the songs, and say the words that their contemporaries wanted to hear, with 1967's *Sgt. Pepper's Lonely Hearts Club Band* album serving as a virtual manifesto for their generation while the single "All You Need is Love" was its anthem. George's visit to the Haight-Ashbury district of San Francisco in August

1967 was viewed as an official endorsement of the hippie movement on America's West Coast, and the whole concept of transcendental meditation was popularized when The Beatles studied TM under Maharishi Mahesh Yogi.

Where they went, millions of others followed, for as John Lennon once said, "One thing The Beatles did was to affect people's minds."

This is Now—The Record-Breaking Statistics

During the years 1963 to 1970, The Beatles not only sold millions of records but, while vinyl was a lot more flexible than shellac, they also managed to break quite a few—sales figures, the speed of sales, the number of prints of *A Hard Day's Night* that were distributed to movie theaters, TV viewing figures, the amount of merchandise, and on and on. The entertainment industry had never known anything quite like it.

Some of the group's achievements were so staggering that they stand to this day, while others were only surpassed in 1996… by The Beatles themselves. Here are the Fab Four's current record-breaking statistics:

- The greatest sales of any group, estimated by EMI, Apple Records, and the RIAA at over 2.3 billion albums worldwide.

- 19 number one albums in the U.S., 13 of them platinum, with a total of 175 weeks spent atop the chart.

- 15 number one albums in the U.K., with a total of 175 weeks spent atop the chart.

- 18 U.K. number one singles.

- The biggest first-week sales of a double album (*The Beatles Anthology 1*, which sold 855,473 copies in the U.S. from November 21 to 28, 1995).

- The most successful songwriters (Lennon and McCartney) in terms of number-one hits. (In the U.S., Paul takes the credit for 32 and John for 26, with 23 of these having been written together; in the U.K., John takes credit for 29 and Paul for 28, with 25 of these having been written together.)

- The most covers of any song (over 3,000 versions of "Yesterday").

- The fastest-selling single ("I Want to Hold Your Hand," with a staggering 10,000 copies per hour in New York City alone after 20 days).

- The biggest advance orders for a single (2.1 million copies of "Can't Buy Me Love" in the U.S.)

- As for The Beatles' own records in relation to their long list of achievements, here are some of the leading statistics:

- Their biggest-selling single was "Hey Jude," which sold more than 8 million copies in the U.S. and U.K.

- Their most-played song is "Yesterday," which has been broadcast more than 8 million times on U.S. radio alone.

- Their greatest volume of sales within a 12-month period is, due to the popularity of all three *Anthology* albums, an estimated 33 million during 1996/97.

Chapter 2

Four Little Lord Fauntleroys—All Bow Down

With the possible exceptions of Elvis Presley and Bob Dylan, no other popular entertainment act has been as influential or as idolized on a long-term basis as The Beatles.

The fans range from the interested to the obsessive (with the adoring somewhere in between), but almost without exception their motives are genuine. They have been taken by the group's music, their personalities, their clothes, you name it.

Then there are the musicians who impersonate The Beatles, as well as those who are influenced by them to the point of looking and sounding like imitators. These comprise a mixture of admirers and profiteers, and there's little middle ground with regard to what they produce. It will either entertain or annoy you. In this chapter, I'll provide you with a potted history of the Beatles' fans and describe their behavior so that you'll be able to spot them a mile away. Then we'll take a look at the professional admirers and imitators, after which I'll give you a run-down of some of the more notable/notorious "tribute" records.

The Beatlemaniacs

The Beatles had fans in Liverpool and Hamburg, Germany (where they played during the early 1960s) even before they were world-famous. Many of those who regularly watched "the boys" playing in their hometown in 1961 and '62 even belonged to the original fan club, yet this was all small-fry compared to the numbers that made up the Official Beatles Fan Club of Great Britain by September 1964: 58,000 of them, along with a special telephone number (COVent Garden 2332) that handled up to 100 inquiries per hour. (What everyone had to inquire about is anyone's guess.)

Meanwhile, there were more than a million registered fans in clubs all over North America, Europe, Africa, Asia, and the Pacific Rim. Rabid Beatlemaniacs from the Netherlands to Nigeria, Mauritius to Mozambique, would do practically anything to get close to their idols, if and when the Fab Four were anywhere near them. So it was that, as the band left the stage of the Seattle Coliseum on August 21, 1964, a girl fell from an overhead beam and landed at Ringo's feet.

On another occasion, at a Dallas hotel on September 18 of that year, a chambermaid was kidnapped by a frantic female and urged at knifepoint to divulge which suite The Beatles were staying in. Apparently the chambermaid held out, but there was more drama in the same hotel when several other Beatle maidens had to be fished out of the air-conditioning shaft. These were the kind of lunatics who were prepared to shell out money to buy bogus merchandise such as "Bottled Beatle Breath."

The Beatles-mad author in 1977 with, at left, a renowned Fab Four expert who would come to be known for far more than his spectacular array of badges.

Quite a few American teenagers who ran away during the Beatlemania years were simply en route to London in the hope of catching a glimpse of John, Paul, George, or Ringo. Others were even more persistent, and when the band's company, Apple, established a London office in the latter part of the 1960s, these fans would wait outside for days and even weeks on end to say, "Hi," "Bye," or perhaps a few more words to their heroes. The Beatles dubbed them the Apple Scruffs and George wrote a tribute song by that name (released on his solo *All Things Must Pass* triple album). Others would simply turn up wherever The Beatles went—familiar faces with names such as Big Sue, Little Sue, Margo Stevens, Carole Bedford, Gayleen Pease, and Lizzie Bravo.

Today, the really mad behavior has obviously subsided. Yet, you'll still see countless people risking their lives on the pedestrian crossing in front of London's Abbey Road Studios (as captured via webcam 24-hours-a-day: http://abbeyroad.com/CrossingArchive). If they survive the speeding cars, chances are they'll also scribble messages on the regularly whitewashed wall in front of the facility's parking lot. Others take assorted "Magical History Tours" around Liverpool and hang around outside the various Beatle homes in London, Sussex, New York, Monte Carlo, and Henley-on-Thames. There's no lack of places to visit for the current generation of Beatlemaniacs.

The Abbey Road crossing that, every day (and night) of the year, serves as the perfect setting for Beatle People from all over the world to emulate their idols.

The Beatles Impersonators

While some bands have copied or been clearly influenced by the Fab Four, others have actually made a living by being straight imitators. They impersonate their sounds, their look, and often even their speaking voices... with varying degrees of success.

The trend really got underway during the 1970s, when public demand for the real Beatles to reunite wasn't met by the people in question.

Others rushed forward to try to fill the void ("try" being the operative word), taking names from albums such as *Abbey Road* and *Revolver.* Then there were the fully fledged stage shows, such as *John, Paul, George, Ringo... and Bert, Sgt. Pepper's Lonely Hearts Club Band on the Road,* and the Broadway show *Beatlemania* (later adapted into a film).

Unabashed imitation aside, in 1978 there was that brilliant spoof of the whole Beatles legend in the form of The Rutles and their TV "rockumentary," *All You Need is Cash.* Musically this was the brainchild of Neil Innes of The Bonzo Dog Doo-Dah Band, who, aside from assuming the Lennonish role of Ron Nasty, ingeniously concocted Beatlesque numbers that made reference to specific Beatles songs without actually infringing copyright. The script was co-written by Monty Python team member Eric Idle, who also starred as both the show's narrator and as McCartney parody Dirk McQuickly. A cameo appearance by George Harrison (a pal of the Pythons) served as the ultimate endorsement.

John Lennon's death in December 1980 ended any hopes of a full Beatles reunion. What it did do, on the other hand, was elevate the group's already-mythical status to yet another level and ensure a steady living for enterprising imitators.

The Beatle-like Bands

The accusation of trying to look and/or sound like the Fab Four has been leveled at countless bands up to the present day. This trend started way before The Monkees were assembled as an American "answer" to The Beatles, echoing the way the Brits manufactured their own Elvises during the preceding decade. In fact, it even started before West Coast folk-rock group The Byrds went to see *A Hard Day's Night* and emerged from the movie theater with a definite idea as to their own future direction. ("Hey, dig those moptop hairstyles, man, and go for that cool Rick 12-string sound!")

Such was The Beatles' impact on the British scene during the summer of 1963, and so clearly different were they from anyone who had come before, there was almost immediately a glut of domestic artists trying to jump on the Beatle buggy. One way, of course, was to be a beat group with that Mersey Sound; another was to just look like the Fab Four. You could, for instance, don those distinctive Pierre Cardin collarless jackets, as worn by The Beatles during the first half of 1963. Then there were the shaggy hairstyles, which acts such as The Dave Clark Five—

and, the following year, The Kinks and Herman's Hermits—were quick to latch onto; or the waistcoat, shirt, and tie look that even The Rolling Stones decided to adopt for a short while.

A few years later, Mick and the boys would take another, equally unsuccessful stab at trying to match John, Paul, George, and Ringo. In the wake of The Beatles' landmark *Sgt. Pepper* album, the Stones recorded *Their Satanic Majesties Request*, featuring overt drug references and psychedelic sounds. However, beads 'n' bells never suited the Stones as much as rhythm and blues, and, despite standout tracks such as "2000 Light Years from Home," "Citadel," and "She's a Rainbow," Keith Richards has himself asserted, "The album was a load of crap."

A few years earlier, on the other side of the Atlantic, some groups gave a nod in the direction of the "Liverpoplians" (as U.K. newspaper *The Daily Mirror* idiotically nicknamed The Beatles) by christening themselves with Brit-sounding monickers such as The Beau Brummels and The Buckinghams. Then, toward the end of the decade, The Beatles seemingly adopted an attitude of "If you can't beat 'em, join 'em," by signing soundalike band The Iveys to their own Apple label, renaming it Badfinger, and issuing singles such as "Come and Get It" and "Day After Day" that were composed and produced by members of the Fab Four.

So, that was the way of things while The Beatles were together, and since then it's been a similar story. Sample the *Revolver*-type sounds of early early-eighties outfit The Jam, or the "Rain"-soaked psychedelia of nineties supergroup Oasis. Both were preceded by the unmistakably Lennon-ish voice and production values of producer/composer/musician Jeff Lynne.

As things turned out, Lynne's tastes and talents benefited not only his band, Electric Light Orchestra, but also Paul, George, and Ringo. George was the first to sit up and take notice, collaborating with Lynne on a number of projects during the late-eighties and early-nineties, including Harrison's smash-hit album, *Cloud Nine*, and two records by all-star group The Traveling Wilburys, featuring Messrs. Harrison and Lynne playing alongside Bob Dylan, Roy Orbison, and Tom Petty. Still, even this lineup paled in comparison to the one featured on one of Jeff's subsequent production assignments—namely, the two Threetles singles, "Free as a Bird" and "Real Love."

Sometimes it pays to emulate your idols.

We Love You Beatles: The Tribute Records

Never mind that there have been more than 3,000 cover versions of "Yesterday." By the end of 1981, just a year after John's death, there had been no less than 357 records produced as "tributes" or novelty items relating to The Beatles. (And that was just in English, because the Swedes, the Germans, and seemingly everyone else on the planet had got in on the act, too.)

Given a particularly strong fad, there will always be eagle-eyed entrepreneurs who are hot out of the starting blocks. At the tail end of 1963, comedienne Dora Bryan started Britain's cash-in craze with "All I Want for Christmas is a Beatle." Thereafter, The Vernon Girls recorded "We Love The Beatles" while, in the U.S., Allan Sherman asserted "Pop Hates The Beatles." Still, for all of the admirable efforts, the only song to crack the Top 80 of the U.S. charts was "We Love You Beatles" by British girl trio The Carefrees, which reached No. 39 in 1964. (One of the vocalists, Lynn Cornell, was married to session drummer Andy White, who had played on the album version of The Beatles' "Love Me Do," as well as the B-side of their first single, "P.S. I Love You.")

Not that all of the tributes came from a bubblegum wrapper. In fact, you may be surprised by the caliber of some of the other artists who jumped on the imitation bandwagon during the height of Beatlemania. How about Ella Fitzgerald recording "Ringo Beat"? Or Cher (under the assumed name of Bonnie Jo Mason) warbling "Ringo I Love You," produced by the legendary Phil Spector? In 1964, Mr. Starr evidently served as a magnet; in Britain, TV entertainer Rolf Harris even recorded "Ringo for President." Then there was singer/composer and sometime member of The Crickets, Sonny Curtis, with "A Beatle I Want to Be," and, in 1967, TV talk show host Steve Allen with "Here Comes Sgt. Pepper" (!)

The following year, the sight of John Lennon and Yoko Ono standing naked on the cover of their *Two Virgins* album distracted future Oscar-winning actress Sissy Spacek from her drama lessons long enough to sing, "John, You Went Too Far This Time."

These days, I'm glad to say, Beatle "tribute" songs are practically non-existent. (The last flurry of activity was immediately after John Lennon's death.) Nevertheless, some of those old discs are still worth searching out, even if their value is more novelty than monetary.

Lennon '64

"This was my first painting of the Beatles series and the only one for which I didn't 'Frankenstein' a particular photo. I had been drawing that image ever since I saw it on the cover of The Beatles' Second Album *as a kid. I'd always loved its composition—a close-up of John that doesn't really focus on his facial features—and for me that was the painting's driving force. Having drawn it a hundred times, I could do it in my sleep..."*

– Eric Cash

Chapter 3

The Band You've Known for All These Years

Like the four points of the compass, The Beatles managed to cover all bases. They had the perfect combination of unique talents and winning personalities with which to conquer the masses, as well as the determination, imagination, and uncanny sense of timing that enabled them to sustain their success.

In this chapter we'll take a brief look at the personal characteristics of John, Paul, George, and Ringo, as well as the trends they set both before and after they established themselves at the top of the pop tree. The Beatles were primarily musicians, yet their charm, sense of humor, and outward appearance all loomed large in their legend

Tip of My Tongue

Whether spoken or singing, the voices of John, Paul, George, and Ringo were easily identifiable. Many people—often professional actors and musicians—have attempted to impersonate them down the years, and even though some have managed to get fairly close, there's nothing like the real thing.

As far as Liverpool accents go, The Beatles' regional nuances gradually became less pronounced—although only slightly—after they left their home city. Accents are very important in England, and in the British Isles in general. A miniscule piece of land when compared to the United States, England has a very large population that's about one fifth of America's. Nevertheless, British accents differ sharply every few hundred miles.

Not only does an accent indicate where you come from in the U.K., but, in an extremely class-conscious society, it also points to your social standing. Liverpool is an industrial city. Not everyone who lives there works in industry or is poor, yet those with the thickest local accents are generally perceived to be "working class." In this respect, the speaking voices of both George and Ringo are a dead giveaway as to their humble backgrounds.

During the early years of The Beatles' success, George still had a Scouse accent. To a lesser extent so did Ringo, although his voice is altogether deeper and somehow suits his sad-eyed face. Paul, on the other hand, has always spoken with less of an edge or an accent than his three colleagues, while, according to John's Aunt Mimi, her nephew's voice originally reflected his middle-class upbringing before he then cultivated a stronger accent as a Beatle. Whether this was true or not, the native accent remained until the end of John's life, even though, during his final years, it was tinged with the faintest of American inflections.

The Four Up Close—Tell Me What You See

Just as with their voices and their individual musical talents, John, Paul, George, and Ringo had four very distinct personalities. Of course, given the nature of the press and media, this led to stereotyping along the lines of the animated Beatles in the *Yellow Submarine* cartoon, yet those simplistic characterizations did have some basis in truth. Here's a brief run-down.

John—The Cynic

John Lennon was a man who could annihilate an opponent with a razor-sharp put-down and fend off all comers with his stoic, myopic glare. There was little point in crossing verbal swords with him; he would usually win.

Intolerant of ignorance and, as he described them, "thick heads," John was a broad-minded thinker who ingested everything around him, from music, art, books, and magazines to radio, film, and—one of his pet loves—television. Still, he was a mass of contradictions: a hard-edged cynic who regularly displayed a heart of gold and an alert skeptic who often left himself wide open to masters of exploitation. Impulsiveness was one of his chief traits—Beatles producer, George Martin, likened him to someone "driving without a clutch"—and even though he worked extremely hard at his career, John confessed to being inherently lazy. Indeed, on several occasions he asserted that, if The Beatles hadn't been successful, he "would probably still be a bum hanging around Liverpool."

That said, John spent the better part of his life trying to improve himself as a human being, evolving from a physically aggressive youth into a man of peace, from a chauvinist into a feminist househusband.

He had, to use his own words, "a grasshopper mind," and to the end of his short life he was an interviewer's dream, full of strong opinions and witty insights. After all, nearly everything that John Lennon ever said or wrote for public consumption made for a great quote.

Paul—The Baby-Face

Adored by female fans as the handsome, "baby-faced" Beatle, Paul McCartney capitalized on gentle looks that hid an iron will and a steely determination. An unabashed "workaholic," he's always had a strong sense as to how things should be done (i.e. his way), and while this has led to friction in several of his professional relationships, it has also helped him remain in the public spotlight for more than five decades.

Paul was always the Beatle most in love with being a member of the Fab Four. He enjoyed performing concerts more than the other three, and he was the last to want to quit touring. His competitive nature spurred both John and himself to greater heights as songwriters, and it was Paul who struggled to keep the band together when cracks started to appear. On the other hand, he's also apt to tread carefully: He was the last member of the group to experiment with drugs, the last one to get married, and, notoriously frugal with money, the only one to be wary of manager Brian Epstein's eventual successor, Allen Klein.

A publicity man's dream, Macca is almost always courteous to fans and eager to do interviews, yet he also treasures the simple privacy of his Sussex countryside home and that at his farm in Scotland's Mull of Kintyre. An astute businessman (at least since his Beatle days), he's one of Britain's wealthiest citizens. What's more, thanks to the influence of his late wife, Linda, Paul is among the nation's most celebrated environmentalists and animal-rights activists.

George—The Quiet One

Behind the lop-sided grin and understated manner, George Harrison was a man of strong opinions and long-standing, deep-rooted beliefs. During the mid-sixties, he was the Beatle who first turned his fellow band members—and then countless others in and outside of the entertainment industry—onto Indian music and Eastern culture. For most this was just a passing fad, but George never wavered. He was a faithful follower and supporter of Hindu philosophy, while sustaining a personal and professional relationship up until his death with legendary sitar player, Ravi Shankar.

While John was largely perceived as the intellectual member of The Beatles and Paul was the pin-up, George charmed the masses with his apparent shyness. However, he rarely missed an opportunity to make an incisive comment or funny aside during interviews and, in several respects, he was also Paul's polar opposite.

For one thing, George almost immediately resented the intrusion on his privacy and freedom exacted by The Beatles' fame. As a result, he was the first member of the Fab Four to make a case for quitting live performances. Thereafter, he largely shunned giving interviews and making public appearances unless he really felt the need (which wasn't very often). And when he did talk about The Beatles, his bittersweet memories were undoubtedly laced with more than a little cynicism.

Ringo—The Clown

Ringo Starr was the oldest Beatle, the last to join the group and, at five foot eight, also the shortest by three inches. Ringo ensured a place in everybody's hearts thanks to his sad eyes and ready smile, yet he's always been more than capable of standing up for himself when the going gets tough. Ringo came closest to John in terms of generating laughs, and it was for that reason—as well as his innate ability to win the sympathy of an audience—that he was singled out for his performance in *A Hard Day's Night* and then given the central role in *Help!*

During the Beatlemania years, Ringo was perhaps the most popular— and certainly most recognizable—member of the group among members of the general public. However, within the group itself he fully acknowledged John's and Paul's greater talents as both singers and composers, and he therefore accepted his more limited role while taking full advantage of whatever opportunities came his way. As a result, through all the ups and downs of The Beatles' relationships with one another, Ringo was probably the best team player.

Don't You Know the Joker Laughs at You?

The Fab Four were no slouches when it came to wisecracks. Neither, for that matter, are their fellow Liverpudlians, who are noted in Britain for their ability to see the funny side in even the most depressing situations. Given the social and economic status of the industrial city in which they live, they have certainly seen their fair share.

The Beatles grew up in an environment where one-liners flew at them from every direction. So, their minds quickly became attuned to dealing with quips and put-downs, as well as to doling out more than a few of their own. The expert in that regard was John Winston Lennon, who not only had a quick brain and a sharp tongue, but who also loved nonsensical wordplay. This was inspired by the radio characters he heard during his youth, including the anarchic British comedy team, *The Goons* (comprising Peter Sellers, Spike Milligan, and Harry Secombe), and he was already putting it to good use by the time he was in his early teens.

At school John would amuse fellow classmates by filling his exercise books with cartoons, nonsense verse, and drawings of the teachers. Each book bore the handwritten title, *The Daily Howl*, and inside there were send-ups of then-popular characters: Davy Crockett, for example, was immortalized in "The Story of Davy Crutch-Head." John would mess with words—switching letters or changing their sound so that they had a double meaning—and this specialized talent would later be given fuller expression in his best-selling books of poetry and nonsense prose, *In His Own Write* and *A Spaniard in the Works*, as well as in classic Beatles numbers such as "I Am the Walrus" and "Come Together."

Lennon's irrepressible sense of humor was laced with both cruelty and natural comic timing—he had a lifelong obsession with (and fear of) physical disabilities. Meanwhile, an ability that all of The Beatles shared was the remarkable speed with which they could fire off the one-liners. They ruled supreme in press conferences, especially the one held at Kennedy Airport just minutes after their initial arrival in the United States on February 7, 1964. It was hard to believe that the questions and answers hadn't been rehearsed beforehand, but they hadn't—and America was won over before The Beatles had even played a note on U.S. soil.

Here's a brief sampling of The Beatles' quips at assorted press conferences:

Q: Do you wear wigs?

John: If we do they must be the only ones with real dandruff.

Q: What did you think when your airline's engine began smoking as you landed today?

Ringo: Beatles, women, and children first!

Q: How does it feel, putting on the whole world?

John: How does it feel to be put on?

Q: Paul, you look like my son.

Paul: You don't look a bit like my mother.

Q: Ringo, why do you wear two rings on each hand?

Ringo: Because I can't fit them through my nose.

Q: What's your reaction to a Seattle psychiatrist's opinion that you are a menace?

George: Psychiatrists are a menace.

Q: Would you like to walk down the street without being recognized?

John: We used to do this with no money in our pockets. There's no point in it.

Q: You were at the Playboy Club last night. What did you think of it?

Paul: The Playboy and I are just good friends.

Q: Does all the adulation from teenage girls affect you?

John: When I feel my head start to swell, I look at Ringo and know perfectly well we're not supermen.

Q: Do teenagers scream at you because they are, in effect, revolting against their parents?

Paul: They've been revolting for years.

Q: What is the biggest threat to your careers? The atom bomb or dandruff?

Ringo: The atom bomb. We've already got dandruff.

Q: The French have not made up their minds about The Beatles. What do you think of them?

John: Oh, we like The Beatles. They're gear.

Q: Do You like topless bathing suits?

Ringo: We've been wearing them for years.

Q: There's a "Stamp Out The Beatles" movement underway in Detroit. What are you going to do about it?

Paul: We're going to start a campaign to stamp out Detroit.

Q: Sorry to interrupt you while you are eating, but what do you think you will be doing in five years time when all this is over?

Ringo: Still eating.

Nothing is Real—Changing Tastes and Trends

Just as quickly as The Beatles' music progressed from album to album, so the guys themselves developed new tastes, altered their appearances, and seemingly led the world in whatever direction they chose to pursue.

When John, Paul, George, and Ringo expressed their liking for recordings by the black Tamla Motown artists, this gave a tremendous boost to the fledgling Detroit label. The same could be said for The Byrds when, in 1965, The Beatles proclaimed them to be their favorite American group, and for the Indian sitar music of artists such as Ravi Shankar. Basically, if The Beatles liked these people it had to be worth giving them the time of day.

Lark cigarettes, scotch whisky, and Coca-Cola—whatever they fancied was all right with practically everyone else. Not so, perhaps, when they began to replace the sugar in their tea with some LSD, but there were still people who chose to follow their example.

Nevertheless, among the many opportunists who profited from our heroes changing like the British weather, the people who arguably owed them the most were those operating within the fashion industry. The Beatles, you see, were never reluctant to copy an appearance that someone else had started, from the greasy ducktail hairstyles and leather outfits they started with in the 1960s to the disheveled scarecrow look with which they ended that decade. Whatever they did was rightly perceived as some sort of endorsement, while in between they set trends that were a sensation, especially among fashion designers, manufacturers, and retailers. Let's take a quick look at some of them.

First off, having refashioned their retro hairstyles into those revolutionary moptops, The Beatles agreed to go along with their manager Brian Epstein's advice and smarten their collective physical appearance. This initially took the form of the kind of mohair suits that were worn by countless pop smoothies of the era—now, at least, you could bring them home to meet the folks. Then, from April to October of 1963, there were those Pierre Cardin collarless jackets that took the world by storm, even though the Fab Four only wore them in Britain and on their autumn trip to Sweden. (More indelible impressions were made via the circulation of publicity photos in which they dressed this way.)

While 1964 ushered in the era of suits with velvet collars, 1965 was the year of military-style uniforms with Nehru collars, as worn by "the boys" in their second movie, *Help!*, by which time the hair was perilously close to covering their ears. They still wore a variety of matching suits for their final world tour the following year, yet the mustaches that they sprouted shortly thereafter marked the last time that they really all conformed to a particular image. Sure, they all hopped into elaborate uniforms for the *Sgt. Pepper* cover shots, but, in line with their different personalities, these were each a different color.

The psychedelic, flower-power era was now underway, and the clothing industry no longer needed to look to The Beatles to gain "an early clue to the new direction." Still, there was one more major fashion statement to be made, and this would last a lot longer than all of the others: those circular "granny glasses," as worn by Mr. Lennon and available from your local optometrist. The fact that this was one of the styles subsidized by Britain's National Health Service made them easily affordable, and the fact that John inadvertently caused a run on them may have accounted for the tax rises that took place shortly thereafter.

Chapter 4

Reelin' and Rockin'—The Beatles' Artistry

Few people would dispute that The Beatles were musical pioneers. However, if the band members had pursued separate careers right from the start, it's fairly certain that none of them would have made as big a splash as they did together. The Fab Four have each met with varying measures of success in their solo work, and the fewer sparks of creative genius lend credence to that saying about the whole being greater than the sum of its parts.

There's a game that some fans like to play in which they try to estimate how successful the band would have been had its lineup been different. How about John, Paul, Eric Clapton, and Ringo? Or perhaps John, Paul, and George, together with The Who's flamboyant drummer, Keith Moon? There will never be an answer to this kind of speculation, but we do know that the four very different characters who made up The Beatles complemented each other brilliantly. In the end, those differences caused tension, but when they clicked there was magic in the air and on record.

And Your Bird Can Sing

Just as The Beatles had distinctive speaking voices, when they sang each of them were very recognizable.

John, with his harsh, razor-sharp tones, was by far the easiest to identify, whether singing lead or backing vocals. Thanks to his tremendous range and incredible power, he was undoubtedly the Beatle—and arguably the artist—with the best rock 'n' roll voice, ripping into numbers like "Twist and Shout," "Slow Down," "Rock and Roll Music," and "Hey Bulldog." At the same time, while his voice couldn't exactly be described as pretty, it had a sincerity and depth of feeling that enhanced ballads ranging from "If I Fell" to the heartfelt "Julia."

John himself never really rated his own singing. In fact, when he eventually produced his own solo recordings, he often tried to cover up what he considered flaws by smothering his vocals in echo. On the other hand, those who worked with him had a completely different opinion, asserting—like Beatles producer George Martin—that he had "a tremendous voice."

If any of the Fab Four did have a "pretty" voice, it had to be Paul, the Beatle best suited to singing romantic numbers like "Till There Was You," "And I Love Her," and "I Will." Like his speaking voice, Paul's singing sounded altogether smoother than his colleagues', but when he sang rock songs such as "Long Tall Sally," "Oh! Darling," and "Helter Skelter," he had nearly as much edge as his Lennonish sidekick. What a unique, winning combination for one band: two lead singers who could rock and serenade with the best of them.

George's voice was not as powerful as John's or as melodic as Paul's, nor could he boast the dexterity or range of either one. Nevertheless, he was still able to inject energy into his performance of a rock standard like "Roll Over Beethoven" while summoning up the necessary wistfulness for tracks such as "While My Guitar Gently Weeps" and "Here Comes the Sun."

Having been heavily influenced by The Everly Brothers, John and Paul learned to harmonize perfectly with each other, whether sharing the lead vocal or blending together for the backing. Paul would take the high harmonies, John would handle the low, and they were expertly accompanied by George. Indeed, songs like "Help!," "The Night Before," and "If I Needed Someone,"—where one would perform the lead vocal and the other two would back him—comprised a large part of The Beatles' unmistakable and much-imitated sound. When all three harmonized together, such as on the track "Because" on *Abbey Road*, the effect was sublime.

As for Ringo, well, his voice was even more limited than George's. Its sound, however, was undoubtedly as distinctive as his style of drumming, whether he was rocking his way through "Boys," crooning "Goodnight," or getting by "With a Little Help From My Friends."

There aren't many four-piece rock bands that share the vocal spoils. The Beatles were an exception. Still, I can't end this description of their singing talents without mentioning the intonation of their voices. You see, as rock 'n' roll was originally an American art form, many non-

American performers—British, Swedish, Australian, you name it—tend to acquire a pseudo-American accent when they sing in English. Just listen to Paul's rendition of Carl Perkins' "Sure to Fall (In Love with You)," featured on The Beatles' *Live at the BBC* album. Macca sounds like he just stepped out of hillbilly country: "Lovin' yooo, is the natural thang t'dooo..."

John, George, and Ringo, on the other hand, were invariably British in terms of their vocal style, and George sometimes emphasized his Liverpudlian roots. In the song "Do You Want To Know a Secret?" he sings, "You'll never know how much I really *cur.*" That last word was his pronunciation of "care," while "alerted" as exaggeratedly sung during the second bridge of the acoustic "While My Guitar Gently Weeps" demo—first issued on *Anthology 3*—purposely sounds more like "a-*lair*--ted." Pure Scouse.

Songs That Fill the Air

In the annals of 20th-century popular music, John Lennon and Paul McCartney composed an unparalleled body of work, ranging from the early naiveté of "Ask Me Why" to the worldly sophistication of "Girl"; from the catchy melody of "Misery" to the meandering nature of "She Said She Said"; from the slickness of "All My Loving" to the disjointed character of "Happiness is a Warm Gun"; and from the straightforward subject-matter of "I'll Follow The Sun" to the quasi-religious psychedelia of "Tomorrow Never Knows."

While John and Paul evolved and progressed as songwriters, they also turned their hands to many different styles of composition. However, when listening to a Beatles recording of a Lennon-McCartney song, it's usually pretty easy to discern which of them played a bigger part in writing it. You see, contrary to the widespread public perception, once they tasted success (and often even beforehand) it was only on rare occasions that John and Paul sat down together and composed a number from beginning to end. Usually, one of them would write most—if not all—of a song, and then the other would perhaps contribute the odd musical or lyrical idea.

The easiest way to tell who wrote a particular song is to listen to who actually performed the lead vocal. (As I've already told you how to identify each of the voices, this should be fairly straightforward.) "Ticket to Ride," for example, was basically John's song whereas "I Saw Her Standing There" was Paul's. Then again, some early numbers on which the two shared the vocal spoils—such as "Misery," "From Me to You," "Thank You Girl," "She Loves You," "I'll Get You," "I Want to Hold Your Hand," and "Baby's in Black,"—were true collaborative efforts for which they *did* sit down and write together. Conversely, numbers like "We Can Work it Out," "A Day in the Life," and "I've Got a Feeling," each consisted of incomplete compositions that were slotted together, so John and Paul just sang the sections that they themselves wrote.

Otherwise, another way of identifying who wrote what is to listen to the lyrics. This applies specifically to numbers not dealing with the standard "I love you, I've lost you," pop format. In such cases John would often write in the first person, relating his own experiences— "I'm a Loser," "Help!," "You've Got to Hide Your Love Away," "In My Life," "Strawberry Fields Forever," and so on. Paul, on the other hand, seemed to enjoy constructing scenarios about other people, as with songs like "Penny Lane," "Rocky Raccoon," "Ob-La-Di, Ob-La-Da," and "Maxwell's Silver Hammer."

While the different composing styles were evident right from the start, these became more marked as time went on, with John, Paul, and eventually George evolving into more accomplished tunesmiths and lyricists. John's songs usually retained a harder edge and, in the case of numbers such as "I Am the Walrus" and "Happiness is a Warm Gun," became more unconventional and lyrically complex.

Paul's songs sometimes matched John's for rawness—"Why Don't We Do it in the Road" is a prime example—but he also composed upbeat pop ditties that his erstwhile writing partner grew increasingly disenchanted with. "Ob-La-Di, Ob-La-Da" and "Maxwell's Silver Hammer" may have been catchy enough, but as John made clear in certain post-Beatles interviews, they definitely weren't his cup of tea.

For his part, some of George's earlier compositions were awkward both melodically and lyrically. John and Paul would sometimes help him out, but he had no real writing partner and therefore had to do much of his learning in public. Still, the opportunity to do so, coupled with the hothouse atmosphere of sharing a creative environment with Lennon and McCartney, eventually paid off. George carved out his own niche with Indian-flavored numbers such as "Love You To" and "Within You Without You," before his Western pop sensibilities blossomed in the form of "While My Guitar Gently Weeps," "I Me Mine," "Something," and "Here Comes the Sun," among other notable "Harrisongs" of the era.

In this climate, even Ringo caught the songwriting bug, penning the solo compositions "Don't Pass Me By" and "Octopus's Garden," which appeared on *The Beatles* (a.k.a. the "White Album") and *Abbey Road*, respectively. Nevertheless, in the *Let It Be* film George can be seen assisting Ringo while he tries to work out the melodic structure of "Octopus's Garden" on a piano. And although "Don't Pass Me By" was recorded in 1968, Ringo had referred to it a full five years earlier when talking about his new song to press and radio interviewers. Obviously, the competition was hot.

Getting Better All the Time

Overall, you can gauge the progress in The Beatles' songwriting from album to album. At the same time, the band's entire body of compositions can be broken down into several distinct periods. First there was the straightforward I've-got-her, I've-lost-her, I've-got-her-back-again era, stretching from 1962 to 1965 and winding down with the *Help!* album. Then *Rubber Soul*, recorded and released later that year, signaled a definite transition, with serious, intricately crafted numbers such as "Nowhere Man," "Norwegian Wood (This Bird Has Flown)," "Girl," and "In My Life," (all John's songs), as well as "You Won't See Me" and "I'm Looking Through You" (both Paul's).

Rubber Soul served as a bridge between *Help!* and *Revolver*, the remarkable 1966 album that signaled the start of The Beatles' experimental/ psychedelic songwriting period. This would flourish with the release of *Sgt. Pepper's Lonely Hearts Club Band* in 1967 and basically end with the tracks recorded for the *Magical Mystery Tour* TV movie later that year. Thereafter, through 1968 and 1969, the floodgates really burst open, with songs ranging from commercial pop to hard rock, country & western to the avant-garde.

It's incredible to think that the same guys who sang "Love Me Do" and "Baby's in Black" were going into the studio with material such as "Eleanor Rigby," "Tomorrow Never Knows," "A Day in the Life," "I Am the Walrus," and "While My Guitar Gently Weeps" just a few years later. In fact, just six months separated the recording sessions for "Run For Your Life" and "Tomorrow Never Knows." But then, that's a large part of what made The Beatles great.

Movin' and Groovin': The Musicianship

Individually, The Beatles weren't the world's greatest musicians, yet the effect of their combined playing, together with their unbridled willingness to keep pushing back the boundaries in this respect, helped make them world-beaters.

The only one of the four to really rank in the upper echelons was Paul McCartney, whose bass playing, although fairly average at the start, became truly innovative by the mid-1960s. A major turning point was the recording of "Paperback Writer" in 1966, on which Paul utilized a Rickenbacker bass instead of his usual Hofner, and played melodic lines that, until then, would have normally been left to a lead guitarist. What's more, just to ensure that everybody shared in the excitement of what he was doing, engineer Geoff Emerick recorded Paul's bass so that it was far louder than on any previous pop record. It was almost as if Paul was playing "lead bass," and much the same applied on tracks such as "With a Little Help from My Friends," "Lucy in the Sky With Diamonds,"and, most notably, "Hey Bulldog," throughout which his bass line dances all over the place.

At around the same time, Geoff Emerick was also boosting the sound of Ringo's bass drum to unprecedented heights on songs like "Tomorrow Never Knows" and "Sgt. Pepper's Lonely Hearts Club Band." In a technical sense, Ringo's drumming wasn't in the same league as some of his contemporaries', yet John and Paul always asserted that he was the best drummer in the world for The Beatles, providing a rock-solid backbeat and a feel that was all his own.

George Harrison's lead guitar playing also had a characteristic sound; inspired by Nashville session man and producer Chet Atkins, George excelled on the Fab Four's more country-flavored performances for the *Beatles for Sale* album. At times, George's shortcomings could be exposed in a live situation or in a recording setup that didn't permit more than one take. This is evident on several tracks on The Beatles' *Live at the BBC* album. However, when he got it right in the studio, he *really* got it right, and standout examples of this are his electrifying solos on songs such as "I Feel Fine," "And Your Bird Can Sing," and "Hey Bulldog," as well as the innovative backwards solo that the two Georges (Harrison and Martin) contrived for "I'm Only Sleeping." (This was achieved by George Martin notating the musical chart for the solo, then writing it out in reverse. George Harrison was recorded playing to this backwards score, and then, when the tape itself was subsequently played back in reverse, the result was a backwards-sounding guitar playing a normal tune.)

The sounds that musicians produce are often an extension of their personalities. This was true with regard to George, whose careful, precise guitar playing didn't have the loose feel associated with, say, an Eric Clapton or a Jimi Hendrix. Likewise, and similar to his vocal delivery, John Lennon's guitar style was altogether more raw than George's. His usual role was to play rhythm and this he did quite adequately. One of his more notable performances was his distinguished, super-fast strumming on "All My Loving." You have to remember that, despite their shortcomings, The Beatles each contributed unique sounds that have served to influence and inspire.

In order to compare the guitar styles of Lennon, McCartney, and Harrison, listen to the instrumental break in "The End" on *Abbey Road*. As well as featuring the only drum solo of Ringo's Beatle career, Paul, George, and John (in that order) can be heard trading guitar solos several times in quick succession. A fitting end to a fantastic career.

Recordings and Technology

As The Beatles took giant strides in their songwriting, they also became more adept as studio musicians, capitalizing on the talents of their producer, George Martin, and engineers such as Norman Smith and Geoff Emerick, in order to realize their artistic visions. What's more, together with the technical staff at EMI Studios in North London, they conspired to break the rules and push back the boundaries of recording technology.

These days, most major artists only release an album every few years, and when they do, the progression in the sound and the material is often marginal. In The Beatles' case, however, the advances were enormous and so was the amount of product: two albums each in 1963, 1964, and 1965, and one each in 1966, 1967, 1968, 1969, and 1970. This, however, does not include the *Long Tall Sally* EP (extended play record) in 1964 that contained four new tracks; the 1967 *Magical Mystery Tour* EP that featured six new tracks; or the *Yellow Submarine* album in 1969 that included four new songs.

Then there were the U.K. singles themselves—22 of them from 1962 to 1970, featuring 44 songs, 25 of which were never included on albums at that time. (In America, Capitol released many more singles, but The Beatles had little say in the matter.) These included such gems as "She Loves You," "I Want to Hold Your Hand," "I Feel Fine," "We Can Work it Out," "Penny Lane," "Lady Madonna," "Hey Jude"... the list goes on and on. So does the one comprising the incredible album tracks that were not even offered up as singles in the U.K. Would you believe "I Saw Her Standing There," "All My Loving," "Eight Days a Week," "Yesterday," "Nowhere Man," "Back in the U.S.S.R.," and "The Long and Winding Road," for example? All could have very easily topped the British charts, giving you just some idea as to how prolific and steeped in quality The Beatles were.

Equally remarkable was the difference in sound from album to album. Easily the most old-fashioned by today's standards was the first one, *Please Please Me*, released in March 1963, and full of heavy echo and "sha-la-la"-style backing vocals. Yet, just eight months later, there was *With The Beatles*, a record that sounds as fresh and full of life today as it did on the day of its release. Of course, the band had producer George Martin and engineer Norman Smith largely to thank for this, but the power of their performances and their own determination to improve also moved things forward.

Likewise, the next four albums each had their own distinctive sounds and advancements: George's highly influential employment of his new

Rickenbacker 12-string guitar on *A Hard Day's Night*, the countrified twang of *Beatles for Sale*, and the Hammond organ and harmonium featured on *Help!* and *Rubber Soul*. As for the string quartet on "Yesterday" and George playing an Indian sitar on "Norwegian Wood (This Bird Has Flown)"—at the time, these were ground-breaking innovations for a rock 'n' roll band.

The next really major breakthrough came with *Revolver* and, most specifically, tracks such as "Tomorrow Never Knows," with its multi-recorded effects, distorted guitars, and John's voice being fed through the revolving Leslie speaker of a Hammond organ. Incredibly, this was the first Beatles recording on which 20-year-old Geoff Emerick served as the engineer. For his work on their next album—the landmark *Sgt. Pepper's Lonely Hearts Club Band*—he would receive a Grammy Award.

A large part of what turned the musical world on its head about *Sgt. Pepper*, in addition to the breathtaking vision of songs such as "A Day in the Life," was the manner in which it was assembled as a concept instead of as a random collection of individual tracks. In this case, the concept was a supposed stage show, and to this end there were numerous sound effects—audience laughter and applause, even a cock crowing, courtesy of the EMI Studios effects library—as well as the device of having some songs segue (fade directly) into one another.

Just a few years before, all that The Beatles needed to make a record were bass, drums, two guitars and, on occasion, a keyboard. Now here they were, enlisting the services of a 40-piece orchestra while utilizing instruments such as a mellotron. Then there were the innovative techniques that the EMI technical staff came up with in order to meet their recording demands, including ADT (artificial double tracking), flanging (time delay), and the linking of tape machines to enable the capturing of more sounds. Never had so much care been taken over the recording and mixing of an album, or so much time (just under five months).

After *Sgt. Pepper*, The Beatles continued to toy with different sounds and techniques—"I Am the Walrus" being a prime example. Then, however, as a reaction to the seemingly endless recording sessions for the "White Album," they decided to revert to the methods of the good old days, when they had completed the entire *Please Please Me* album in under 10 hours. All of the songs were to be recorded live in the studio, with no additional overdubbed effects. Unfortunately, group squabbles ensured that the new project lasted months rather than mere hours, while the shoddy state of the recorded material necessitated editing and overdubbing, as well as changing the name of the album (and film) from the hopeful *Get Back* to the more philosophical *Let It Be*.

And in the end... there was *Abbey Road*, a polished production and one of The Beatles' finest works. Still, producer George Martin did have to strike a compromise between the artistic desires of Lennon and McCartney. Whereas Side One of the record featured individual tracks that appeased John's way of thinking, Side Two reflected Paul's acceptance of George Martin's suggestion to "try to think in symphonic terms, and think in terms of having a first and second subject, put them in different keys, bring back themes," and even have some intricate vocal harmony work. John wasn't overly enthused about this approach.

"*Abbey Road* was really unfinished songs all stuck together," he told P*layboy* magazine in 1980. "Everybody praises the album so much, but none of the songs had anything to do with each other, no thread at all."

You can't please everyone...

Starr Quality

"This is adapted from a photo-and-a-half, merging part of a 1964 shot of Ringo—cropping out guitars and amps—with the foreground cymbals to provide a more interesting composition. Still, for me the driving force behind this painting was his expression and the shaggy hair. It's pure Ringo."

– Eric Cash

Chapter 5

All These Friends and Lovers

While there are obviously four central characters in the story of The Beatles, they are easily outnumbered by the cast of supporting players. So outnumbered, in fact, that it would be almost impossible—and just plain boring—to list them all here.

Therefore, in this chapter I plan to start off by telling you how some of the band members' friends actually played a role in the shaping of their career. Many of these people can only be credited with cameo appearances; others remained on the Fab Four scene a little longer, and a few lasted through the halcyon years and beyond.

Next, I'll explain the functions of two of The Beatles' closest and most faithful assistants: Mal Evans and Neil Aspinall. Of course, countless other helpers served the group in a variety of ways: press officers such as Derek Taylor, Tony Barrow, and Brian Sommerville; their driver, Alf Bicknell; and associates of manager Brian Epstein, such as Peter Brown and Alistair Taylor. Yet, Mal and Neil were the two men who, through the years, were seemingly always by their side, both on the road and in the studio.

Finally, this chapter will wind down with brief summaries of how John, Paul, George, and Ringo met their various wives, and what has become of them and the children that these unions produced.

Buddies, Friends, and Pals

None of the young Beatles were classmates or childhood chums. Paul and George certainly knew each other from an early age and they both attended the Liverpool Institute during their teens. A year apart, they eventually struck up a friendship of sorts by way of their mutual love of rock 'n' roll. As for the rest of the group, they all eventually became firm friends, but only as a result of having formed a musical alliance rather than the other way around.

During the first explosion of rock music in the mid-1950s, thousands of British teenagers decided to form their own bands, and it was easy to collaborate with close friends or casual acquaintances. Ringo, for example (then still going by his real name of Richard—or Richy—Starkey), got together with a fellow engineering apprentice named Eddie Miles and assembled the Eddie Clayton Skiffle Group.

16-year-old John Lennon, on the other hand, was truly the founder of the musical unit that would become known as The Beatles. The first person he turned to in his new venture was his best buddy at Quarry Bank High School, Pete Shotton.

By 1957, Lennon and Shotton were notorious at school as two of its most disruptive and unruly students. (Don't take the word "students" too literally here—neither of them did that much studying.) Other mates would join The Quarry Men (so named because of a line in the school song, "Quarry Men, old before our birth..."), among them Bill Smith, Rod Davis, Colin Hanton, Eric Griffiths, Len Garry, Nigel Whalley, and John "Duff" Lowe. Yet, although Pete would be among the first to leave, he would also be one of the very few to remain in John's circle of friends.

George Harrison knew the meaning of loyalty—throughout the years he would stay in touch with boyhood acquaintances such as Arthur Kelly and Tony Bramwell— and in 1965 he and John set Pete Shotton up in a supermarket business. Later on, Pete would also be employed within The Beatles' Apple empire and as John's personal assistant. For his part, Tony Bramwell worked for Brian Epstein before being appointed Apple's head of production.

Filling Pete's shoes as John's fellow crony when he went to art college was an unconventional individual by the name of Jeff Mahomed. Yet, it was with another college student that John would form one of his very closest friendships: Stuart Sutcliffe. An artist of prodigious talent, Stu would become John's trusted confidant and, at John's insistence (despite a conspicuous lack of musical ability), even a member of the fledgling Beatles. Unfortunately, what looked like being a lifelong friendship was cut short by Sutcliffe's premature death from a brain hemorrhage.

Stu's girlfriend, photographer Astrid Kircherr, remained in touch with the group over the years, as did another friend from their Hamburg days, artist Klaus Voormann. In fact, Voormann put his talents to good use for The Beatles, coming up with the imaginative sleeve designs for their 1966 *Revolver* album and, three decades later, the *Anthology* box-set. Meanwhile, as a bass guitarist, the groups he played for in the 1960s and '70s included John and Yoko's Plastic Ono Band and Manfred Mann.

For all that, perhaps the person who could claim to have made one of the most significant contributions to the whole Beatles story was yet another of the part-time Quarry Men. His name was Ivan Vaughan. A pal of both Paul (whose birthdate he shared) and John, Ivan was the one who took Paul to see John's group playing at a church fete in Liverpool on July 6, 1957. That was the day when Lennon and McCartney first met. Within a couple of weeks they had joined forces, and the rest of the story...well, I'll be telling you about that a little later on.

Helping Out—Mal and Neil

In The Beatles' first film, *A Hard Day's Night*, John, Paul, George, and Ringo are constantly ordered about by their onscreen "road manager," Norm (played by Norman Rossington). Partly aided by his dimwitted but likable sidekick, Shake (John Junkin), Norm struts about like a principal badgering a bunch of naughty schoolboys. Back in the real world, there's no way The Beatles would have put up with this kind of nonsense, yet the roles of Norm and Shake were undeniably based on a pair of individuals who were far more competent in real-life: Mal Evans and Neil Aspinall.

Big Mal was working as a bouncer at Liverpool's Cavern Club when he first encountered the band. On August 11, 1963, he quit his day job as a post office engineer to become their assistant and, during the next three years, he could be seen setting up their amplifiers and instruments on concert stages all over the world. At the same time, Mal also doubled as The Beatles' personal bodyguard, and he often accompanied one or more of them when they went on private vacations.

In the studio, Mal was called upon not only to help set up the equipment (as is evident in the *Let It Be* documentary), but also make cups of tea and even help out on some of the recordings. What's more, he made cameo appearances in the movies *Help!* (in which he portrays a long-distance swimmer who has trouble finding his way) and *Magical Mystery Tour*, as well as in the 1968 Beatles Christmas message.

In 1968, Mal was appointed assistant general manager of The Beatles' company, Apple, and, after their split, he both managed and produced the group Badfinger. On January 5, 1976, Los Angeles police were called to Mal's home when, due to mounting problems in his personal life, he was threatening suicide. In his confusion, Mal pointed an air rifle at three of the officers—who presumed it was a rifle—and when he refused to put it down they shot him dead. Mal Evans was just a few months short of his fortieth birthday.

When Mal took over the chore of lugging The Beatles' equipment from one venue to the next, he was also giving a well-earned break to Neil Aspinall. Neil had been doing this job in the less-than-savory atmosphere of Liverpool's dingier clubs. There, local thugs would keep a beady eye on him as he walked to and from the van that he also drove the group around in.

Having attended the Liverpool Institute with Paul and George, Neil was also a close friend of The Beatles' drummer, Pete Best. When Pete was fired in August 1962, Neil was so outraged that he considered turning his back on the band that had recently signed a recording contract. In the end, however, he made what turned out to be a profitable decision. He quit his accountancy studies and went to work for The Beatles full-time as their chief road manager (while continuing his relationship with Pete's mother, Mona, that had resulted in the birth of their son, Vincent "Roag" Best, just three weeks before Pete's sacking). In turn, his loyalty and intellect were rewarded in 1968 when he was appointed managing director of their Apple Corps company. It's a position Neil (or "Nell" as John liked to call him) would hold until shortly before his 2007 death from cancer at age 66.

Fab Wives

Four Beatles, nine wives, with an even spread of two marriages for John, George, and Ringo, while Paul came from behind in that regard to snatch the lead. Still, they've so far shared the spoils in terms of divorces, with just one each.

The first—and youngest—Beatle groom was John Winston Lennon. He married Cynthia Powell on August 23, 1962, when he was still 21 and she was 22. The two had met just a little under five years earlier at Liverpool College of Art, and it really had been a case of opposites attracting. For one thing, Cyn was a diligent student. She spoke nicely, dressed conservatively, and was seemingly no match for loudmouthed Lennon, with his greasy Elvis-style hairdo, devil-may-care attitude, and bunch of equally rowdy friends. At first, sending up her air of quiet civility, John referred to Cynthia as "the posh Miss Powell," but soon they hit it off and their friendship turned into love.

Ye Cracke, the Rice Street pub close to the art college that was frequented by John and his cronies, and which was the scene of his first date with Cynthia Powell.

John relied on Cyn's emotional strength and honesty, yet it's arguable whether they would have ever married had she not become pregnant. It was a sign of the times, and of John's honorable instincts, that he viewed marriage as the only option in such circumstances. At the subsequent civil ceremony, Paul and George were the only friends in attendance. That night, the band fulfilled a concert booking in nearby Chester.

Cynthia set the tone for the first generation of Beatle wives, largely staying out of the spotlight. In fact, there was initially a concerted effort to keep the marriage a secret due to a fear that, if John wasn't "free and single," it might hurt his reputation with the female fans. That soon proved to be a joke, as word leaked out and the press spread the news. The adoring girls didn't seem to care either way.

Stability was, seemingly, the main feature of the Lennon marriage, but in many ways John came to realize that he was looking for more; he wanted someone less conventional and more in tune with his wayward tastes and ideas. Enter Yoko Ono, the Japanese avant-garde artist who he first met in December 1966 when visiting an exhibition of her work at Central London's Indica Gallery. He didn't initially view Yoko as the realization of his dreams, but when he did—some 18 months later— the resultant explosion blew away the union with Cynthia and put an immense strain on The Beatles.

John and Yoko's love for one another was all-consuming and made them inseparable. He grew his hair long to resemble hers and, soon after their wedding on March 20, 1969 (which was Yoko's third), changed his middle name from Winston to Ono. Surviving a 15-month "trial separation" that, according to John, "didn't work out" during the mid-seventies, the union lasted until his death in December 1980.

During the latter part of their relationship, Yoko, nearly seven years John's senior, took care of all the couple's financial dealings while he stayed home to tend to their baby, Sean. Born into a wealthy banking family, Yoko's background has served her well since her husband's death, as she has kept a tight rein on the multi-million dollar Lennon estate. For her part, Cynthia has been married three more times, divorced twice, and recently widowed.

Ringo's first wife, Maureen Cox, was only 18 when she married The Beatles' 24-year-old drummer on February 11, 1965. Previously, she had been among the locals who watched the group perform at Liverpool's Cavern Club, and she and Ringo had started dating in 1962. While the Fab Four toured the world, "Mo" stayed in Liverpool and worked as a hairdresser. Then, after their marriage, she and Ringo moved to a house situated close to that of John and Cynthia, in Weybridge, Surrey.

Maureen answered her husband's fan mail and attended Beatles concerts whenever possible. She's the one Paul is talking to when he says, "Thanks, Mo," at the end of "Get Back" on the *Let It Be* album. Nevertheless, by 1973 the marriage was faltering (not least due to Mo's affair with George), and Ringo spent a lot of time in Los Angeles while Maureen stayed at home in England with their three children. The couple divorced in 1975, but they remained friends up until her death from cancer on December 30, 1994.

During the interim, Ringo had taken actress Barbara Bach as his second wife. Bach's biggest claim to fame was her starring role opposite Roger Moore in the 1977 James Bond movie, *The Spy Who Loved Me*. Three years later, she met Ringo on the set of the film, *Caveman*. Having survived a really bad car crash without injury in London on May 19, 1980, Ringo and Barbara evidently felt they were destined to be together. They were married on April 27 of the following year and, despite some difficult times (including Ringo's much publicized—and winning—battle against alcoholism), they have remained together ever since.

Present at Ringo and Barbara's London wedding in 1981 were the two other surviving Beatles and their wives. Like Ringo, George was with his second wife, his first marriage having been to Patricia Ann Boyd, a London model who had a bit-part in *A Hard Day's Night*. Beatlemania was at its height, yet in the beginning Pattie actually had the cheek to reject George's advances; she was engaged to somebody else, but the youngest Beatle was nothing if not determined.

Both George and John, you see, shared a passion for the actress Brigitte Bardot, and Cynthia had even dyed her dark hair blonde to please goggle-eyed Lennon. Well, when George caught a glimpse of Pattie he was convinced that she bore a resemblance to the French sex kitten. On January 21, 1966, the two of them tied the knot, with Paul and manager Brian Epstein sharing best man honors while John and Ringo were away in Trinidad.

Pattie became just as involved as George in the study of Indian culture—in fact, it was she who first introduced her husband to the Transcendental Meditation teachings of the Maharishi Mahesh Yogi. Still, while they appeared perfectly compatible as the archetypal swinging, mystical '60s couple, Pattie felt increasingly alienated by George's near-obssessive pursuit of spiritual enlightenment and physical recreation with other women. Eventually, she embarked on an affair of her own with her hubby's best friend, guitarist Eric Clapton, whose 1970 recording of "Layla" with Derek and the Dominos described how he'd fallen in love with Pattie "when your old man had let you down." George and Pattie split up in 1974 and five years later she and Eric began a short-lived marriage. Still, any bitterness on George's part was also short-lived. At the wedding party, he, Paul, and Ringo reunited for an impromptu jam session.

In the meantime, George had hooked up with Olivia Trinidad Arias, a secretary for his Dark Horse record label in Los Angeles. The two of them first met in 1974, and shortly afterwards Olivia moved to England and into the Harrison Friar Park residence in Henley-on-Thames. When the couple's plans to marry in May 1978 were cancelled due to the death of George's father, the wedding was rescheduled for September 2, a month after the birth of their son, Dhani.

In the marital sweepstakes, that's three Fabs down and one to go: Paul, the longest-lasting bachelor Beatle. Throughout much of the 1960s his most serious relationship was with British actress Jane Asher, leading to constant rumors that they were about to get married or had already done so. The speculation appeared to be at an end when they became engaged on Christmas Day of 1967, but then, just seven months later, Jane announced on TV that their relationship was over. This cleared the way for Linda Louise Eastman (and was the result of Jane having caught Paul with her).

Born into a wealthy Jewish family in Scarsdale, New York, Linda had already been married and had a child by the time she first came face-to-face with Paul. That was in her capacity as a rock photographer—The Beatles, The Rolling Stones, Traffic, Jimi Hendrix, and Jim Morrison were just some of the famous names that Linda would eventually be able to count among her subjects. Nevertheless, on May 15, 1967 it was a social encounter at London's Bag O'Nails nightclub that initially stirred up interest between her and Paul, and four nights later they met again at the launch party for the *Sgt. Pepper* album. Still, this didn't dissuade him from getting engaged to Jane, so in May 1968 Linda tried again.

At a New York press conference held by John and Paul to announce the setting up of their Apple business venture, Linda slipped the baby-faced

Beatle her phone number. This time he took the bait, and in October 1968, with Jane Asher firmly off the scene, Linda made a permanent move to England. She and Paul were married on March 12, 1969, with Paul's brother Mike as best man. None of the other Beatles attended.

Paul and Linda stuck together through thick and thin. Some of the thinnest moments included drug busts, as well as press and public criticism for her inclusion in Paul's musical ventures despite her obvious "lack of experience." On the up side, Linda continued to take great photos—she took the official pics when Paul, George, and Ringo reunited for the *Beatles Anthology* project—and she and Macca were also among Britain's leading spokespeople for the preservation of the environment and eating of vegetarian food. Linda actually authored two best-selling vegetarian cookbooks, and Findus also launched a line of frozen veggie food with her face on the packet.

During the mid-nineties, Linda had to battle breast cancer, an illness that had taken the life of Paul's mother when he was in his early teens. Linda wasn't even able to stand by her husband's side when, on March 11, 1997, he went to Buckingham Palace to receive his knighthood from the Queen, and on April 17, 1998, following a brief period when her cancer appeared to be in remission, Lady Linda succumbed to the disease at age 56.

Devastated by the loss, Paul did his best to put his life back together and within a couple of years he was in a new relationship that would lead to marriage… and a relatively quick yet highly public divorce.

Paul first encountered Heather Mills just 12 months after Linda's passing, when they were both presenting awards at a Pride of Britain event at London's Dorchester Hotel. A former nude model, Heather had had her left leg amputated below the knee following a road accident in which she was hit by a police motorcycle, and she'd set up the Heather Mills Trust with some of the £200,000 that she had been awarded as compensation. This organization provided prosthetic limbs to victims of landmine explosions and, following their initial meeting, Paul provided backing vocals for a song that Heather and her sister had written and recorded to raise funds for the charity. He also donated £150,000, and it wasn't long before Britain's tabloid press began reporting about their relationship.

Unlike his registry-office marriage to Linda, Paul pulled out all the stops for his second wedding, which took place at an Irish castle on June 11, 2002. His bride, wearing a £15,000 diamond and sapphire ring, was 34; he was one week shy of turning 60. Their daughter Beatrice was born in October of the following year, but by May of 2006 it was all over, with Heather demanding a £125 million settlement while accusing Paul of having been physically and mentally abusive. This, in turn, incurred the wrath of not only Paul's kids but also the British press—it's never a good idea to publicly attack a Beatle—and after having her old nude pics trotted out for everyone to see, the second Lady McCartney was eventually awarded just over £24 million. Not bad for a marriage that was officially terminated in May 2008.

Still, remember that saying about the third time being the charm? Far from being deterred by his bad experience, Paul began dating one Nancy Shevell in November 2007. The vice-president of her family's New England Motor Freight business and a board member of New York City's Metropolitan Transportation Authority, Nancy shared Linda's Jewish heritage and, just like his first wedding, Paul married her at London's Old Marylebone Town Hall... on October 9, 2011, which would have been John Lennon's 71st birthday.

Gear Kids

Being that all four Beatles can never get back together, how about forming a group consisting of some of their kids? Say, John's oldest son Julian on rhythm guitar, Paul's son James on bass, George's son Dhani on lead guitar, and Ringo's oldest son Zak on drums. Now, doesn't that sound like a good idea? I hope not, and I'm sure it doesn't to the parents concerned (or concerned parents). But it has been suggested... by certain hacks in the media, not by The Beatles themselves.

John, Paul, George, and Ringo all kept their children from the full glare of the publicity spotlight. The first to be born, on April 8, 1963, was Julian (named in honor of John's late mother, Julia). Aside from some official family photographs, his parents made every effort to keep Julian away from the press, yet during his early years he actually had a hard time gaining the attention of John himself. Too busy recording and touring with The Beatles to be a constant presence in his son's life,

John only wanted to deal with the youngster on his own terms when he did return home. Later on, after his parents' divorce, Julian lived with Cynthia and visited John during school holidays, although this became a little more difficult when John and Yoko moved to America in 1971.

Following some tough times, John and Julian did grow increasingly close toward the end of the decade, and this made things even more difficult for the elder son when his father was murdered in December 1980. Julian subsequently enjoyed short-lived chart success as a musician in his own right, but it appears that the interest that he initially sparked was due more to his name than anything else.

Meanwhile, another junior Lennon has attempted to step out from under his father's musical shadow. This is Sean, who was born on October 9, 1975, John's 35th birthday. Sean is the Irish version of the name John (Julian's first name is also John), and the first five years of the infant's life coincided with his father's temporary retirement.

Having been absent for much of Julian's childhood, and having tried so hard with Yoko to actually have a child, John was determined to make a better effort the second time around. This effort extended to not only being at home more, but actually being ever-present. Yoko took care of business while the former chauvinist Beatle assumed the role of househusband, cooking the meals and taking care of the baby.

From Sean's perspective, John's death not only deprived him of a doting father, but it also brought him to the public's attention on a scale unmatched by any of the other Beatle kids. Sure, Zak Starkey is now a successful professional drummer in his own right (having toured with his father and with The Who), Dhani Harrison is a George look-alike with musical pursuits of his own who's overseen the promotion of his father's work, James McCartney played guitar on his dad's 1997 *Flaming Pie* album, and Paul's daughter Stella is now one of the world's top fashion designers. But, on the whole, most of the Fab Four's offspring could walk down any street largely unnoticed.

Reputable author that I am, I'm not about to disrupt the kids' privacy by giving you a full physical description of each and every one of them. What I will do, however, is provide you with a comprehensive list of names and birth dates. (This does not include stepchildren or any unofficial claimants to The Beatles' dynasty.)

Beatle Parents and Kids

The Parents	The Kid	The Birth Date
John and Cynthia	John Charles Julian	4-8-63
John and Yoko	Sean Taro Ono	10-9-75
Paul and Linda	Mary	8-28-69
	Stella Nina	9-13-71
	James Louis	9-12-77
Paul and Heather	Beatrice Milly	10-28-03
George and Olivia	Dhani	8-1-78
Ringo and Maureen	Zak	9-13-65
	Jason	8-19-67
	Lee Parkin	11-11-70

As you can see, coincidence was certainly on the menu when Sean Lennon was born on John's birthday, just as it was when Stella McCartney came into the world precisely six years after the grand entrance of Zak Starkey. James was just a day too early to turn Zak and Stella's shared anniversary into a triple play, yet he did ensure the continuance of a particular family tradition: James was the name of Paul's father, who died on March 18, 1976, and it is also the first name of... yes, Paul himself. Not that this has ever been a secret—in 1973, he made a song-and-dance TV special titled *James Paul McCartney*.

PART 2

CRYING, WAITING, HOPING—YEARS OF STRUGGLE

And in the beginning... There were four young guys, born into a depressed city, but not altogether miserable surroundings. The Beatles had close relatives who cared, some who didn't, and the limited prospects of many war babies growing up in the north of England during the 1940s and early-fifties—a basic education and, hopefully, a steady job. That is, unless they had the talent to make something of themselves, or perhaps even the luck to... no, Liverpudlians didn't take too much stock in luck back then.

Well, in the story that's about to unfold, talent certainly played a part. First, however, we must look at the other factors that grabbed the spotlight before ability took center-stage: the social and cultural influences, the barely adequate early musical excursions, the disappointments, the disasters, and the people who never quite made it. The Beatles had to go through all of these phases before they began to taste the fruits of their labors.

Chapter 6

The Baby Beatles

Outside of India and its caste system, Britain is one of the most class-conscious societies in the world. Much of the population consists of the working and lower-middle classes, with the remainder comprising the affluent upper-middle class (millionaire businessmen, for instance), privileged upper class (such as the late Princess of Wales when she was Lady Diana Spencer), and, of course, the aristocracy.

Now, a working class Brit can certainly climb up the ladder, just as an upper class one can slide down the slippery slope. Yet, among many citizens, there is an underlying belief that, while you can take the person out of the social class, you can't take the social class out of the person. I'm not about to discuss the rights and wrongs of that philosophy, but it did help shape the social attitudes of John, Paul, George, and Ringo. However much success changed their lifestyle, it didn't really alter their take on the world around them, and in 1970 John even wrote and recorded a song in which he referred to himself as a "Working Class Hero." While that may have reflected how he felt, his self-appraisal was a little wide of the mark…

There's a Place (Up and to the Left a Bit): Liverpool

Located in the northwest corner of England, Liverpool is positioned above Wales and across the sea from Ireland. Consequently, there's plenty of Welsh and Irish blood to be found in Liverpudlians, as well as some sharp tongues and a sardonic sense of humor.

Among the city's major claims to fame during the 19th century were the world's first passenger railway, in 1830, and the world's first ocean liners, which were launched by the Cunard Steamship Company at the start of the following decade. (In time, the local sailors who traveled back and forth between Liverpool and the United States would become known as "Cunard Yanks.") Lancashire, the county in which Liverpool is situated, was then a center of the thriving cotton industry, and so the ships served everybody's purposes by bringing in the cotton for the mills.

For the next 100 years, as one of the world's major seaports, Liverpool thrived with activity, yet to Londoners and others living close to Britain's seat of government it was still just "up north"; one of the cities—along with places such as Newcastle and Manchester—in which many of the country's biggest wheels of industry turned, yet which few southerners would care to visit. After all, what was the point? There were plenty of jobs down in London, and that's where all national decisions were made.

Liverpool, like many British cities, suffered the effects of heavy German bombing during the Second World War, and that period also coincided with the decline of the cotton industry. Therefore, by the time John, Paul, George, and Ringo had joined the local scene, large sections of it were already run down.

In the city center, imposing but grimy-looking 19th-century public buildings mirrored Liverpool's declining fortunes. Nearby, the endless rows of "terraced" public housing reflected the cramped living conditions that were afforded the industrial classes. The front door of each house opened directly onto the sidewalk; at the back, a tiny yard accommodated an outside toilet.

To people living "down south," Liverpool was the place that spawned many of the nation's best-loved comedians, yet for Liverpudlians the early post-war years were not always a laughing matter. A focal point where they would gather was the Pier Head. There, lining up at the central bus terminal, they could see ships sailing across to Ireland and America, and a few of them would dream—dream about someday leaving their home city and making a name for themselves out there in the big, wide world. A fleeting thought, perhaps, but nonetheless some sort of ambition.

Those Were the Days: The Historical Perspective

Though no one could have known it at the time—and few would have believed it—the end of World War II signaled the start of the longest period of peace Western Europe has known in centuries. For once this meant that young men wouldn't grow up just to die at a front where their ruling elders sent them. Still, there *was* the Cold War to contend with, including fear of the hydrogen bomb which was a thousand times more powerful than the one dropped on Hiroshima.

While the Cold War raged on throughout the 1950s, there was also a general rise in the standard of living. This was more true for America than Britain, and still more true for Britain's southern and rural areas than its industrial north. There were more cars on the road and more TV sets in the homes, while advances in medical science—such as the development of a polio vaccine—meant that people in the West now had the chance to lead healthier lives. As an added bonus, Brits also benefited from the free medicine, attention, and facilities provided by the new state-run National Health Service.

This was all good news, yet for Western teenagers there could be no denying that the early 1950s were also pretty boring. I mean, think about it: all that the "hit parade" had to offer were antiseptic records like "How Much Is That Doggie in the Window?" And as for sex—the basic message from parents, TV, and the movies seemed to be that it didn't even exist. Could every birth be the result of an immaculate conception? During the 1950s, *repression* was a key word, yet things were about to change. Dr. Alfred Kinsey's reports on sexual behavior, as well as the surgical transformation of Denmark's George Jorgenson into Christine Jorgenson, brought sex out into the open. And so, for that matter, did a sideburned young punk from Memphis, Tennessee, named Elvis Presley.

Cry Baby Cry?—Childhood Days

Like most cities, Liverpool has its good areas and its tough areas, its blue-collar districts and its white-collar neighborhoods. All of The Beatles were born into working-class surroundings during the years that German bombs were raining down on the city, yet in three of the four cases—and one in particular—their living conditions definitely improved as time went on.

The one whose lot in early life remained the same was Ringo Starr. Born Richard Starkey on July 7, 1940, Richy was brought up in the Dingle, by far the worst of any of the neighborhoods in which The Beatles were raised, and also among the roughest in Liverpool. Situated in the center, not far from the docks, the Dingle was drab compared to the newer suburbs where Richy's future colleagues grew up.

The Madryn Street house in which he spent the first five years of his life was a terraced three-up, three down (rooms, that is). However, the rent was too expensive for his hard-working single mother, Elsie, so they moved around the corner to a two-up, two-down in Admiral Grove. They were still living there when The Beatles took Britain by storm in 1963.

At the age of five, Richy enrolled at nearby St. Silas primary school, but after only a year he was hospitalized when his appendix burst and he came down with peritonitis. Two operations followed at Myrtle Street Children's Hospital, and then a 10-week spell when Richy was in a coma. He would remain in the hospital for just over a year. At that point he was still not able to read and write.

When he was 11, Richy wasn't even allowed to take the "eleven-plus" exam which, at that time, would entitle those who passed to enter the higher caliber grammar schools. Instead, he went to Dingle Vale Secondary Modern, and within two years he was back in the Myrtle Street hospital with pleurisy and a shadow on the lung. From there he was moved to Hezzle Children's Hospital and, when 15 year-old Richy finally emerged after two years, his school days were at an end.

12 Arnold Grove in Wavertree, the birthplace of George Harrison, where the meager facilities included an outside toilet, a solitary coal fire, and a small hen house.

George Harrison, meanwhile, began life on February 25, 1943 in yet another tiny two-up, two-down terraced home, although this was in the relatively better neighborhood of Wavertree. Just like Ringo's house and many others across Britain in those days, 12 Arnold Grove had very little in the way of heating. In fact, in the winter it was freezing. The family was on a seemingly endless re-housing list, and it wasn't until George was six that he, his parents, and his siblings finally moved to Upton Green in Speke. The home there was on an estate owned by the Liverpool Corporation, and although it was larger and more comfortable than the one on Arnold Grove, the area was still rough. The Harrisons eventually went back onto the housing list and, in 1962, they moved to 174 Macket's Lane near Woolton, not far from Menlove Avenue where John grew up.

Dovedale Road Primary School in Wavertree, attended by John and George three years apart.

As a five-year-old in Wavertree, George also happened to go to the same infant and junior school as John, in Dovedale Road near Penny Lane. Not that they met then, since George was over two years younger. A person he did meet at his next school—Liverpool Institute—was Paul, who was a year above him. Paul was fairly studious until rock 'n' roll took over his life, but George—who, like Paul, had passed the eleven-plus—never really studied and left school with no qualifications.

20 Forthlin Road, the Allerton house that became home to Paul, his brother, and their parents in 1955. It was here that, skipping their studies, John and Paul wrote many of their earliest songs, and where one of their rehearsal sessions with an early lineup of The Beatles—including Stu Sutcliffe on bass—was taped sometime in the spring or summer of 1960.

James Paul McCartney was the only Beatle baby born in the luxury of a private ward. This was on June 18, 1942, at the Walton Hospital, where his mother Mary earned that privilege by having previously worked there as a nurse. During his earliest years, Paul also lived in Speke, in a small council house on Western Avenue. At five, he went to the nearby Stockton Wood Road Primary School, and then Joseph Williams Primary in an area named Gateacre. In 1955, the McCartneys moved to a semi-detached council home at 20 Forthlin Road in the more pleasant Allerton neighborhood and this brought Paul into the orbit of one John Winston Lennon.

Liverpool Maternity Hospital on Oxford Street, adjacent to the University of Liverpool campus, where John Lennon entered the world on October 9, 1940.

Born in a general ward at the Liverpool Maternity Hospital on October 9, 1940, John initially lived in his mother's tiny terraced house on Newcastle Road, near the now-famous Penny Lane. Again, it was the kind of place where the front door opens onto the street, but John wasn't there for long; moving, when he was five, to a distinctly middle-class area and the only privately owned home that any of The Beatles ever lived in as children.

9 Newcastle Road in Wavertree, around the corner from Penny Lane, was the modest home that John shared with his mother Julia during his earliest years. In October 2013, it sold at auction for £480,000 ($770,000).

This was "Mendips," the relatively spacious semi-detached house on Menlove Avenue in Woolton, where John lived with his Aunt Mimi and Uncle George after his parents had split up, and which was in a different league to the homes of Paul, George, and Ringo. So much for the Working Class Hero: as John's Art College friend, Bill Harry, told me in 1992, "He didn't know what it was like to live in a really tough area. I mean, Menlove Avenue?"

'Mendips' at 251 Menlove Avenue in Woolton, where John was raised by his Aunt Mimi and Uncle George. His bedroom was directly above the front door porch where, during his mid-teens, he'd play his guitar to capitalize on the reverberant sound.

Despite his genteel upbringing, young Lennon "fought all the way through Dovedale [Primary School]," and relied on his innate intelligence to get him through the eleven-plus exam. This would have qualified him for the highly respected Liverpool Institute, but Aunt Mimi instead opted for Quarry Bank Grammar School, partly because it was nearer to home, and also because it was in a nicer area than the bohemian city-center Institute location. Not that this altered her nephew's attitude.

Mosspits Lane Primary School in Wavertree, the first place to experience the academic talents of John Winston Lennon.

"I looked at the hundreds of new kids," John told Beatles biographer Hunter Davies in 1968, referring to his first day at Quarry Bank, "and thought, 'Christ, I'll have to fight my way through all this lot!'"

He never quite managed that feat, but, together with Pete Shotton, his friend from Dovedale, Lennon did cause untold mayhem. The offenses are too numerous to list here, but among some of the charges on his school reports were "insolence," "cutting class," and "throwing blackboard out of window."

John had the ability to succeed as a student, but not the initiative. During his first year at Quarry Bank he was high up in the A-stream class, but by the end of his graduation year he was 20th in the C-stream. That meant bottom of the bottom class, and things didn't improve at the College of Art.

The Family Way—Who's Who Among the Relatives

The only Beatle who had a professional musician for a parent was Paul. His father, James McCartney, had played the piano in a ragtime outfit named Jim Mac's Band during his late teens and early twenties, and his son evidently inherited Jim's ability to pick up an instrument and produce a tune.

Jim married Mary Patricia Mohinn when he was a 39-year-old cotton salesman and she was a 30-year-old nurse. Both were of Irish descent.

The following year, 1942, Paul was born, and he was followed a couple of years later by his brother Michael. Jim, meanwhile, was too old for active duty in World War II. So, when the Cotton Exchange closed, he took a day job at the engineering works and served as a firefighter at night. Next he was employed as a garbage inspector (checking up on the collectors, not the trash), and, as he was now bringing in a fairly small pay-packet, Mary paid the larger portion of the bills by becoming a midwife.

Jim and Mary ran a settled, tight-knit family home, investing it with an atmosphere that Paul would later recreate with his own wife and children. Then, one day in 1956, Mary felt pains in her chest and, after visiting the doctor, she was diagnosed with breast cancer. Within months, she was dead, and Jim, Paul, and Michael were devastated.

While Jim managed to support the household on his meager wage, Paul found solace in music. Accordingly, his dad bought him a trumpet for his birthday, but when the budding vocalist realized that he couldn't sing with the brass instrument stuck in his mouth, he traded the trumpet for a guitar.

Jim McCartney lived to see his eldest son become a world-famous superstar and his other son find British chart success as Mike McGear, lead singer with Liverpudlian novelty group, The Scaffold. Mike McCartney would subsequently publish his late-fifties, early-sixties photos of Paul and The Beatles in book form and Jim would remarry; helping new wife Angie to raise her daughter, Ruth. James McCartney died in 1976.

The two other Beatle dads to remarry did so after deserting and divorcing a pair of Beatle mums. One of these was Ringo's father, Richard Starkey, who married Elsie Gleave in 1936 when they were both working at a bakery. He was 24, she was 22, and four years later Richy was born. Three years after that, the elder Richard was out the door, and his son would subsequently see him on just a handful of occasions.

Elsie, one of 14 children, was accustomed to poverty, and to make ends meet she worked as a barmaid while Grandma Starkey often looked after young Richy. Then, when her son was 12, Elsie married Londoner Harry Graves, a painter and decorator who immediately hit it off with the only child and bought him his first drum kit. Both Harry and Elsie would be around to witness Ringo's fame and fortune; appearing in the photographs of his 1965 wedding to Maureen Cox.

The other deserter-divorcee Beatle dad was Alfred Lennon. The son of an Irishman named Jack who had toured America as a Kentucky minstrel, Alf had been orphaned at the age of five. Ten years later, while he was an office boy, he met John's mother, Julia Stanley. That was in 1928, and they would continue to see each other on and off for the next ten years. The reason for the off periods was that in 1929 Alf went to sea, initially working as a waiter. He sometimes sang on board and, according to him, taught Julia to play the banjo during one of his visits home.

In December 1938, the two of them married and a couple of years later John was born. Nevertheless, Alf continued to sail the seven seas and, while he was away, Julia did play. An outgoing, free-spirited soul, she enjoyed the company of men and therefore handed the responsibility of raising John to her far more upstanding sister Mimi and brother-in-law George Smith.

When John was five, Alf returned home and tried to save his faltering marriage. This attempt quickly failed, so the boy's parents then discussed who should have custody of the child and, after Julia won the day, she promptly handed John back to Mimi and George. Mimi was a strict, no-nonsense woman, and with Julia only making the odd visit from her home in nearby Springwood, things ran fairly smoothly for John until Uncle George died in 1952. (It was this gentle man who bought John his first musical instrument, the harmonica.)

1 Blomfield Road in Allerton, the home that Julia shared with her boyfriend John Dykins, nicknamed 'Twitchy' by John due to his facial tic. It was here that, while waiting for Julia to return from visiting Mimi, John and Twitchy learned that she'd been killed in a road accident.

Thereafter, Julia began to show up more often at Mendips, and John would also visit her at the Blomfiield Road home that she shared with John Dykins who, due to a facial tic, was charmingly nicknamed "Twitchy" by the increasingly unruly teenager. Teaching her son to play the banjo, Julia also encouraged him to be more rebellious like her. The two of them shared the same disdain for authority and offbeat sense of humor, and although Mimi disapproved of the unsettling influence that her sister had on John—often allowing him to stay home from school—the problem was massively compounded when Julia was killed in a road accident on July 15, 1958. A car driven by an off-duty policeman knocked Julia down as she walked across Menlove Avenue after visiting Mimi. John never really recovered from the loss.

Menlove Avenue, as viewed from 'Mendips.' After visiting her sister Mimi on the evening of July 15, 1958, John's mother Julia crossed one half of the road en route to a nearby bus stop, and she was then struck and killed by a car when stepping from the central reservation to cross the other half.

Alf, meanwhile, was off on his travels, and after 20 years he made his grand return. By then, of course, John was a famous Beatle and his father was washing dishes in a hotel not far from the younger Lennon's upscale home in Weybridge, just outside of London. Looking like a hobo, Alf turned up on John's doorstep one day and tried to angle for some cash. At the same time, he told a tale of misery and woe to the national newspapers and, wouldn't you know it, was quickly hustled into a studio to record a lousy song titled, "That's My Life (My Love and My Home)." It bombed and John's embarrassment was complete, as was his resentment. Despite initially appearing to patch things up with the man he'd later refer to as "The Ignoble Alf," John revisited his childhood pain during an intensive course of "primal scream" therapy and subsequently shocked and scared his father by unleashing all of his bottled-up anger in a scathing verbal attack.

By then, 56 year-old Alf had married 19 year-old Pauline Jones, and in 1969 they had a son, David Henry Lennon. John bought them a home and set them up with a modest weekly allowance. Four years later, Robin Francis Lennon was born, but when John died in December 1980 he had still never met his seven-year-old half-brother. Alf passed away on April 1 (April Fools' Day), 1976. For her part, Mimi outlived them all, dying on December 5, 1991, at the age of 88.

And so we arrive at the happy Harrisons, for at least George didn't suffer any of the childhood traumas that his fellow Beatles experienced. Indeed, among all of the Beatle parents and guardians, his mother Louise was the only one to really support the whole notion of a musical career for her teenage son, and so it was often a case of "Let's go over to George's" when the pre-fame Beatles needed a place to rehearse.

Yet another Fab Four relative with Irish blood in the veins, Louise French was a greengrocer's assistant when she met Harold Harrison in 1929. He was a steward in the merchant navy, and they were married the following year. In 1931, their first child, Louise, was born, and three years later came a son, Harold. Peter, born in 1940, just under three years before George, was in the same class as John Lennon at Dovedale Primary School.

Harry senior left the navy in 1936 and, after being out of a job for 15 months, he became a bus conductor, taking the passengers' money and handing out the tickets. Then, in 1938, he actually got to drive the bus. Years later, when George was fantasizing about what he would do with his money if he became famous, he vowed to buy his dad his own bus...

That little ambition was never realized, but both parents did have the satisfaction of seeing their youngest kid make it to the top of the showbiz tree. Louise, who had sprung for her son's first guitar, died in July 1970, but her husband visited the United States during George's 1974 concert tour and even accompanied him to see President Gerald Ford at the White House. Harry, Sr. died in May 1978.

Country Gentleman

"This is one of the images for which I myself did some modeling. George's face was adapted from a Dezo Hoffman photo, but that's my arm and my body. George's hand and his guitar were taken from a totally different photo of him, and so, even though there are no bolts in his neck, this is a prime example of 'Frankensteining.'

"That said, the painting is less about the composition than about the color palate. I used a more muted brown to portray George as the 'Quiet Beatle'—not brooding, but a 'Dark Horse' who was a subtle force in the group, playing a huge role that was vital to its existence. I wanted the palate to speak to that."

– Eric Cash

Chapter 7

Long Distance Information—Early Influences

In the decades before TV took over as a multi-purpose medium, radio was king. A lot of people got their entertainment and up-to-the-minute information by way of the "wireless," as it was then known, and John, Paul, George, and Ringo were no exceptions.

That well-known Beatle sense of humor came about partly because of the radio comedians they listened to as kids. At the same time, it was also via the airwaves that they first heard the strains of rock 'n' roll. In this chapter you'll learn about some of the personalities The Beatles idolized during the 1950s, as well as the effect these people had on our Fab heroes. Next, I'll explain the skiffle music craze that swept Britain in 1956 and 1957. Lastly, I'll reveal how The Beatles came to know all the songs they covered during the early part of their career; not just the golden oldies, but also the numbers from the 1950s and early-sixties that they didn't write, but which you probably don't recall hearing elsewhere.

From Luxembourg to The Goons—Radio in the Fifties

None of The Beatles' families were exactly made of money; food, clothing, and roofs over their heads were the first priorities, and after that everything else was a bonus. Public transport was often a necessity and TV sets were a definite luxury, but one commodity that found its way into all of their homes was the radio.

For George and Ringo, that radio probably consisted of a small wooden box with a pair of twiddly knobs, a cloth-covered speaker, and a large tuning dial. Over at the McCartney household things were a little more up-market, with Jim accommodating his sons by rigging up the radio to two pairs of headphones in their bedroom. Meanwhile, at Mendips, John would sit in his bedroom listening to the flashy radiogram located in the living room downstairs. This was achieved by way of an extension speaker connected to a wire running down the staircase.

John would sit in his room for hours, reading the *Just William* series of mischievous-schoolboy books by Richmal Crompton, Lewis Carroll novels such as *Alice in Wonderland*, and the writings of Balzac. At other times he would shout out, "Change the program on the wireless, Mimi," and have her tune the radio to *Up the Pole*, featuring British vaudeville-style comedians Jimmy Jewel and Ben Warris, the thriller serial *Dick Barton, Special Agent*, or his all-time favorite, *The Goon Show*.

Showcasing the talents of Peter Sellers, Spike Milligan, Harry Secombe, and, on occasion, Michael Bentine, *The Goon Show* was an inspiration to millions of Brits, both old and young alike. Certainly, its outrageous characters, way-out scenarios, and anarchic humor were a revelation to The Beatles and others of their generation. John would often mimic the characters' voices, but neither he nor Paul, George, or Ringo could have ever dreamed of one day collaborating with the man behind some of Sellers' and Milligan's comedy records: Beatles' producer George Martin.

Another influence on John, both in terms of his humor and his penchant for word play, was comedian Stanley Unwin, who almost created his own language by transforming English into gobbledygook. It's important to highlight this, because later on such influences would be evident in John's books of poetry and nonsense prose, *In His Own Write* and *A Spaniard in the Works*, as well as in the words to several of his songs. As a lyricist, John Lennon was far and away the most imaginative and creative of The Beatles.

Meanwhile, all four guys got their first taste of rock 'n' roll via the airwaves, and that's where Radio Luxembourg came in. During the mid-fifties, the only British channels that most people tuned into were those of the government-controlled British Broadcasting Corporation. The BBC may have produced some classic comedy shows, but the "popular" music they transmitted was basically what the adults wanted to hear: "easy listening," all the way from Vera Lynn to Frankie Laine. No way would there be any of that new-fangled rock nonsense, because many adults didn't even regard it as music.

So, what to do? Well, if you turned that dial really carefully to 208 meters at night, you could just about pick up the pop sounds being broadcast from the tiny European state of Luxembourg. The reception was poor and the sound faded in and out, but the music captivated the people who really mattered in terms of future record sales: the kids.

It was on Radio Luxembourg that John, Paul, George, and Ringo almost certainly heard Elvis Presley's "Heartbreak Hotel" for the first time, and after that nothing was the same again, either for themselves or for the world around them.

Strawberry Field, the Salvation Army children's home in Woolton, around the corner from 'Mendips,' where John attended summer garden parties and played with his friends as a child, and which later lent its name to his composition 'Strawberry Fields Forever.'

Rock 'n' Roll—Grow Those Sideburns!

As children, The Beatles were raised on the music of their parents' generation and those before them. All they knew, it was pleasant enough, but then came the first flourishes of rock 'n' roll in the form of Bill Haley and His Comets. The use of his smash-hit recording, "Rock Around the Clock," over the opening credits of the 1955 juvenile delinquency picture, *Blackboard Jungle*, immediately aligned Haley's rhythmic, jazz-based music with rebellious youth. The same, however, couldn't be said for Haley's appearance—a chubby man in a plaid sports jacket with hair that was styled into an old-fashioned "kiss-curl" at the front, he didn't inspire the pre-Fab Four to follow in his footsteps.

Instead, Elvis Presley started the ball rolling and his legion of teenage disciples—including John, Paul, George, and Ringo—ran with it. At the same time, courtesy of their talents, their music, and the sexual innuendo inherent in many of the songs they performed, many other rock artists had a major impact on The Beatles during these formative years. Among them were Fats Domino—whose "I'm In Love Again" was the first rock 'n' roll record that George Harrison recalled hearing—as well as Eddie Cochran, Carl Perkins, Gene Vincent, and non-rock acts such as Ray Charles. The list goes on and on, but following are some of the main artists who influenced The Beatles, along with the major reasons for that influence.

Elvis Presley

The King. The teenage messiah. The guy who lit The Beatles' fuse. Elvis had the sound, the look, the hip clothes, the stage moves—the whole nine yards as far as John, Paul, George, and Ringo were concerned.

When, around May 1956, they each heard the strains of "Heartbreak Hotel" coming out of their radios, it was like a call to arms. I mean, who was this guy, his voice swamped in echo, singing as if he were stuck in the most desolate place on earth? "Waaall, since ma baybeh left me, ah foun' a noo place to dwell..." Yeah, down at the end of some lonely street—not near the Liverpool docks, but probably in the darkest recesses of the singer's mind. Stacked up against the likes of Perry Como telling people to "catch a falling star and put it in your pocket," this was pretty heavy stuff.

Many people assumed Elvis was black. None of the popular white artists would ever have the nerve to sing like that, communicating that kind of emotional pain. This guy knew what it was like to feel lonely, to feel angry, to feel depressed. So did plenty of caucasian kids living in an environment where parents and teachers made the rules, but they could never translate their frustrations into music. No, he had to be black. Then they saw his picture—in a magazine, on a poster, somewhere—and they were hit with culture shock number two: he was *white*. What's more, he was white with plenty of attitude—hair slicked back into a DA, long sideburns like a truck driver, top lip curled into a sneer that said, "Go hang yourself," and moody, heavy-lidded eyes that invited all of womanhood into his bed.

When Elvis sang "Good Rockin' Tonight," his suggestive phrasing alluded to more than just a spot of dancing. And when he belted out the lyrics to "Hound Dog," it was with a venom and a spirit that were completely liberating. Almost instantly, kids all around Britain began styling their hair like his, wearing flashy clothes (or, at least, what they considered to be flashy clothes), taking an insolent attitude toward adults, and trying to play a musical instrument. Among them were the teen Lennon, McCartney, Harrison, and Starkey.

While taking the Western world by storm, Elvis also laid the foundations for those who would succeed him.

Chuck Berry

Although Elvis served as the future Beatles' main inspiration, he wasn't quite the complete package. He sang brilliantly, he looked fantastic, and he delivered great songs, but he didn't actually write them. That task was taken care of by professional composers, some of them specially commissioned, yet other artists coming onto the scene also wrote their own material, and this kind of self-sufficiency really appealed to the young Lennon and McCartney.

At the top of that particular tree was one Charles Edward Berry from St. Louis, Missouri. Chuck, as he was known, was one of the few African American performers to get across to white teenage audiences during the 1950s, and he did so largely on the strength of a charismatic stage demeanor (enhanced by his trademark "duck walk"); his distinctive, rocking, and widely imitated guitar licks; his infectious tunes, and his ingenious lyrics.

"Maybellene," "Roll Over Beethoven," "Johnny B. Goode," "Sweet Little Sixteen," "Memphis Tennessee," "Brown Eyed Handsome Man"—each featured witty, sometimes acerbic words and, thanks to the uncluttered instrumentals and Berry's clear vocal delivery, listeners could actually understand them.

The subject matter often dealt with young love and teen rebellion, and it did so in a poetic style that particularly appealed to John Lennon. In fact, if any one aspect of Chuck Berry's tremendous influence should be highlighted, then it's the way he introduced a more sophisticated and disciplined form of lyricism to rock music. At the same time, he also inspired the likes of Lennon and McCartney to write their own songs and become a self-contained unit.

Buddy Holly

Whereas Elvis Presley had looks to die for, Buddy Holly gave Joe Average a sense of hope. As Paul McCartney stated, "Suddenly, here was a rock and roll hero who had glasses."

That's right: black, horn-rimmed glasses that near-sighted John Lennon normally only wore in private. And they sat on a face that belonged more to your next-door neighbor than some matinee idol. Yet, that was part of the Holly charm—the everyman who proved talent alone could sometimes be enough.

Charles Harden Holley—he dropped the "e" as part of his stage name—had plenty of ability, and he used it to help craft some of the late-fifties' best pop songs; catchy melodies with a driving beat such as "Rave On," "Peggy Sue," and "Maybe Baby"; simple teen ballads like "Everyday"; and, toward the end of his tragically short career, the melodic string arrangements of "True Love Ways" and "It Doesn't Matter Anymore."

When Buddy and his band, The Crickets, appeared on British TV's *Sunday Night at the London Palladium* in 1957, thousands of budding Brit rockers paid close attention to his solid-bodied, ultra-modern-looking Fender Stratocaster guitar. It would help inspire a craze for the instrument that lasts to this day. Holly died in a plane crash at age 22 on February 3, 1959, yet this only heightened his popularity, especially in Britain. The Beatles' name would be a play on that of the insect-like Crickets, and they would cover his songs—their earliest known recording is a 1958 rendition of "That'll Be the Day" (on *Anthology 1*). During the 1970s, Paul actually acquired the publishing rights to Buddy's music, and in 1976 his "Buddy Holly Week" celebrations became an annual tradition in the U.K.

The Preacher and The Killer: Little Richard and Jerry Lee Lewis

Two men—one black, one white, both from the American South, both innately religious, yet compelled to perform "the devil's music." The wild guys of early rock 'n' roll, Little Richard and Jerry Lee Lewis left a lasting impression on the soon-to-be-Fab Four by way of their onstage energy and dynamic hit records.

Richard Penniman, from Macon, Georgia, honed his rasping gospel style singing in church choirs, and this helped electrify songs such as "Tutti Frutti," "Good Golly Miss Molly," "The Girl Can't Help It," "Rip It Up," "Ready Teddy," "Lucille," and "Long Tall Sally." Likewise, his live performances set audiences on fire. White crooners such as Pat Boone had far greater chart success than Richard did with his own songs; recording insipid, toned-down versions that were more acceptable to—and therefore encouraged by—many white parents. Fortunately, The Beatles and their British peers never paid attention to them. It was Richard's, not Pat's version of "Long Tall Sally" that they emulated onstage and on record, and in 1962 they also shared Liverpool and Hamburg concert bills with the Man from Macon. Richard would subsequently take credit for teaching Paul McCartney to sing the high-pitched "ooohs" that can be heard on Beatles tracks such as "She Loves You."

Louisiana's Jerry Lee Lewis, meanwhile, was definitely not in the Pat Boone mold. A one-time student minister, Jerry Lee displayed an arrogance and aggression never previously seen in a white performer. Combining raucous, country-flavored vocals with manic, boogie-style piano playing, "The Killer" tore his way through songs such as "Whole Lotta Shakin' Goin' On" and "Great Balls of Fire," leaving listeners and concertgoers almost more exhausted than he was.

As John Lennon asserted in 1970, "There is nothing conceptually better than rock and roll. No group, be it Beatles, Dylan, or [the] Stones has ever improved on 'Whole Lotta Shakin',' for my money."

The Everly Brothers

Don and Phil, from Brownie, Kentucky, were always more country than rock. However, during the late 1950s and very early-sixties their tight, widely acclaimed vocal harmonies made them one of the most important acts in the early evolution of rock 'n' roll.

A string of perfectly produced pop hits, including "Bye Bye Love," "Wake Up Little Susie," "All I Have to Do is Dream," and "Cathy's Clown," had a major impact on fledgling artists on both sides of the Atlantic. These ranged from Simon and Garfunkel to Lennon and McCartney, who all learned a thing or two listening to how the Everlys' voices blended so perfectly with each other. Just listen to any of the above-mentioned Everly Brothers hits and then play The Beatles' recordings of "If I Fell" and "Baby's in Black."

So, there it is—the demeanor of Elvis Presley, the lyricism of Chuck Berry, the commercial appeal of Buddy Holly, the unbridled energy of Little Richard and Jerry Lee Lewis, and the vocal harmonizing of The Everly Brothers. These were some of The Beatles' major musical influences—but not all of them.

All Fingers and Thumbs—The Skiffle Boom

At around the same time that rock 'n' roll swept Britain in early 1956, a similar form of music came along and simplified the task of forming a band for cash-strapped British teenagers. For that matter, it also did the same for *talent*-strapped British teenagers.

Skiffle was really an amalgam of American jazz, blues, and folk music, and it had been surfacing in various guises for quite some time. The reason money and skill weren't of paramount importance is that band members only needed a cheap acoustic guitar ("guaranteed not to split"), and a bunch of items that were still common in households across Britain during the 1950s: thimbles, a broom handle, a length of string, and a tea-chest.

One musician, wearing thimbles on the fingers and thumb of one hand, would run these up and down the washboard in order to create a percussive rhythm. Meanwhile, the broom handle would be poked through a hole in the upturned tea-chest, and the cord attached between the two, in order to create a crude imitation of an upright bass, known in this case as a "tea-chest bass." As for the guitar: "Skiffle King" Lonnie Donegan had a basic three-chord style, but even that wasn't important. For most newcomers, the instrument was little more than a prop.

So, that was the core of the skiffle band—guitar, percussion, bass—and then, if money was growing on trees, the lineup could be augmented with drums, an accordion, a ukulele, you name it.

In January 1956, the Lonnie Donegan Skiffle Group's recording of the old Huddie "Leadbelly" Ledbetter blues song, "Rock Island Line," entered the British charts and took the teen scene by storm. Other acts quickly followed in Donegan's wake: among them, Tommy Steele, The Vipers Skiffle Group, and the Chas McDevitt Skiffle Group featuring Nancy Whiskey.

The real skiffle craze only lasted about 18 months or so, from the start of 1956 until the latter part of 1957. Yet, during that relatively short time, more than 5,000 such groups came into existence around Britain, several hundred of which were in Liverpool, and one of which—The Quarry Men—instigated the events responsible for you reading this book.

Back in the U.S.A.—Imported Records

The previously-mentioned "Cunard Yanks"—sailors who, in the old days, used to spend their time traveling between Liverpool and the United States—also played a role in The Beatles' story. Some of the American records that they brought back to Merseyside were by less-than-mainstream artists: bluesmen such as Muddy Waters and Big Bill Broonzy; country guitarists like Chet Atkins and Jimmie Rodgers; and, as the 1950s turned into the sixties, the acts out of Detroit who were recording for a small, independent label named Tamla Motown.

Many of those records were sold or passed around, and among the teens who either heard or laid their hands on them were the pre-Fab Four. Atkins and Rodgers were subsequently big influences on George's guitar playing and he often sounded more comfortable when dealing with country material, as evidenced by his consummate solo work on *Beatles for Sale*, the group's most country-flavored album.

At the same time, Ringo was a huge fan of C&W artists such as Gene Autry, Hank Williams, and a couple of singer-songwriters whose compositions he recorded (and sang lead vocals on) with The Beatles: Buck Owens and Carl Perkins. In interviews, John Lennon alluded to

Perkins' influence in the fields of both country and rock 'n' roll, with "Sure to Fall (In Love with You)"—which the Fab Four perform on *both* volumes of BBC live recordings—and "Matchbox" (on their *Long Tall Sally* EP) as respective examples of each genre. John also cited Hank Williams' "Honky Tonk Blues" as a favorite of his while admitting that he could never quite achieve the unique Williams yodeling effect.

The artists mentioned in this chapter comprise just a tiny fraction of the recorded talent that The Beatles were exposed to during their pre-fame days, but here's the point: despite their inability to read or write music, John, Paul, George, and Ringo had a pretty comprehensive musical education. They breathed in the sounds and the feel of all the different influences that came their way and, when they exhaled, the result was a remarkable depth and variety to their work, both as composers and as performers.

Furthermore, there were the songs of other artists that The Beatles chose to record on their earlier albums. These were often lesser-known B-sides of singles or just tracks that many fans were plain unfamiliar with. "Anna (Go to Him)" by Arthur Alexander, "Chains" by The Cookies, "Devil in Her Heart" (originally "Devil in His Heart") by The Donays, "Bad Boy" by Larry Williams—none were massive hits. Yet, The Beatles' had the ability to creatively interpret such material for performances that were often better than the originals.

The Introduction

"We don't have any pictures of Lennon and McCartney's first meeting at the St. Peter's Church fete on July 6 1957, but the famous photo that Geoff Rhind took of The Quarry Men that day shows us what they were wearing, and Jim O'Donnell's book The Day John Met Paul *provides us with a moment-by-moment account of what happened. The TV film* In His Life: The John Lennon Story *also depicts the scene inside the actual church hall, so I combined all that information with what I learned from a 2007 interview that I did with the surviving members of The Quarry Men to come up with this painting.*

"They told me they were just hanging around, waiting for the next show, and like many musicians they probably gravitated toward the piano. It was late in the afternoon, hence the long shadows, and I painted the scene as a sort of homage to the artist Norman Rockwell, who's been a big influence on me. Without a photo, I couldn't go for photo-real, but I did find some 1962 shots in which John and Paul were standing in the positions I wanted. So, I turned back the clock on them, making them both younger and Paul a little chubbier in the face. Then again, there aren't many photos of Ivan Vaughan, who introduced them to one another, but an out-of-focus black-and-white snap of him happened to be perfect for what I needed.

"Like Rockwell, I hired models; in this case, teenagers who posed as the band members while I spent about an hour photographing them and capturing their body language. That painting took me a year to complete, and it wasn't until I met The Quarry Men in 2007 that I added some of the finer details while also employing a little artistic license to achieve the desired end result. For example, it has been contended that John and Paul met on the stairs leading to the stage, but although it's possible they spoke there, I just couldn't imagine the other teenagers all sitting on those stairs to witness what happened when Paul first walked in. So, I went with what I believed and what I'd heard from everyone else in order to piece together the puzzle.

"I had to be constantly aware of the story I was trying to tell. We see teacups and cigarette butts, and it looks like the band members have been there for awhile. Paul, on the other hand, is the only one wearing a jacket and his guitar is still on his back, illustrating that he's just shown up. What's more, the painting's composition has all of the Quarry Men overlapping each other, signifying that they're together, whereas Paul is off to the side and separate from them. The guitar in the foreground, leaning against the table, is once again an homage to Rockwell, providing the feeling that we could have been there, too. It gives us perspective and puts us in the picture, and although it was a huge challenge I had a lot of fun doing it."

– Eric Cash

Chapter 8

The Pre-Beatles—Thinking of Linking

Imagine going to see one or more of The Beatles perform at your local church or social club, and watching them do so with cheap or battered instruments. Well, everyone has to start somewhere, and there was a time when our not-yet-Fab heroes would take any gigs that were offered to them. Sometimes there were a few hundred people in attendance, sometimes only a handful, but they all shared one thing in common: an inability to realize they were witnessing the birth of a phenomenon that would forever change the course of popular music. Those earliest efforts were nothing to write home about, but they were the vital starting point.

In this chapter, we'll take a look at how John, Paul, and George each started playing music, how they met, and how they joined forces. These three were the nucleus of The Beatles; as Ringo didn't enter the picture until a bit later, we'll get to him in a later chapter. The story began a full six years before the band rose to national prominence and seven years before it arrived in the U.S. During that time its members really struggled for their success and, in spite of what the media said when Beatlemania finally exploded, they were certainly not *overnight* sensations.

Quarry Men, Old Before Our Birth

Although John Lennon's life turned around the moment he heard Elvis Presley sing "Heartbreak Hotel" in May 1956, it wasn't until the following year that he actually did something about it. First, he persuaded Aunt Mimi to shell out £17 (equal to about $50) for an acoustic guitar. Then he turned to his mother, Julia—who he was now beginning to see more often—for instruction on how to play it. The fact that she taught him banjo chords didn't seem to matter at that point. He practiced relentlessly and drove Mimi so crazy that she would banish him to the front porch of their house. There he could strum tunelessly to his heart's content.

Next, in March 1957, John teamed up with his best friend, Pete Shotton, to form a skiffle group named The Black Jacks. That lasted for all of a week before they morphed into The Quarry Men in recognition of their school, Quarry Bank High, and its song containing the line, "Quarry Men, old before our birth." Friends and acquaintances soon joined the lineup—John on guitar and vocals, Pete on washboard, Rod Davis on banjo, Eric Griffiths on guitar, Colin Hanton on drums, and Bill Smith, Len Garry, Ivan Vaughan, and Nigel Whalley all taking turns on tea-chest bass.

The first proper rehearsal took place in Eric Griffiths' house, after which the location shifted to the upstairs bathroom at the home of John's ever-encouraging mother, Julia. Although a few engagements were quickly secured, they largely consisted of parties and school dances. Nevertheless, by the start of June, with barely three months of experience under their belts, The Quarry Men felt ready for the big time.

Caroll Levis was then the host of a popular talent show on British TV, and in order to discover budding jugglers, magicians, singers, sword-swallowers, or whoever, he would run *Star Search* shows up and down the country. A preliminary audition took place at Liverpool's prestigious Empire Theatre on June 9, 1957, and among the long list of hopefuls were The Quarry Men, but the try-out didn't lead to their inclusion on the short list of qualifiers for the finals.

At this point, fame and fortune didn't exactly come knocking on their door (or even make it to the sidewalk), but John and his fellow band members stuck with it. A couple of weeks later, on June 22, they performed atop a stationary coal truck at an outdoor party in Roseberry Street, Liverpool 8. Everything was going fine until a couple of local thugs decided that, instead of listening to the music, they should "get that Lennon." John's loudmouth reputation preceded him, and this meant that, after the gig, he and several other Quarry Men took refuge in the party organizer's house. They were then given a police escort to the nearby bus stop.

Such were the risks of being famous. Next up: a nondescript gig at a local church...

St. Peter's Church in Woolton where, on Saturday, July 6, 1957, Paul first saw John perform with The Quarry Men and, after being introduced to him, made enough of an impression to be asked to join the band.

A Fateful Church Fete—John Meets Paul

St. Peter's Parish Church in Woolton isn't far from the Menlove Avenue home where John grew up. On Saturday, July 6, 1957, its annual garden fete/party took place in the field behind the church, attended by several hundred people who were there to see the crowning of the local Rose Queen, as well as a parade featuring boy scouts, girl guides, youth club members, and kids in fancy dress. Throughout the afternoon, musical entertainment was provided by the Band of the Cheshire Yeomanry and by "the popular Quarry Men Skiffle Group," the engagement having been secured by Pete Shotton's mother.

The lineup on that sunny summer afternoon featured John on guitar and vocals, Pete on washboard, Eric Griffiths on guitar, Len Garry on bass, Rod Davis on banjo, and Colin Hanton on drums, while the audience included a couple of notable observers. One was Aunt Mimi who, apparently, had been unaware of the band's existence until she heard their sound blasting through the refreshment tent as she sipped her tea. Looking toward the field to figure out where all the noise was coming from, she saw a group onstage, including John and "that Shotton" (as she would warmly refer to him).

John and Mimi had argued that morning over his Teddy Boy appearance (comprising an Elvis hairdo and clothes reminiscent of an Edwardian dandy, including a long drape jacket, tapered trousers, and crepe-soled shoes). Now, as he saw his aunt approaching, John began ad-libbing the words to the song that he was singing: "Mimi's coming... Uh-oh, Mimi's coming down the path..."

In The Quarry Men's repertoire that day were numbers such as Elvis's "Baby, Let's Play House"; the traditional Liverpool number "Maggie May," which had recently been popularized by The Vipers Skiffle Group; Lonnie Donegan's "Cumberland Gap," "Railroad Bill," and "Putting on the Style"; and The Del-Vikings' "Come Go with Me." Incredibly, an amateur recording of two of those July 6, 1957 performances—"Baby, Let's Play House" and "Putting on the Style"—would later surface.

John's rendition of "Come Go with Me" particularly caught the attention of the other notable observer on that fateful afternoon: 15-year-old Paul McCartney. Standing next to Liverpool Institute schoolmate Ivan Vaughan, Paul was intrigued by John's substitution of the song's barely decipherable second line, "Please don't send me 'way beyond the sea," with the more bluesy, somewhat confusing "Down, down, down to the penitentiary." Paul also couldn't help noticing that the few chords John played looked a little strange—hardly surprising since they were the banjo chords that Julia had taught him. So, even though Paul was blown away by the charismatic, 16-year-old Teddy Boy group leader, he also probably viewed John as a more rudimentary guitarist, and this played no small part in the events that followed.

Having already tried his hand at the piano and his mouth at the trumpet, Paul had focused on the guitar after going to a Lonnie Donegan concert at the Liverpool Empire the previous November. Now, as Ivan Vaughan introduced him to The Quarry Men while they set up for the evening dance inside the church hall, Paul picked up a guitar and displayed his virtuosity. He played one of John's favorite contemporary hits, Eddie Cochran's "Twenty Flight Rock," and impressed everyone with not only his adept performance, but also his knowledge of the words. John was lousy at memorizing lyrics and grateful when Paul wrote down those to not only "Twenty Flight Rock," but also Gene Vincent's "Be Bop A-Lula." Next, his gratitude turned to pure (if concealed) admiration when Paul showed him and Eric Griffiths another trick he had up his sleeve: how to tune a guitar. (Until then, John and Eric had been paying someone to do this for them.)

Quit while you're on top—always sound advice, and that's exactly what Paul did. He walked out of the church hall that evening and left John Winston Lennon impressed but confused. After all, what should he do? Improve the band but threaten his own supremacy by recruiting someone who was, at the very least, his equal in the talent department? Or should he just hang onto his unrivaled leadership?

A couple of weeks later, Pete Shotton happened to meet Paul while cycling in Woolton. There and then he asked him on behalf of John and the group if he'd like to join. After weighing his options and giving it some serious thought (for about five seconds), Paul accepted the offer. However, although he began rehearsing regularly with The Quarry Men from July onward, he didn't make his concert debut with them for another three months. It was at Liverpool's New Clubmoor Hall on October 18, 1957, that Paul played lead guitar onstage for the first and only time. Thereafter, he was relegated to rhythm. The reason? First-night nerves that caused him to fluff his long-awaited solo during a rendition of "Guitar Boogie."

Play "Raunchy" for Me—George Jumps on Board

Soon after Paul joined The Quarry Men, things began to change. For one thing, the professional bookings became more frequent and a little more prestigious (even if one of the venues was a slaughterhouse). For another, the demise of skiffle just happened to coincide with the departure of several band members.

The Quarry Men now comprised John, Paul, Eric Griffiths, Len Garry, and Colin Hanton, with John "Duff" Lowe sometimes sitting in on piano. Then, on February 6, 1958, they encountered a 14-year-old school friend of Paul's at a gig they played in the suburb of Garston. His name was George Harrison.

To 17-year-old John, George was little more than "a kid." However, afterwards, while they were taking a ride on the top deck of a late-night bus, John's eyes were drawn toward the flashy guitar that George had "coincidentally" brought along with him. Egged on by Paul, George performed "Raunchy," an instrumental that he was adept at playing on the bass strings. Again, John was suitably impressed, and thereafter he constantly teased his gaunt-looking admirer by saying, "Come on, George. Give us 'Raunchy'," aware that, no matter where they were, the young guitarist would oblige.

George was not the most natural of musicians, but he worked hard at his craft. He and his brother Peter had taken up the guitar at about the same time, and together they had formed a skiffle group named The Rebels whose only gig was at the British Legion Club near their home in Speke. Meanwhile, on their bus journeys to and from school each day, George and Paul became increasingly friendly due to their shared passion for the guitar. They even practiced together in the bathroom of the Harrison home, and that's precisely what The Quarry Men began to do soon afterwards.

George's hero worship of John irritated the chief Quarry Man. Still, the kid did have a great guitar, undoubted technical ability, and a convenient place to rehearse, so his persistence soon paid off. Eric Griffiths was unceremoniously bumped from the lineup and George Harrison took his place.

The Pre-Fab Three

Sometime in the spring of 1958, John, Paul, George, Colin Hanton, and John Lowe made what could loosely be described as the first ever Beatles recordings. I say *loosely*, because two of those participants would soon play no further part in the group's musical ventures. And besides, they were still named The Quarry Men. However, three of the Fab Four were now firmly in place, forming the nucleus of the band we've known for all these years.

Turning up at the home studio of an old Liverpudlian named Percy Phillips, the five young guys parted with a small amount of money in return for the privilege of taping two songs: Buddy Holly's "That'll Be the Day" and a Harrison-McCartney composition titled "In Spite of All the Danger." John sang lead on both recordings, and these were then transferred to a two-sided shellac disc. Percy Phillips wiped the tape, but John Lowe held onto the disc, and in 1981 he sold it to Paul McCartney for a tidy sum. 14 years later the two cuts would be included on the CD set, *Anthology 1*.

So, even though he hadn't written either song, John Lennon still asserted himself as the head honcho and took care of the lead vocals. That practice didn't last much longer, and neither did the Quarry Men careers of Messrs. Lowe and Hanton. Len Garry had already vacated the bass player's position thanks to a bout with meningitis, and John Lowe was never a full-time member anyway. Colin Hanton, on the other hand, may not have been Liverpool's greatest drummer, but he did have an expensive kit, so he lasted until the spring or early summer of 1958. Then a drunken row after a gig ensured that he wouldn't see John, Paul, or George ever again.

In October 1958, drummer-less, bass-less, and, in John's case, guitar-less (after heavy-handed playing had demolished his cheap Gallotone Champion), the trio took another shot at auditioning for the TV talent show, *Star Search*, hosted by "Mr. Star-Maker" Caroll Levis. Performing at a Manchester theater as Johnny and the Moondogs, they not only qualified for the grand final, but Johnny also found a quick solution to his lack of a musical instrument. As Paul put it in 1995, "I believe that day some unfortunate person in that theater was relieved of his guitar."

The final itself took place at the Manchester Hippodrome during the last week of November 1958, and John once again showed up without a guitar in case somebody recognized the one he had stolen. Still, far from feeling embarrassed, he subsequently stole the limelight by standing center stage and singing Buddy Holly's "Think It Over" with his arms draped around the shoulders of his strumming, harmonizing Moondogs. Being that George was right-handed and Paul left-handed, their guitar necks pointed outward, so the visual effect was pretty good. And if anyone happened to ask why there wasn't a drummer, they'd assure them, "The rhythm's in the guitars…"

Unfortunately, we will never know what the audience thought of that rhythm because John, Paul, and George didn't stick around to take a bow at the end of the show and have the crowd's applause measured by the all-important *clapometer*. Instead, the schoolboys had to leave early to catch the last train home, and their disappointment was compounded during much of 1959 when, despite a change of name to Japage 3 (as revealed by Mark Lewisohn more than five decades later in his definitive *The Beatles: All These Years, Volume One—Tune In*), the live gigs dried up.

Never slackers when it came to their music, John and Paul made the best of this fallow period by honing their songwriting skills via numbers with titles such as "I Lost My Little Girl," "Thinking of Linking," "Years Roll Along," "Too Bad About Sorrows," "Just Fun," "Keep Looking That Way," and "That's My Woman." Additionally, there were other, slightly more familiar songs: "Love Me Do," "Hello Little Girl," "The One After 909," "I'll Follow the Sun," and "When I'm Sixty-Four."

George, meanwhile, started to find alternative musical outlets, including a band named the Les Stewart Quartet. When a row between Stewart, Harrison, and bassist Ken Brown relating to an August 22, 1959 gig resulted in the group's leader canceling an engagement for the following week, Brown asked George if he knew anyone who could fill in. This was for the opening night of a new venue named the Casbah Coffee Club, located in the basement of a house owned by a go-getting woman named Mona Best. George's suggestion: how about teaming up with that modestly talented duo of Lennon and McCartney?

Ken Brown went along with the idea, and for the next four-and-a-half months the resurrected Quarry Men/Quarrymen not only had a bass guitarist but, with the weekly Casbah bookings, a regular venue in which to play. Then Ken fouled things up by having another row, this time with his new and soon-to-be-former band mates. The cause of all the unhappiness was Brown's "audacity" in accepting his share of the fee from Mrs. Best, when he had a cold one night in January 1960 and was too ill to perform. Talk about all being friends together—Paul was having none of it: no play, no pay. Ken dug his heels in—he was keeping his portion of the £3 ($8) fee and that was that, resulting in a not-so-fond farewell to Ken Brown, short-lived member of The Quarrymen.

That night, it was back to the Fab Threesome of John, Paul, and George, as well as a brief upturn in their fortunes. (Which wasn't difficult, being that they were at rock bottom.)

You Know My Name... Well, Maybe Not—Naming the Band

The Black Jacks, The Quarry Men, Johnny and the Moondogs, Japage 3—how many names, you may well ask, did those guys actually go through before they arrived at The Beatles? Well, the answer is quite a few, and now, at the risk of getting slightly ahead of ourselves in terms of the story, here's the whole shebang: the names, the relevant periods, and, where necessary, the reasoning...

- The Black Jacks: March 1957

- The Quarry Men: March 1957—November 1958

- Johnny and the Moondogs: November 1958

- Japage 3: November 1958—August 1959

Pronounced "jay-page," this was an amalgam of John, Paul, and George, although it isn't clear why the first two letters of John's name weren't used to form the name Jopage 3.

- The Quarrymen: August 1959—March 1960

- The Beatals: March 1960

It's unclear whether John Lennon or his friend Stuart Sutcliffe (who, by this time, had joined the band as bass player) concocted this name—they possibly did so together. Either way, both Paul and George would later recall meeting John and Stu at their flat in Gambier Terrace and being told that they had just come up with a great new name for the group. Basically, it was a play on that of Buddy Holly's band, The Crickets; another variety of insect, with the added bonus of misspelling the word so that it contained "Beat." From this point on, for the next few months, they toyed around with variations of the same name until settling on you-know-what.

- The Nerk Twins: April 23 & 24, 1960

During an Easter break in the south of England, John and Paul stayed and worked at the pub of Paul's cousin, Elizabeth Robbins, and her husband Mike. In return for serving behind the bar at the Fox and Hounds in Caversham, Berkshire, Lennon and McCartney were generously allowed to perform live. (Imagine that—"If you work for us, we'll permit you to give a couple of free performances.") Still, John and Paul were so desperate for any kind of musical outlet that they sat on stools, played acoustic guitars, and sang without microphones. It was Mike Robbins who named them The Nerk Twins.

- May 10—early June, 1960: The Silver Beetles

While readying themselves for an audition to back singer Billy Fury (who you'll read all about in the next chapter), the would-be Beatals were informed in no uncertain terms by a member of another local band that their name was "ridiculous." That man was Brian Cassar of Cass and the Casanovas, who went on to suggest that they call themselves something a little more logical... like Long John and the Silver Beetles. (As in Long John Silver, get it?) According to Lennon, the Long John part never made it as far as the audition, and The Silver Beetles also didn't succeed in backing Billy Fury. However, they did secure a small tour of Scotland behind the lesser-known Johnny Gentle, and for that sortie into the big time they went all out.

Paul chose the stage name of Paul Ramon because he thought it was "very exotic" and "French-sounding"; George transformed himself into Carl Harrison as a tribute to his American rockabilly idol, Carl

Perkins; and Stuart Sutcliffe became Stuart de Staël in acknowledgment of Russian painter, Nicholas de Staël. Meanwhile, even though John would later insist that he retained his own name, Paul would assert that, for the duration of the Scottish tour, the group's leader was definitely known as Long John.

- May 14, 1960: The Silver Beats

We jump backwards here to a single Liverpool engagement and a sort of aberration in the middle of being Silver Beetles. They just weren't sure about that name.

- Early/mid-June 1960: The Beatles

Could this have been inspired by the identical name of one of the gangs in the 1954 Marlon Brando/Lee Marvin biker movie, *The Wild One?* Highly unlikely, as the film was banned by the British Board of Film Censors until November 1967. Still, it's quite a coincidence.

- Mid-June—early July 1960: The Silver Beetles

One step forward, two back.

- Early July—early August 1960: The Silver Beatles

Okay, that's good... Now come on, just one more little adjustment...

- August 16, 1960—eternity: The Beatles

Chapter 9

Too Much Monkey Business

1960 really marked a turning point for The Beatles. Not only did they settle on a permanent band name, but, after an uneventful start, they also began to secure more worthwhile bookings. They undertook their first tour; started to build a local following; made their initial, arduous, exciting trip to Hamburg (in what was then West Germany); and topped things off on their return to Liverpool by experiencing their first real taste of fan mania.

More than anything, as 1960 wore on, The Beatles began to get the feeling that, just maybe, they could make a living doing all of this. Sure, there had been problems fleshing out the lineup, but by the year's end they had at last found someone who was willing and able to back them full-time on the drums, as well as a man who was prepared to kick-start their career.

Before we get to that, let's begin by taking a look at what our boys were doing (or, more to the point, *not* doing) in terms of their studies and sensible employment. It was the dawn of an exciting new decade, but only a psychic could have foreseen that these dead-end kids were going to have any sort of impact on it.

Studies and Not-So-Steady Jobs

Quarry Bank Grammar School in Allerton, where the adolescent Lennon and best buddy Pete Shotton terrorized students and teachers alike.

Back in 1957, the writing had clearly been on the wall for John Lennon in terms of his career prospects. Aunt Mimi had done her best, overseeing her nephew's studies at home and trying to pull him back into line when he misbehaved at nearby Quarry Bank High School. But then along came Elvis Presley and it was all over.

Entered for nine GCE O-level exams, John failed the lot, including art which was his best subject. (O/ordinary-level exams precede the A/ advanced-level exams required to enter British universities.) Still, in the fall of 1957, John's impressive portfolio of drawings did gain him entry to Liverpool College of Art and he immediately stood out... for all the wrong reasons. Picture the scene: arty young intellectuals, in their casual coats and chunky sweaters, mingling with a sneering, greasy-haired Teddy Boy wearing a pale blue drape jacket, tight black "drain-pipe" jeans, lilac shirt, bootlace tie, and crepe-soled shoes. Not a conventional sight in those surroundings, and neither was the Lennonish behavior that everyone had to endure. Having expected free rein to express himself with pencil and paintbrush, John quickly discovered that he had to take courses in geometry, architecture, object drawing, and lettering. Just as quickly, he gave up and spent most of his time fooling around.

The Liverpool College of Art on Hope Street, adjacent to the Liverpool Institute, where John, Paul, and George used to rehearse their music repertoire in the basement canteen. It was also here that John, dressed in full 'teddy boy' regalia, hooked up with best friend Stuart Sutcliffe, future wife Cynthia Powell, and future *Mersey Beat* editor Bill Harry, while doing his level best to flout all the rules. The building is now part of the Liverpool Institute for the Performing Arts (LIPA).

Having observed the bohemian lifestyle of fellow students Stuart Sutcliffe and Rod Murray, John soon decided that he wanted to move out of Mimi's Mendips home and into Stu's run-down room within a large Georgian house on Gambier Terrace, close to the college. Not only did Stu share John's love of art and poetry; he'd now also be able to spend more time with his girlfriend, Cynthia, and far less listening to his aunt's persistent nagging. "I feel like a baby living at home," he told Mimi, before sweetly adding, "Anyhow, I can't stand your food."

Fine—he could go. And go he did, with his full college grant. Four weeks later, he was broke and starving. The money that was supposed to last three months had already been spent, the Gambier Terrace flat was a shambles, and by the middle of winter, John, Stu, and Rod reportedly had to burn furniture in the middle of the room to keep warm.

Occasionally, when his hunger got the better of him, John would turn up on Mimi's doorstep and she would oblige with a meal that he evidently was able to tolerate. She would also plead with him to give up the guitar and concentrate on his drawing, but all to no avail. "I'll be okay," he'd say. "I don't need the bits of paper to tell me where I'm going."

Hillary Mansions on Gambier Terrace, around the corner from the art college, where struggling students/musicians John Lennon and Stu Sutcliffe shared a studio room within a large, filthy, shambolic Victorian flat that was also occupied by Rod Murray and several other students.

Where John was going was Scotland, for which he cut class in May 1960 in order to tour with The Silver Beetles. Soon afterward, having ended his course and failed his lettering exams, he felt free to do as he liked.

Paul's teen education consisted of a somewhat similar story to John's—plenty of initial promise that eventually faded. There, however, the similarity ends. Paul was always far more studious, conscientious, and better behaved than his Lennonish friend. Yet, being about 20 months younger, he also abandoned his education at an even earlier stage when things started to get interesting for The Beatles.

Having passed enough O-levels at the Liverpool Institute to study for his A-levels in English and Art, Paul didn't exactly over-extend himself in that regard. In the spring of 1960 he should have been deep in revision for the forthcoming exams. Instead, he was packing his bags for Scotland, having somehow convinced his vigilant but kindly father, Jim, that—now get this—the break would help his chances by giving his brain a rest.

The Liverpool Institute High School for Boys, attended by Paul McCartney, George Harrison and, during the same era, Paul's brother Mike, future Beatles road manager Neil Aspinall, Len Garry of The Quarry Men, and Ivan Vaughan, who introduced Paul to John shortly after the latter began 'studying' at the art college next door. Closed in 1985, the school was reopened by Paul and Mark Featherstone-Witty in 1996 as the Liverpool Institute for the Performing Arts.

After Scotland, after A-levels, the plan was still on for Paul to go to teacher training college. However, the Hamburg trip was looming and, for P McC, the offer was just too good to pass up. Once again his persuasive powers did the trick on his father, who reasoned that it would be good for his son to get this whole business "out of his system." Then he could settle down and go to college...

Meanwhile, what about George? Well, here we're really beginning to slide down the academic scale (as we head toward Ringo). George, like John, ended up with zip O-levels. George, unlike John, quit all forms of studying right there and then. (In fact, he had basically quit them long before.) That was in 1959, when Japage 3 was going through a particularly lean period.

For several months George just played his guitar whenever and wherever the opportunity arose, surviving financially with a little financial help from his hard-working dad. Then, when pressure from his father and his own sense of embarrassment resulted in George trying to get a job at the Liverpool Corporation. he failed the test. A short time later, he visited the Youth Employment Centre and was told he could work as a window dresser at Blackler's, the Liverpool department store. However, the job was gone by the time he arrived, so he was instead employed as an apprentice electrician. And there he remained... until that tour of Scotland was offered to The Silver Beetles.

This brings us to Ringo, whose education was decimated by illness, and whose first job at age 16 was as a messenger boy for British Rail. It could have been a nice, steady vocation—not too demanding, regular wage increases, two weeks vacation each year. But Richy was disgruntled. His lowly status didn't qualify him for a proper uniform, so he walked out after six weeks and tried his luck as a barman aboard a Mersey River ferry boat making regular trips between Liverpool and New Brighton. This ended in his dismissal after he apparently became confused as to whether he should be serving the drinks or consuming them, at which point stepfather Harry Graves intervened to set up Richy with what could have been another steady job for life. This was as an apprentice fitter at Hunt's engineering firm, which is where, as previously mentioned, the future Beatle joined forces with fellow apprentice, Eddie Miles, to form The Eddie Clayton Skiffle Group.

Stuart Sutcliffe: The Fifth Beatle

Several people have been referred to as "the fifth Beatle," from manager Brian Epstein and aide Neil Aspinall to record producer George Martin. New York disc jockey Murray the K latched onto the group following its February 1964 U.S. arrival and anointed *himself* "the fifth Beatle," apparently hoping some of the silver would rub off on him.

In truth, of course, John, Paul, George, and Ringo were the only Beatles who shook the world, but there was also a time when the group featured a five-man lineup by choice. (At least, John Lennon's choice.) This consisted of George on lead guitar, John and Paul on rhythm, Pete Best and various others on drums, and Stuart Sutcliffe on bass. Stu was John's closest friend at the Liverpool College of Art, and if anyone could justifiably be called "the fifth Beatle," it was Stu.

Born to Scottish parents in Edinburgh on June 23, 1940 (exactly two weeks before Ringo), Stuart Fergusson Victor Sutcliffe moved to Liverpool with his family as a toddler. From an early age, he displayed a precocious, unconventional talent for art and he was subsequently accepted into the art college before he had even reached the normal age of admittance.

In early 1959, the quiet, thoughtful, slender Sutcliffe ran into John Winston Lennon, and although the two may have appeared to be polar opposites, they were actually spiritual soulmates. Each had a passion for art and literature, especially the stream-of-consciousness writings by then-popular beat poets such as Kerouac and Ferlinghetti, which expressed their need to break free from life's constrictions.

In John, Stuart saw the literate, witty, extrovert character that he admired but could never be; in Stuart, with his arty, tight-fitting clothes, swept-back hair, dark glasses, and undeniable mystique, John saw the understated qualities that he himself admired but could never aspire to. At the same time, he also recognized a vulnerability and a sensitivity with which he could identify, in addition to a deep-rooted knowledge of art and literature that fascinated him.

The whole idea of playing in a rock 'n' roll band appealed to Stu. He possessed little innate musical ability, but the image would give even greater resonance to his artistic status and John evidently agreed. If he was the band's hard-edged rocker and Paul its handsome, romantic type, then Stu could be its James Dean: sensitive, wounded, a man of mystery.

From November 19, 1959 to January 17, 1960, the second biennial John Moores Exhibition took place at Liverpool's celebrated Walker Art Gallery. A painting submitted by Stu was among the few selected to hang there, and it made such an impression on Moores himself that, once the exhibition was over, he bought it for £65 (about $160).

Now, according to John, Paul, and George, what better way to use that hard-earned cash than to spend it on a bass guitar? Stu was quickly persuaded; instead of purchasing art materials, he invested in a Hofner President bass and joined the group. His musical skills were questionable, but he looked great, and whenever he feared being exposed onstage he'd just turn his back to the audience.

Stu skipped college to go with The Silver Beetles on their tour of Scotland, and he was with them when they made the first trip to Hamburg. Girls in the audience would swoon when he stepped up to the microphone to croon the Elvis Presley ballad, "Love Me Tender," and among them was a local photographer by the name of Astrid Kirchherr. When The Beatles returned to Liverpool toward the end of 1960, Stuart remained with Astrid in Hamburg until February '61 and was back there the following month, before The Beatles arrived to commence their second round of German concerts. By now his membership in the group was basically over. He'd occasionally join them onstage and was always around to see them perform. However, due to the other band members' merciless criticism of his playing (especially Paul's), his own lack of musical interest, and his all-consuming love for Astrid, his attentions lay elsewhere.

Stu was the first Beatle to have his hair styled into a "moptop" by Astrid. Unfortunately, he also, according to legend, received a crushing kick to the head from a local thug outside a Liverpool venue sometime in 1960. Whether or not this was the cause of his blinding headaches is not clear, but they steadily grew worse, and on April 10, 1962, Stu collapsed in the Hamburg apartment that he shared with Astrid. He had suffered a brain hemorrhage and died in her arms as an ambulance sped them to a nearby hospital. He was 21.

Unaware of the tragedy, The Beatles arrived for their third stint in Hamburg the very next day. Astrid met them at the airport and they were devastated by the news, yet the show had to go on. On April 13, Stuart's mother, Millie Sutcliffe, arrived in Hamburg to formally identify her son and take his body back to Liverpool. That night The Beatles opened at the soon-to-be legendary Star Club.

Failed Auditions: Part I

At the end of the rooftop concert that provides the finale to the Beatles documentary movie, *Let It Be*, John wryly thanks the makeshift audience and expresses his hope that the group has "passed the audition." A seemingly blasé comment, this may have been a little more pointed than most people realized because, over the years, The Beatles had their fair share of auditions and fair share of failures. A few of these have already been documented in this book and more are to follow, but among the most notable of their early try-outs was one that took place at Liverpool's Wyvern Social Club on May 10, 1960.

The Wyvern was owned by Welsh-born businessman, Allan Williams, who had recently teamed up with top British impresario, Larry Parnes, to promote an all-star concert in Liverpool. Parnes had been impressed by some of the local musical talent, and he was now interested in auditioning groups that could back his own stable of touring artists.

Thanks to Larry, these singers had been re-christened with potent stage names such as Billy Fury, Tommy Steele, Duffy Power, Marty Wilde, Georgie Fame, Lance Fortune, Vince Eager, Nelson Keene, and Dickie Pride. Fury, a native Liverpudlian whose real name was Ronald Wycherley, desperately needed a band for a nationwide tour, so Williams set up the auditions and invited many of Liverpool's top beat groups, including Derry and the Seniors, Cass and the Casanovas, and Gerry and the Pacemakers. The newly renamed Silver Beetles turned up as well, decked out in matching black shirts and pants as well as white-top shoes, yet they had a problem: Tommy Moore, who had recently been drumming with the group, still hadn't arrived when his colleagues commenced their 10-minute spot. Johnny Hutchinson of the Casanovas was therefore persuaded to sit in with them until Moore showed up halfway through, but although the boys gave it their all, this wasn't quite enough.

Allan Williams would later recall that, despite Billy Fury loving The Silver Beetles, Larry Parnes wasn't fooled by Stu Sutcliffe turning his back to them while fumbling around on bass. They could tour if they were four, but not with Stu in the lineup. John, Paul, and George flatly refused, and Parnes himself subsequently refuted this version of events, asserting that his main problem lay with 36-year-old Tommy Moore arriving late and looking way older than his four bandmates.

Either way, no backing group was found for Billy Fury on that occasion, yet The Silver Beetles were still awarded the opportunity to tour Scotland behind one of Parnes' lesser known artists, Johnny Gentle. Considering that the guys could have been asked to support an artist with a name like Fury, Steele, Power, or Wilde, the limp moniker of Gentle came as a profound disappointment. And so, for that matter, did the tour.

The Silver Beetles were each paid £18 (about $45) per week and partial expenses for the seven-engagement, nine-day jaunt, but before long they were broke, starving, disheveled, and freezing cold while crammed together inside a battered van as it zig-zagged around Scotland's northeast coast. So much for the glamorous rock 'n' roll lifestyle. By the time the tour was over, they were fed up with each other and disillusioned with the business.

The Man Who Gave it All Away: Allan Williams

Allan Richard Williams may have been, by his own admission, only a small cog in the giant wheel of The Beatles' career, yet the role that he did play was an absolutely vital one.

Aside from securing the band gigs around Liverpool, Williams was also the man who took them to Hamburg. There, among other things, they became seasoned stage performers and made a professional recording that would eventually bring them to the attention of manager Brian Epstein. Had The Beatles never visited Hamburg, there's no telling how their fortunes would have fared, and so for that reason alone they should be extremely grateful to Allan Williams...

Bumping 'n' Grinding

Of course, the entrepreneurial Williams didn't assist The Silver Beetles for charitable reasons, and why should he? He was running a small Liverpool coffee bar named the Jacaranda at the time he first set eyes on them, sitting at a corner table sharing a solitary Coke and jam *butty* (as a sandwich is often referred to on Merseyside). When things got really desperate, they agreed to redecorate the Jac's bathrooms in return for some free meals, but then Williams found the band a drummer in the shape of Tommy Moore and, after they went on the Scottish tour, he began to take them more seriously.

Through his company, Jacaranda Enterprises, Williams booked The Silver Beetles into venues on either side of the River Mersey. What's more, in return for a very generous round of Coca-Colas and plates of baked beans on toast, they'd play in the basement venue of the Jacaranda when the resident Royal Caribbean Steel Band had the night off. Not that this was the lowest point of the future Fabs' career.

In the early summer of 1960, Williams engaged them to play at the New Cabaret Artistes, yet another venue he had recently opened. The fact that the NCA was an illegal strip club meant that, in the eyes of the breathless customers, the group's performance could never match that of the artiste they were backing: a class act named Janice who insisted on exhibiting her talents to live music, not crackling records. So, once again drummerless, but with three guitars and a bass piled onto the tiny stage, John, Paul, George, and Stu gave Janice what she'd asked for—well, almost. She had provided them with sheet music to works by Beethoven and Khachaturian but, unable to read notation, they instead strummed their way through "Summertime," "Begin the Beguine," "Harry Lime (Third Man Theme)," "Moonglow and the Theme from Picnic," "September Song," and— you'll love this—"It's a Long Way to Tipperary." Paid £2 (about $5) per night, they played for a week and it's just a pity that no one filmed any of the performances...

For his part, Allan Williams promised that things would get better.

(What else could he say?) However, not even he could have foreseen what his own enterprise and some incredible luck would soon achieve.

Playing for Hamburgers

After Allan Williams discovered that his Royal Caribbean Steel Band had been secretly lured away to a club in Hamburg, some of the band's members called to tell him about the exciting German nightlife and suggest that he visit there with other groups. The tireless businessman's response was to make a recording of several local outfits, including The Silver Beetles, and play this in Hamburg for one Bruno Koschmider. The owner of a club named the Kaiserkeller, Koschmider was impressed by Williams' boast that he managed some of "the greatest rock bands in the world," yet he was less than enthused when he heard the tape. Somewhere along the journey from Liverpool it had become demagnetized, and the audible result was noisy gibberish.

Williams returned home with egg on his face, only to be confronted by another of his acts, Derry and the Seniors. Having quit their day jobs when Larry Parnes promised them work backing some of his singers, the band members were ready to kill him after Parnes suddenly canceled his plans. In desperation, Williams drove Derry and the boys directly to London's famous Two I's Coffee Bar, where acts such as Tommy Steele had been discovered, and persuaded the venue's manager to let them perform. Meanwhile, who should be there but Bruno Koschmider—do the words "incredible" and "coincidence" spring to mind?

Despite the useless tape that Williams had taken to Hamburg, Koschmider had been so impressed by the Welshman's outlandish boasts that he decided to pay England a visit—*London*, England. Now, impressed by Derry and the Seniors' impromptu Two I's performance, he immediately signed the band to play at the Kaiserkeller.

Soon after the Seniors started appearing at his club, Koschmider wrote to Williams, informing him that he was about to open a second venue, the Indra, where he would like to engage another of the 29-year-old entrepreneur's terrific groups. When local outfits such as Rory Storm and the Hurricanes and Gerry and the Pacemakers proved to be unavailable, Williams offered the booking to The Silver Beatles, so long as they could come up with a drummer. This they did in the form of Pete Best.

AllanWilliams, his wife Beryl, brother-in-law Barry Chang, business partner Harold Philips (known as Lord Woodbine due to his penchant for smoking Woodbine cigarettes), and an interpreter all accompanied the newly renamed Beatles to Hamburg, arriving there on August 17, 1960. From that point on the group would never look back, and neither would they honor their verbal agreement with their manager-cum-booking agent. After negotiating the terms of their club contract just prior to their second Hamburg visit in early 1961, the band members decided that Williams no longer deserved his commission. He threatened to sue—and probably would have won—but eventually didn't bother. Fourteen years later, Allan Williams co-authored the colorful, highly entertaining memoir, *The Man Who Gave the Beatles Away*.

Allan Williams, The Beatles' first manager, standing on Mathew Street just steps from the site of The Cavern, four years after its 1973 demolition.

The Search for a Drummer

Okay, so now we arrive at the real problem for the early Beatles (or whatever their name was at any given moment): finding someone to put behind the skins. After all, you needed money to own a full kit, and that wasn't always easy to come by in the Liverpool of those days. Which is why Colin Hanton, for all of his technical shortcomings, was still a handy chap to have around. When a drunken squabble resulted in his departure, John, Paul, and George probably assumed they could "find more where he came from," but soon realized that was easier said than done.

Hanton had been a founding member of The Quarry Men and, as such, he was basically in it for the long haul. Several of those who succeeded him, however, had a different attitude. Tommy Moore was brought on board by Allan Williams, who heard about him sitting in with various bands at a club run by local concert promoter, Sam Leach. Moore had little in common with his fellow Silver Beetles, but he needed the money, which was one reason for him being so fed up after returning virtually penniless from the Johnny Gentle tour.

Another factor had been a crash involving the van in which the group traveled around Scotland, causing Tommy to suffer a concussion and the loss of several front teeth. Dragged out of hospital to help the band fulfil its engagements, he then found himself on the receiving end of John's malicious humor, mocking the drummer's gap-toothed appearance. As he himself put it, by the end of the tour he'd had "a bellyful of Lennon," and soon after that he was an ex-Silver Beetle with a job at the Garston bottle works.

One evening, John, Paul, George, and Stu tried to persuade Tommy to climb down from his forklift and help them with a gig that had already been booked. When he flatly refused, they found themselves in a sticky situation. Then, just to make matters worse, Lennon's loose tongue sprang into life and, according to Allan Williams, things got even stickier.

You see, the band still had Tommy Moore's kit. Therefore, when they took to the stage that night, John decided to tell the audience about their predicament while half-jokingly asking if any drummers present would like to help out. This was at the Grosvenor Ballroom in Liscard, a venue notorious for its naked violence and vicious thugs. One such individual, a hefty Teddy Boy who Williams and his co-author Bill Marshall named "Ronnie," reportedly took Lennon up on his offer and seated himself behind the kit, where he proceeded to thrash away at the drums like a mad gorilla. Only Williams' hasty intervention in response to John's frantic phone call ensured that the band got out of the Ballroom with their lives, as well as with their equipment.

Not surprisingly, John didn't bother to ask if anyone cared to drum with them when they played at the New Cabaret Artistes strip club. Soon afterwards, however, they did manage to recruit an excellent drummer named Norman Chapman. He played with the group for a few weeks before finding himself among the last young Brits conscripted into the Army for National Service.

Which brings us back to August 1960 and Allan Williams' offer to send The Silver Beatles to Hamburg if they could find themselves a more permanent drummer. The only gigs that they'd been able to secure without one were the regular Saturday night bloodfests at the above-mentioned Grosvenor Ballroom. That was until August 6, when residents' complaints about all of the hooliganism forced the local council to cancel that week's "swing session." With nothing better to do, John, Paul, George, and Stu turned up at the Casbah Coffee Club run by Mona Best, and there they saw her handsome 18-year-old son, Pete, playing drums with a band named The Blackjacks.

The Silver Beatles were interested to hear that The Blackjacks were on the verge of disbanding, and that Pete Best, having recently left Liverpool Collegiate Grammar School with several O-level exam passes, was looking for a full-time career as a professional drummer. Equally fascinating to them was his gorgeous new kit. After a quick audition, Pete was offered the chance to join them in Hamburg. He was on his way.

Backbeat

"This painting was adapted from a shot of Ringo taken during The Beatles' first American concert, at the Washington Coliseum on February 11, 1964. I moved the sticks around a little bit, his arms are in a different position, and I originally had jelly beans flying around him, thrown by hysterical teen girls in the audience, as well as the movement of his hair and the cymbal. I have never seen another performance by Ringo where he tore up the kit like he did on that occasion. He was knocking it out, and I wanted to portray that with a greater sense of motion, but over time I came to dislike too many things looked blurred. It's not something you'd typically see in fine art— which is my field of activity, as opposed to abstract—so I stripped away all the movement with the exception of his drumsticks.

"For the jellybeans to look like they were flying through the air instead of hanging motionless, suspended by strings, there had to be tracers—a pink streak, a blue streak, an orange streak—and that was really distracting. So, I eliminated the jellybeans and then I decided, 'If I'm not going to do that, I'd better not have the cymbal or Ringo's hair moving.' Only at the last minute did I choose to convey at least some of the energy via his drumsticks, and I think that worked out okay because it's relatively subtle. Painting that movement has to be done spontaneously. It's all about the brush-stroke, so I had to get just the right brush and I had to fan it because you can't overwork those motion lines. You'll notice there's a slight bending of the sticks, and while that may be impossible since they're made out of hard wood, getting into the realm of a photographic blur meant I did have to go all the way and bend them just a little bit..."

– Eric Cash

Chapter 10

Leather and Liquor—Live in Hamburg

One of the most significant turning points in The Beatles' career occurred in Hamburg, in what was then West Germany. Before the first trip, the band had no permanent drummer and was basically a ramshackle collection of part-time musicians who had little idea about how to perform onstage. Their Hamburg experience changed all that.

The incessant nightly routine of playing long hours before demanding audiences ensured that The Beatles expanded their repertoire and evolved into a tight-knit musical unit; refining, innovating, and crafting the sound that would one day rock the world. At the same time, playing in nightclubs where the patrons' expectations appeared to rise along with their blood alcohol level, our heroes really had to put on a show. Standing like statues while performing limp renditions of other people's songs just wouldn't cut it in front of these crowds. No, for them the Liverpool lads had to jump around and belt out rock numbers like "Long Tall Sally" and "Sweet Little Sixteen" in a style that was light years away from their tame 1958 recording of "That'll Be the Day" (as heard on *Anthology 1*).

Between August 1960 and December 1962, The Beatles made five trips to Hamburg and performed more than 800 hours onstage. During that time they also found plenty to do away from the clubs, being situated, as they were, smack in the middle of the city's red-light district. Hamburg was where "the boys" grew up in more ways than one...

Up and Down the Reeperbahn

Loud night-clubs, oceans of booze, brawling sailors, gaudy women, gangsters, transvestites, pimps, prostitutes... For a bunch of horny young guys, Hamburg's St. Pauli neighborhood was the place to be back in the early 1960s.

Like Liverpool, Hamburg is a seaport populated with plenty of no-nonsense, hard-nosed individuals, and during the Second World War both cities endured heavy bombing. The major similarities end there, however. Basically, John, Paul, George, Stu, and Pete had never seen anything like the sights that greeted them on August 17, 1960, when their van rumbled down the Reeperbahn and made its way to the Grosse Freiheit. Sure, they may have taken trips to the English seaside resort of Blackpool to look at the Disney-like illuminations, but now, late at night, they were attracted by lights of another kind: flashing neon ones, with signs boasting about the entertainment—musical and otherwise— that the numerous bars and clubs had to offer.

An altogether smaller and pokier venue than the comparatively plush Kaiserkeller, the Indra at least provided John, Paul, George, Stu, and Pete with somewhere to bed down for the night: its red leather bench seats. Things then got worse the next day when club owner Bruno Koschmider led them to their full-time sleeping quarters: a decrepit little room behind the flimsy screen of a nearby flea-pit cinema. Named the Bambi Filmkunsttheater (careful how you pronounce that) and known as the Bambi Kino, this Koschmider-owned joint specialized in old American Westerns. Its filthy "bathroom" was where The Beatles were told they could wash, and they probably debated which would be more hygienic to bathe themselves in—the sink or the toilet.

At least they didn't have to worry about taking girls back there. After all, their usual acquaintances—an assortment of strippers and other career women—invariably had their own accommodations arranged. So, here was the social setup: the Gretel and Alphons or Willi's Bar when they fancied a few dozen beers, the Reeperbahn or Grosse Freiheit for some early morning action, and then all down to the British Seamen's Mission at around noon for steak, eggs, and fries, or some refreshing bowls of Cornflakes *mit milch*. The place they saw the least of was the Bambi Kino, and who could blame them? Not only was it a hell hole, but they often only had an hour or two to crash there.

Later on, when The Beatles played at the Top Ten Club, they slept in bunk beds in the overhead attic—not exactly the Ritz, but at least they were moving up in the world...

Band on the Run

The Beatles' time at the Indra was short-lived, and so, for that matter, was the Indra. To start with, this tawdry strip club-turned-music venue was hardly suited to live bands. It was poorly lit, had a tiny stage, and was shabbily decorated. Consequently, few people turned up to dance to the sounds of some unknown Liverpudlians, and when the group did try to create some excitement by cranking up the volume, the old woman in the upstairs apartment complained to the police. Precisely 48 days after opening the Indra, Bruno Koschmider closed it down.

This turned out to be a decent break for The Beatles. On October 4, 1960, Koschmider moved them into the Kaiserkeller to alternate with one of Liverpool's top bands, Rory Storm and the Hurricanes, featuring a certain Ringo Starr on drums. Things went well there, and on October 16 their contract was extended until December 31. Then trouble raised its ugly head in the form of yet another new club and, for Koschmider at least, some unwanted competition.

The Top Ten was that new venue, and its owner, Peter Eckhorn, struck an immediate low blow against the Kaiserkeller by luring away its chief bouncer, Horst Fascher. With hard-drinking hoodlums regularly visiting the St. Pauli district, a good bouncer was a prized possession. So, Bruno Koschmider was not a happy man, and his anger turned into outright fury when he learned that his newly beloved Beatles had been moonlighting at the Top Ten, jamming onstage with resident singer/guitarist Tony Sheridan. This was in direct contravention of a clause in their contract, stipulating that they couldn't play anywhere within a 25-mile radius without Koschmider's permission. The Beatles were therefore given a month's notice, and things then went from bad to worse.

The band members apparently weren't aware of the West German curfew that prevented anyone under the age of 18 from even being in a club after midnight. George was just 17, and not only frequenting the night spots well into the wee small hours of the morning, but also working in them. Somehow the authorities learned about this, and on November 21 The Beatles' lead guitarist was deported back to Liverpool.

As if that wasn't enough, Paul and Pete then fell foul of the law, too. Together with John and Stu, Pete Eckhorn had offered them the room above the Top Ten— infinitely better than the rotten old Bambi Kino. Since they were already on the outs with Bruno Koschmider, they really didn't care what he thought and, just to prove the point, Messrs. McCartney and Best indulged in an innocent—yet untimely—prank. As they were leaving the Bambi with packed bags, they stuck a rubber condom on one of the walls, set fire to it, and watched as it made a small, black scorch mark. No big deal, yet word of the incident immediately reached the vengeful ears of Koschmider, causing Paul and Pete to be thrown behind bars for "attempting to set fire to the Bambi."

After a night in the slammer, both Beatles were temporarily released, only to be rearrested several hours later and informed that they were being deported on the midnight flight to London. The next morning, December 1, they boarded a train from London's Euston Street station to Lime Street in Liverpool, and nine days later a dejected John arrived home, too. Only Stu remained behind in Germany, to be with his new love, Astrid Kirchherr.

This whole debacle could have spelled the end for the group, but instead the guys turned adversity to their advantage and capitalized locally on their Hamburg stage experience. Furthermore, subject to the lifting of their deportation bans (and without Allan Williams' knowledge), The Beatles had already negotiated a one-month booking at the Top Ten Club for the following April. So, things weren't as bad as they initially seemed.

Mach Shau! The Hamburg Clubs

John, Paul, George, Stu, and Pete were each paid 210 DM ($43) per week to perform at the Indra: four-and-a-half hours every night during the week, between 8:00 p.m. and 2:00 a.m.; six hours between 7:00 p.m. and 3:00 a.m. on Saturdays; and another six hours on Sundays, between 5:00 p.m. and 1:30 a.m. The small financial reward for this heavy workload was matched by little audience enthusiasm (or just a plain lack of audience), so switching to the Kaiserkeller was a welcome relief.

A basement venue with unusual nautical decor, the Kaiserkeller afforded The Beatles one of the largest stages they had ever performed on, and after a week there they finally learned how to use it. Allan Williams, making a return visit to Hamburg, decided during their October 10 show that he'd had enough of watching his protégés stand around like store-window dummies. "Make a show, boys!" he urged them, and when Bruno Koschmider and his customers heard this, they decided to follow suit. "Mach shau!" they shouted in their best broken English, and this was all the encouragement that The Beatles needed. With the exception of Pete Best, every one of them started jumping around onstage, gyrating like Elvis and, in John's case, limping like the crippled Gene Vincent. The Kaiserkeller's audiences responded in kind, shouting "mach shau!" night after night—but for Lennon the contortions weren't quite enough. Determined to dent German pride, he took to performing *Sieg Heil* salutes, goose-stepping around the stage, and screaming at everybody that they were "fucking Nazis." Naturally, some patrons objected, but others just guzzled their beer and continued to cry "mach shau!" Fair enough—if *shau* was what they wanted, *shau* was what they'd get, courtesy of Herr Lennon turning up onstage in a pair of bathing trunks with a toilet seat around his neck, shouting, "I'm wearing this because that's what this club is: *shit!*"

Although Bruno Koschmider wasn't enchanted by such pleasantries, the antics of Lennon and his fellow Beatles began attracting an increasing number of locals, many of whom would not only buy drinks for themselves, but also pay for a crate or two of beer for the band members to enjoy. The fact that, with the exception of Pete Best, The Beatles were taking Preludin stimulant pills meant that, after washing the "Prellies" down with all of the free alcohol, John, Paul, George, and Stu would be quite literally foaming at the mouth.

The stage at the Kaiserkeller may have been large, but it was also rotten, and a competition soon developed between The Beatles and Rory Storm and the Hurricanes to see who could demolish it first. When Rory won the bet by way of a leap and heavy landing during a rendition of "Blue Suede Shoes," a seething Koschmider docked the costs from Rory's pay packet. However, he was also aware of The Beatles' role in the vandalism and, when they defected to the Top Ten, that was the last straw.

Like the Indra and many other venues in and around St. Pauli, the Top Ten had been a strip joint in a previous incarnation, yet it was also located within a building that, until recently, had housed a circus. Naked girls riding horses and doing the splits on the high trapeze—few forms of entertainment were *verboten* on the Reeperbahn, the main Hamburg thoroughfare where The Beatles had always wanted to play. The Top Ten was large enough to accommodate huge crowds, yet the contract that they negotiated without Allan Williams' knowledge still earned each of them only 35 DM ($8) per day in return for a brutal schedule: performing from 7:00 p.m. to 2:00 a.m. during the week, and 7:00 p.m. to 3:00 a.m. on weekends, with a 15-minute break each hour.

By the time The Beatles took to the Top Ten stage in their tight black leather pants and jackets on March 27, 1961, George Harrison was old enough to stay out after midnight, the deportation bans had been lifted, and Stu Sutcliffe had left the group. Now a tight-knit quartet of hard-edged rockers, they remained at the club, courtesy of a twice-extended contract, until July 2, clocking a staggering 535 hours onstage and returning to Liverpool with newly fashioned "moptop" hairstyles. The following year, The Beatles would outdo themselves with three separate Hamburg stints, yet none would be at the Top Ten.

In November 1961, Brian Epstein began managing the band, and part of his guarantee to them, aside from securing a recording contract, was to ensure that they played better venues for higher fees. Accordingly, when Pete Eckhorn arrived in Liverpool that December to sign acts for the coming year, his generous offer to nearly double The Beatles' weekly salary to 450 DM ($100) per man was rejected by Brian. He wanted 500 DM ($112) each, but still agreed to consider Eckhorn's proposal before, in late January 1962, former Kaiserkeller and Top Ten bouncer Horst Fascher also arrived in Liverpool. Having recently quit Eckhorn's venue in order to manage a huge new Hamburg rock establishment, the Twist Club, Fascher had been dispatched by the venue's owner, Manfred Weissleder, to sign up what he considered to be the best possible act for opening night that spring: The Beatles.

Brian Epstein duly got the 500 DM per man that he had been looking for, and his clients were booked for a seven-week engagement, from April 13 to May 31. Now able to travel in style, John, Paul, and Pete flew to Hamburg on April 11 and, on arriving at the airport, learned that Stu Sutcliffe had died the previous day. George, who was unwell, flew there with Brian on the 12th. By then, the Twist Club had been renamed the Star-Club and The Beatles subsequently became a major attraction, even sharing the bill with Gene Vincent for a couple of weeks.

When the band members returned for a two-week engagement on November 1, 1962, it was with the prized recording contract under their belts, a certain Starr sitting behind the drum kit, and yet another increased weekly salary of 600 DM ($135) per band member. This time they shared the bill with Little Richard. Then, for their last visit, from December 18-31, their weekly pay packet rose to 750 DM ($170) per man, meaning that, due to their improved musicianship, increased following, and the invaluable help of Brian Epstein, they had managed to triple their Hamburg fee within the space of a year. Yet, by then that hardly mattered. The Beatles now wanted to focus on their burgeoning career back home and long hours onstage were about to become a thing of the past.

The Hamburg Recordings

During the course of their five Hamburg stints The Beatles made several recordings, some amateur, others professional, and the first of these actually captured a 1960 performance by John, Paul, George, Ringo... and Wally.

It was on Sunday, October 15, just under two years before Ringo joined the group, that he filled in for Pete Best when the others cut some tracks at a small facility named Akustik Studio. Ringo was there as a member of Rory Storm and the Hurricanes, playing alongside his future Beatle colleagues as they backed the vocalizing of Hurricanes bass player Walter "Wally" Eymond (stage name Lu Walters). The fruits of their efforts—which, according to Allan Williams, included "Fever" and, according to Walters, also included "September Song"—were nine 78-rpm discs, featuring the group's rendition of George Gershwin's "Summertime" on one side and an ad for leather handbags and shoes on the other. Only one of the nine discs reputedly survived, but its whereabouts remain unknown.

Meanwhile, The Beatles' first professional recording took place during the group's second trip to Hamburg. At that point, in addition to their own performances at the Top Ten Club, they were also backing Tony Sheridan there. Word of this successful union reached the ears of Bert Kaempfert, the German composer, producer, and orchestra leader who, in January 1961, had topped the American charts with the instrumental "Wonderland by Night." Kaempfert subsequently visited the Top Ten and a buzz went around; play well and it may result in a recording contract. Sheridan was already signed to the Polydor label and, when Kaempfert heard The Beatles' energetic performances, they were invited to his office and promptly signed to record for him as an independent producer. The results would be assigned to Polydor.

Expectations were running high on June 22, when two taxis transported the band members and their equipment to the studio. This, however, turned out to be no more than a screened-off stage inside the main hall of a school, and the guys' disappointment was compounded when they realized that they were only there to back Tony Sheridan. This they did on five numbers (without Stu Sutcliffe, who was just an observer): the standards, "My Bonnie Lies Over the Ocean" and "When the Saints Go Marching In"; Sheridan's own "Why (Can't You Love Me Again)"; the Hank Snow country song, "Nobody's Child"; and Jimmy Reed's "Take Out Some Insurance on Me, Baby."

Once this was completed, the four Beatles then recorded a couple of numbers on their own: the old Roaring Twenties hit, "Ain't She Sweet," treated to a rock arrangement and a distinctively raw-edged Lennon lead vocal, and a Harrison-Lennon instrumental composition, which they initially considered naming "Beatle Bop." This was eventually retitled "Cry For a Shadow," a send-up of Cliff Richard's backing group, The Shadows, who were then enjoying chart success of their own with a string of guitar-based instrumentals.

In August 1961, Polydor issued a single featuring "My Bonnie" coupled with "The Saints" (as they were trendily retitled), and credited the recordings to Tony Sheridan & The Beat Brothers because the label execs felt that Beatles sounded uncomfortably similar to *peedles*, a German slang word for penis. Regardless, the record reached number five on the local charts and sold about 100,000 copies in the process. Back in Liverpool it would also serve to bring The Beatles to the attention of Brian Epstein.

The following year, when Brian was trying to attain a U.K. recording deal for his clients, he asked Bert Kaempfert if he would release them from his own contract. Kaempfert agreed to this, as long as he could still have the opportunity to once again record them himself after they returned to Hamburg that April. Consequently, on May 24, 1962, at a facility named Studio Rahlstedt, The Beatles—together with piano player Roy Young—recorded backing tracks to Tony Sheridan's covers of "Swanee River" and "Sweet Georgia Brown." The "Swanee River" recording was subsequently lost, and the reasoning behind the session remains puzzling since alternate versions of both numbers had already been issued on Sheridan's *My Bonnie* album.

Still, while all of the aforementioned Hamburg recordings were made with decent equipment, in many ways the most interesting one is that which boasts by far the poorest audio quality. The reason? It just happens to capture The Beatles' final performances at the Star-Club, and as such it's a priceless piece of history. Never again would the band play gigs of this duration and with such a diverse selection of material—from Lennon-McCartney originals and rock 'n' roll standards to curios such as "Falling in Love Again (Can't Help It)" and contemporary pop hits like "I Remember You." Within a few months they would be treating their fans to just tightly formatted half-hour concerts.

Given how The Beatles' early-sixties image is now inexorably tied to manic screaming and mass adulation, it's fascinating to hear the informality of these Star-Club shows. The audience talks while the band plays, bottles and glasses clink, and John and Paul engage in casual banter with the customers and club staff. It's late December 1962 and The Beatles are clearly tired, yet there's an energy to some of the performances that is hard to ignore, helping to illustrate why they were already held in such high regard both in Hamburg and their own home town.

The Beatles were captured over several nights on a portable Grundig recorder owned by Ted Taylor, the hefty leader of Liverpool group Kingsize Taylor and the Dominoes, who were also playing a residency at the Star-Club. The man operating the machine was Big Three lead guitarist/Star-Club sound man Adrian Barber, and the tape was reportedly offered to Brian Epstein during the mid-sixties, but at that time, with the ability to make much better recordings of the band's then-current concerts, he turned it down. The Beatles would later regret that decision.

In 1977, the original mono master was transferred to 16-track, cleaned up, and, against the Fab Four's wishes, released to the general public as a double album. It has since been re-issued on several occasions, although in 1998 The Beatles finally obtained a court ruling granting them ownership of the lo-fi recording and exclusive rights to its use. Consequently, it is now only available as a bootleg.

By the time of their fifth and final Hamburg stint, The Beatles had a recording contract and were poised for the big time. They no longer needed to play the grueling hours and were thankful to move on, yet in many ways their Hamburg days represented a golden period for them, both in a personal and a professional sense. They could never go back, but they would never forget.

Chapter 11

From a Keller to a Cellar

The Beatles made giant strides as musicians when they were in Germany and they also learned how to make an impression on their audiences— not always the best kind of impression, but a lasting one nonetheless.

Fun in Litherland: The First Rumblings of Beatlemania

When The Silver Beatles had played in Liverpool prior to their first Hamburg trip, they were a pretty desperate bunch. The only weekly gigs they had were at the violent Grosvenor Ballroom, where they faced heavy competition from other local bands and were largely considered something of a joke. In fact, things were so desperate that, when the group had no one to fill in for them, Paul would play the drums. Then they went to Hamburg with Pete Best, and when they returned home in mid-December 1960 it was a different story.

For one thing, they were now renamed The Beatles; for another, their overseas performances appeared to stir up interest on the home front. Never mind that three of the band members had actually been deported; they pretty much kept that to themselves, re-grouped, and immediately capitalized on some new bookings. One of these engagements proved to be a turning point.

The Beatles were added to the bill of a December 27 gig at the Town Hall Ballroom in Litherland, a northern Liverpool suburb where they had only appeared on one previous occasion. Few people there had even heard of the group, and so when the locals saw The Beatles billed as "Direct from Hamburg," they naturally assumed they were German. That night, Beatlemania was born.

As Paul commenced the set by belting out the opening lines to Little Richard's "Long Tall Sally," the effect was instantaneous. The large crowd rushed to the front of the stage and went crazy, almost mesmerized by the musicians who, just a few months earlier, had been largely ignored while they played. Normally, The Beatles were used to a lot of idle chatter while they sang; suddenly they were faced with a horde of kids either shaking their heads to the beat or staring at them goggle-eyed.

The band must have been bewildered by all of this, but among the many lessons The Beatles learned during more than 500 hours onstage in Hamburg was how to pounce on the moment. If the customers were ready to rock, they'd give them every reason to, jumping around to a solid, well-rehearsed repertoire of songs that would blast their ears and blow their minds.

In one fell swoop, The Beatles forever shut the door on playing for baked beans on toast or backing some stripper with "It's a Long Way to Tipperary." From now on, the fees improved and, with increasing regularity, the fans went wild. The promoter of the Litherland gig, Brian Kelly, immediately booked the band for no less than 35 engagements during the next two-and-a-half months, and this, in turn, helped The Beatles become Merseyside's number one rock attraction.

The Town Hall in Litherland, where The Beatles' first performance, on December 27, 1960, established them as *the* musical force on Merseyside. The gig was secured for them by deejay Bob Wooler and promoted by Brian Kelly, whose posters advertising the band as "Direct from Hamburg" led many locals to believe they were paying to see a German outfit. This was forgotten as soon as John, Paul, George, Pete, and bassist Chas Newby commenced the show with a storming Reeperbahn-style rendition of 'Long Tall Sally,' at which point everyone rushed toward the stage in what would subsequently be viewed as the first instance of Beatlemania.

Oh, Mr. Bass Man

Playing bass guitar with The Beatles at the Litherland Town Hall was Chas Newby, replacing Stu Sutcliffe whose interests now focused on pursuing his art career and his Hamburg-based relationship with Astrid Kirchherr. John and Paul had constantly mocked Stu's lack of musical ability, and Paul had pressured him—sometimes not too subtly—to quit the group. Now the job was up for grabs, and with ex-Quarry Men bassist Ken Brown down in London (and out of favor), Pete Best thought of Chas, who had played rhythm guitar in his former band, The Blackjacks.

Chas Newby was on a Christmas break from college when he was asked to join The Beatles, and, after borrowing a bass guitar and the obligatory leather jacket, he made his debut with them at the Casbah Coffee Club on December 17, 1960. Thereafter, the lineup of John, Paul, George, Chas, and Pete gave performances at the Grosvenor Ballroom on Christmas Eve, Litherland Town Hall on the 27th, and again at the Casbah on New Year's Eve. Then Chas went back to college, at which point John probably concluded that the four-man lineup was sufficient so long as one of the three guitarists would take over on bass. He himself he wasn't interested in switching from rhythm and George didn't want to give up the lead, but Paul was another matter. Since flunking his lead solo during his debut as a Quarry Man just over three years earlier, Paul had doubled on rhythm guitar while also dabbling on piano and, when the need arose, drums as well. Now, with no one else willing to assume the role of Beatle bass man, he capitalized on the opportunity to carve out his own instrumental niche.

At first, Paul borrowed Stu's giant Hofner President 500/5 bass, which apparently boasted strings that had been snipped from an accommodating piano. Being left-handed, he played this upside down and initially stuck the guitar cable into his pocket instead of his amplifier for fear that his shortcomings might be audible. Still, as Paul was by far the most adept all-round musician in The Beatles, it wasn't long before he began plugging that cable into the amp and invested in a left-handed, violin-shaped Hofner 500/1 bass guitar.

Paul bought the Hofner during the course of The Beatles' 1961 stint at Hamburg's Top Ten Club and he would later acquire another model with differently arranged pickups. Today, along with a Fender bass, Paul still plays the Hofner in concert. And having established himself as one of rock's premier bassists, the "Beatle bass guitar" is the instrument with which he is most closely identified.

Going South: Alone in Aldershot

Let's jump forward a year to the night of December 9, 1961, and the occasion of The Beatles' first-ever live performance in the south of England.

Liverpool promoter Sam Leach bravely decided to venture there by booking five consecutive Saturday nights at the Palais Ballroom in Aldershot, a town 37 miles southwest of London. Then he invited some of the top pop impresarios to see his grandly titled "Battle of the Bands," pitting a rock outfit from Merseyside against a combo from London. A fine idea in principle, but in reality Sam was wide of the mark.

The most appropriate aspect of the whole "battle" concept was Aldershot being one of Britain's largest military bases. Aside from its army connections and a perennially struggling soccer team, Aldershot had little else to offer, and so it was unlikely that London's music biz bigwigs would travel there. (It was enough trouble getting them to leave their offices and go *anywhere* without the lure of free food and drink.) Why Leach didn't book his battles in London was anyone's guess, but Aldershot's Palais Ballroom was his chosen venue and the first "Battle of the Bands" featured The Beatles versus a totally unknown London group named Ivor Jay and the Jaywalkers.

The "Big Beat Session," as it was headlined on posters, wasn't properly advertised. According to Leach, he placed an ad in the local *Aldershot News* but, unbeknown to him, the paper rejected his check because he wasn't a regular customer. Furthermore, he hadn't supplied his address or phone number, so he couldn't be contacted and, therefore, the ad didn't appear. The Beatles, however, *did* show up, after traveling all day down from Liverpool.

When they realized that they faced playing to a completely empty house, John, Paul, George, and Pete undertook a lightning tour of the town's pubs and coffee bars, informing everyone about "a dance going on at the Palais tonight." Imagine knocking back a pint of beer or cup of Brazilian Blend on a cold Saturday night and seeing John Lennon, Paul McCartney, and George Harrison pop their heads around a door to ask if you'd like to come and hear them play (for free). Within a few years, girls would be hiding out in hotel air-conditioning shafts just to get a glimpse of them, but in December 1961 only 18 Aldershot locals took them up on their offer.

Those adventurous Saturday nighters who witnessed The Beatles' first-ever show "down south" weren't disappointed. Professional to the last, John, Paul, George, and Pete gave their audience the full works, and the patrons responded by spreading out across the ballroom floor and dancing to their heart's content without fear of bumping into anyone. No rushing the stage, no wild scenes, just a sedate and cozy get-together.

Afterwards, with the place cleared of the thronging masses, The Beatles broke open the beer bottles and started kicking bingo balls around the huge floor. Aldershot didn't take kindly to that kind of out-and-out hooliganism. The police arrived and ordered the Liverpudlians to leave their pleasant town. Which they did, heading for the brighter lights of London.

Although there are no surviving scorecards to indicate who won the battle between The Beatles and Ivor Jay's outfit, the Jaywalkers probably got the nod because they returned to the Palais Ballroom the following week for "Battle of the Bands II" against Rory Storm and the Hurricanes. 210 paying customers attended that event after an ad did actually appear in the local paper. Then Sam Leach decided that he'd had enough of Aldershot and his three remaining battles were canceled.

Ringo's Roots: Clayton Skiffle and the Raving Texans

There's one other mildly interesting footnote to the whole "Battle of the Bands" fiasco, and that concerns the fact that, for the second of those star-spangled events, the drummer with Ivor Jay and the Jaywalkers had to cross sticks with Ringo Starr. Again, even though Ringo wasn't yet a Beatle, his and The Beatles' paths kept crossing.

As mentioned earlier, Richy Starkey's first musical venture was with The Eddie Clayton Skiffle Group, who played around the same kind of small Liverpool venues as The Quarry Men. Whenever a band was in need of a drummer, anyone who owned a shiny new kit was often a prime candidate, even without an abundance of percussive skill. Fortunately for Richy, his grandfather lent him £50 ($120)— a considerable sum in those days—to purchase a brand-new set of drums, and in 1959 he joined a band led by vocalist Alan Caldwell.

Caldwell's five-piece group went from Al Caldwell's Texans to The Raving Texans, Al Storm and the Hurricanes, Jett Storm and the Hurricanes, and finally Rory Storm and the Hurricanes. At the turn of the 1960s, the Hurricanes were, briefly, Liverpool's most popular rock band—not The Beatles—and "Rory," with his blonde bouffant hairdo and flamboyant stage movements, was Merseyside's number one attraction. This success was reflected in the Hurricanes' dress code: instead of scruffy jeans and leather jackets, they decked themselves out in sharp-looking suits—Rory, perhaps, in powder blue, the others in hot pink—along with white-and-black winkle-picker shoes.

Richy first drummed with the group on March 25, 1959, before joining on a permanent basis that November. His fellow band members started calling him "Rings" because of all the rings on his fingers, and this was then amended to Ringo to not only reflect his love of country & western music, but to also make him sound like a cowboy such as nineteenth century outlaw Johnny Ringo or John Wayne's Ringo Kid character in the classic 1939 movie, *Stagecoach*. Starkey was then abbreviated to Starr so that the spot in each show when Ringo took care of the vocals or a drum solo could be billed as "Starr Time."

In May 1960, Rory Storm and the Hurricanes were booked for an entire summer season at Butlin's holiday camp in the Welsh town of Pwllheli (pronounced "poohh-helly"). Then, that November, they joined The Beatles at the Kaiserkeller in Hamburg, during which time John, Paul, George, and Ringo made their first amateur recording together, backing the Hurricanes' Lu Walters. Thereafter, whenever Pete Best wasn't feeling well or didn't turn up for a gig, Ringo would sit in with the front-line Beatles. Impressed by the mustachioed drummer's rock-solid playing and the flashy Ford Zephyr Zodiac that he drove back in Liverpool, they also clicked far better with his outgoing personality than that of the introverted Pete.

Ringo continued playing with the Hurricanes, but he soon became bored with their unvarying routine of gigs around Merseyside and summer seasons at Butlin's. In October 1961, he actually wrote to the Houston Chamber of Commerce with a view to emigrating to America, but then lost interest when he realized how much red tape he'd have to deal with. So, that December, he returned to Hamburg— not with the Hurricanes, who he had just quit, but as part of the house band backing Tony Sheridan at the Top Ten Club. This stint lasted until March 1962, when Sheridan's argumentative nature prompted Ringo to re-join Rory and the boys on a French working holiday.

Coming next was another summer season at Butlin's, this time in Skegness, and it's there that Ringo's life would be changed forever by a single phone call...

Sweat and Grime: Let's Go Down The Cavern

If one concert site has become synonymous with The Beatles, it's The Cavern Club, the dingy Mathew Street basement venue located 18 steps below a former fruit and vegetable warehouse on a run-down city-center back street of Liverpool.

The Cavern is where The Beatles took up residency, where they truly bonded with a hardcore following of die-hard fans, where the adoring girls in the front rows would go out of their way to look their best for their heroes, where Brian Epstein had his initial glimpse of them, and where the group's legend officially started. It was also at The Cavern that TV cameras captured The Beatles for the first time. Yet, the place itself was little more than a hole in the ground.

With bare brick walls and stone floors, the venue was something of a death trap. There was no ventilation, the electrical system would have failed the most basic safety inspection, and in the event of a fire the means of escape would have been desperate to say the least. Thanks to an off-the-scale humidity factor, sweat quite literally dripped down the walls, producing not only a foul atmosphere but also a threat to the onstage musicians.

"Either the amps would pack up or there would be a complete power cut," recalled Keef Hartley, former drummer with Rory Storm and the Hurricanes, John Mayall's Bluesbreakers, and his own Keef Hartley Band, when I interviewed him in 1981. "If this happened, John would immediately jump up onto the piano and go into his routine: 'Here we have Paul McCartney, in a string bag, no arms, no legs...' It was completely unrehearsed, but at the same time it was 'instant Lennon,' with that sick, sick humor of his. That gave The Beatles a tremendous advantage over all of the other bands, and I'm sure that people who went regularly to The Cavern were almost more entertained by that than by the live music."

Indeed, the intimate setup at The Cavern provided John with ample opportunity to sharpen his cynical, razor-like wit, while Paul made eyes at the girls, the girls made eyes at Pete, and George focused on his fingers during the guitar solos. The audience, seated on wooden chairs or standing crammed together, were only a couple of feet away from the tiny wooden stage, which itself was just a few feet above the floor. Positioned at the end of a central archway, this was lit by several plain white 60-watt bulbs, while in an adjoining archway there was just enough room to dance. The third main archway, over on the other side, was where the money was taken. Meanwhile, the rest of the club, with its various interconnecting tunnels and Bambi Kino-type "bathroom" facilities, was largely in the dark.

That said, while The Cavern made for a somewhat dodgy rock venue, it had originally been designed as a typical late-1950s jazz cellar. Named after Le Caveau Français Jazz Club in Paris, it had opened in January 1957 and immediately began attracting an assortment of name artists and unknowns. Among the latter, believe it or not, were The Quarry Men. Given skiffle's jazz roots, John and his cronies managed to secure a gig there on the night of August 7, 1957, after Paul had agreed to join the group but before he was ready to make his debut.

The McCartney-less Quarry Men took to The Cavern stage and kicked things off with an acceptable rendition of "Come Go with Me" (no doubt "down, down, down to the penitentiary"). So far, so good— polite applause and approving smiles. Then Lennon launched into Elvis Presley's "Hound Dog" and "Blue Suede Shoes" and the smiles began to disappear. Outraged, club owner Alan Sytner sent a note up to the stage and the message was brief yet straight to the point: "Cut out the bloody rock!"

All of that changed on February 9, 1961, when the renamed Beatles made their Cavern debut during a lunchtime session. By then, Alan Sytner's accountant, Ray McFall, had bought the club and, with the trad jazz (traditional/Dixieland) boom having peaked in Britain, McFall acknowledged the beat groups' rising impact on the city while recognizing the potential income. This resulted in some of them being allowed to perform, much to the regular clientele's annoyance, during the intermission.

Just after the disastrous end to The Beatles' first Hamburg trip, Pete Best's mother, Mona, had telephoned McFall and told him about "my son's group," which had been playing at venues such as her own Casbah Coffee Club. Next, The Cavern's resident deejay, Bob Wooler, had weighed in by lauding the band's performances at a number of local dances where he had been the emcee. McFall took the bait and The Beatles were in, at an initial fee of £5 ($12) for a lunchtime session and £15 ($37) for a nighttime one. Initially, however, they still didn't meet with the approval of the ever-present jazz and blues aficionados. So, they resorted to introducing "a song by Leadbelly" before launching straight into Little Richard's "Long Tall Sally"…

Mona Best, mother of Pete, talking with Beatles fans in 1977 outside her Hayman's Green home in West Derby that, within its basement, had housed the Casbah Coffee Club.

Eventually, the jazzies could see that their haunt was a lost cause and they moved out, to be replaced by the rock 'n' roll brigade. And so, every lunchtime and evening, Bob Wooler, a genial man with an in-depth knowledge of the Liverpool beat scene, would kick things off by smoothly announcing, "Hi, all you Cavern-dwellers, welcome to the best of cellars."

Over the course of the next two years, during which Wooler introduced The Beatles nearly 300 times, he and the adoring fans saw the band evolve from scruffy leather boys who smoked, drank, and turned their backs onstage into disciplined, smart-suited chart-toppers who were rapidly taking the nation by storm. Whereas the exhausting stints in

Hamburg helped shape The Beatles as stage performers, The Cavern Club provided the band with a devoted fan-base whose word of mouth would eventually spread around the world. In return, its connection with the band invested The Cavern with a legendary status, although, typically, it was only after the club's demise that its status was fully appreciated.

Once The Beatles departed Liverpool and dragged many other Merseybeat groups along with them, things went into rapid decline. The energy, heart, and soul appeared to vanish from the local scene and, on February 28, 1966, The Cavern was closed with debts of £10,000 ($24,000). It eventually re-opened, only to be closed down a second and final time in June 1973, when it was demolished to make way for—now hear this—an underground railway air vent.

A tribute to "Four Lads Who Shook the World" beneath the Cavern sign was, for many years, the only Beatles-related artifact on Mathew Street.

Not until 1984 would there be a worthy tribute constructed on the site. This would be The Cavern Walks Shopping Centre, an indoor mall that resulted from the global attention focused on Liverpool and its "favorite sons" in the wake of John Lennon's death. Underneath the assortment of stores, bars, and dining areas, there is a near-perfect—although more health-and-safety-conscious—replica of the cellar club, positioned just a few feet away from the original and even boasting some of its old bricks.

The entrance to the new Cavern Club, which occupies 75 percent of the original site and was reconstructed with many of the original bricks.

This has hosted assorted artists including, on December 14, 1999, a band comprising Pink Floyd guitarist Dave Gilmour, Deep Purple drummer Ian Paice, Johnny Kidd & the Pirates/Billy J. Kramer with the Dakotas guitarist Mick Green, and keyboardist Pete Wingfield… fronted by Paul McCartney to promote his eleventh solo studio album, *Run Devil Run*.

300 people crammed into the venue that night to see a Beatle perform at "The Cavern" for the first time in more than 36 years. Yet, for those able to recall visiting the club during its glory years, nothing, no matter how clean and modern it is, could replace the look, the feel, the vibe, or indeed the smell of the real thing.

In addition to being a prime tourist attraction, the new Cavern is also a live venue that hosted a 'return' concert by Paul McCartney on December 14, 1999, in support of his album *Run Devil Run*.

PART 3

A TASTE OF HONEY—THE RISE OF THE BEATLES

In this part of the book, The Beatles—having served their apprenticeship the hard way—finally get their act together and reap unimaginable rewards. However, they don't reach that light at the end of the tunnel without some invaluable assistance, a few lucky breaks, several disappointments, and a lone casualty.

Fortune smiles on our heroes in the form of two men who, although totally inexperienced in the field of rock 'n' roll, have the artistic vision and priceless ability to turn raw material into rare treasure. At that point events start to accelerate and John, Paul, George, and Ringo head for the stars while saying some fast goodbyes and rapidly leaving their old world behind.

Chapter 12

Baby, You're a Rich Man—That Posh Mr. Epstein

Brian Epstein's role in The Beatles' success cannot be overestimated.

Without a doubt, John, Paul, George, and Pete were already making a name for themselves in both Liverpool and Hamburg before Brian ever appeared on the scene. However, given their general lack of discipline and organizational skills, those cities may well have remained the only places to hear of them. As they were presenting themselves, The Beatles were in no way marketable on a national basis, let alone an international one. Brian almost immediately solved that problem and, by way of a strong vision and sheer determination, he helped fulfill his clients' wishes beyond their wildest dreams.

Beautiful Dreamer: The Man and His Aspirations

Brian Samuel Epstein was born in a private Liverpool maternity hospital on September 19, 1934. His parents, Harry and Queenie, lived in a five-bedroom house in Childwall, one of the city's smartest suburbs, as befitting a very comfortable middle-class lifestyle that included a maid as well as a nanny after their second son, Clive, was born in 1935.

Harry, together with his father, Isaac, ran a popular and very prosperous furniture store, in addition to an adjacent shop that sold sheet music, gramophones, and radios. Known as NEMS (for North End Music Stores), this name would one day loom large in The Beatles' legend. Brian enjoyed a privileged childhood, yet his performance at some of Merseyside's best private schools was no better—and often worse—than that of his future charges. Classified as a "problem child" by some of his teachers, he basically hated academia and didn't get along with his fellow pupils, some of whom taunted him for being Jewish. Harry and Queenie paid huge sums to send their eldest son to no less than eight different establishments, but the results were invariably the same—he hated the schools and the schools were none too keen on him.

Not that Brian was a bully or troublemaker. Rather, he was overly sensitive, with a love for the finer things in life: the theater, painting, ballet, and classical music. In fact, his performances in school plays finally won him plaudits from teachers and pupils alike, and during the final stages of his formal education he actually came top of his class in art and design—which led to his first flight of fancy. Quitting school with no qualifications at age 15, Brian announced that he was going to London to become a dress designer.

Harry Epstein would have none of it, and neither, for that matter, would he listen to Brian's next big idea: studying art. This was fanciful nonsense as far as Harry was concerned and no way for a young man to be thinking. So, in September 1950, Isaac and Harry quickly installed 16-year-old Brian in I. Epstein & Sons as a furniture salesman and, while they hoped for the best, he immediately showed he was up to the task by selling a dining room table to a woman who had come in to buy a mirror. With his smooth demeanor, sophisticated voice, and quiet charm, Brian was a natural born salesman. Yet, he didn't manage to charm old Isaac for very long.

Organized and efficient, Brian displayed a flair for the unusual when it came to dressing the store's windows, arranging dining room chairs with their backs to the street because he felt they looked "more natural" that way. At that point, Grandpa Epstein decided it would be more natural if his grandson took his flair elsewhere, so Brian became an apprentice with the Times Furnishing Company for six months, during which time he again excelled at selling and window-dressing. Soon afterwards, he was drafted for National Service in the Army (where he received his basic training in the sleepy town of Aldershot—scene of The Beatles' under-attended Saturday night gig). Yet, instead of being selected as officer material, Brian was assigned a clerical position and posted to London, where an innocent mistake resulted in him being charged for impersonating an officer, confined to barracks, and put under medical and psychiatric supervision. Then, less than half-way through his two-year military stint, he was discharged on "medical grounds."

Back in Liverpool, Brian reverted to wearing expensive, dapper clothes and returned to the family business, although this time around Harry put him in charge of running the new record department at NEMS. Brian's organizational skills and love for classical music proved to be a surefire recipe for success, but shop life didn't fulfill the artistic aspirations that had him secretly yearning to enter the theater. On the advice of an actor friend he auditioned for London's Royal Academy of Dramatic Art and to his astonishment he was accepted. Once again, Harry and Queenie were more than a little disappointed, but Brian was now 21 and they could no longer stand in his way.

Although not especially endowed with acting talent, Brian did fairly well at RADA. However, just as in Liverpool, Brian never felt that he really fit in with the people around him, not least because of the double life that he led as a closet homosexual. The dapper sophisticate of the day pursued activities by night that very nearly resulted in a jail term while leaving him prey to blackmailers and extortionists. A decade later, worldwide fame would only increase his fear of being outed.

After just over a year at RADA, Brian returned to Liverpool to run another small furniture outlet that his family had recently opened. Shortly thereafter, with the electrical business continuing to expand, he moved to a new NEMS store in the center of Liverpool, taking charge of the record department while younger brother Clive looked after the household appliances division. Then, the following year, 1959, saw the launch of a much vaster NEMS store in the city center business district of Whitechapel.

With sales departments, stock rooms, and offices spread over four floors of a sizable building, this branch of NEMS was able to offer "The Finest Record Selection in the North." The classical discs were on the ground floor, pop was in the basement, and Brian devised a system whereby colored strings attached to cardboard folders informed him as to which records were in stock and which needed re-ordering. In fact, he made it a company policy to never turn down customer requests without exploring every means of locating a rare disc; something which, within a short time, would pay off in a way that neither he or anyone else could have possibly foreseen.

Summary Tour '66

"This is based on two slightly different concert photos; the image of Paul taken about three frames and a couple of seconds after the one of John. I really liked the shot of Paul, but John was laughing in that photo and I thought it worked better to just have both of them singing. I also changed their stage outfits a little to make them more colorful. The Beatles were about to get into their psychedelic period and I wanted to foreshadow that, while seeing John and Paul perform up-close at this stage of their career provides us with a vantage point experienced by very few people—most of them photographers."

– Eric Cash

There is some dispute as to how Brian Epstein first heard about The Beatles. According to Epstein's own account, Stuart Sutcliffe had sent several copies of the Tony Sheridan/Beatles record, "My Bonnie," from Hamburg to Liverpool, and on a Saturday night in August 1961 George Harrison handed one of these to Cavern deejay Bob Wooler. Since Wooler MC'd shows all over Merseyside, he was able to play the record to a fairly wide local audience, encouraging people to ask for the disc at record stores in the hope that it would be officially imported.

So it was that 18-year-old Raymond Jones, from the Liverpool suburb of Huyton, walked into NEMS in Whitechapel at 3:00 in the afternoon of Saturday, October 28, 1961, and asked the manager for a copy of "My Bonnie." Brian was puzzled, as he'd apparently never heard of either the record or The Beatles, but, true to his policy, he promised Jones that he would try to locate the disc for him. When the store re-opened on Monday morning two girls also asked for "My Bonnie," and now, with his curiosity piqued, Brian set about calling specialist record importers. None of them had heard of the disc either, so he next turned to Bill Harry, the editor of local pop paper *Mersey Beat*. Brian learned that, far from being German, The Beatles were a Liverpudlian group who regularly performed at a club named The Cavern, which was located just around the corner from NEMS.

There are, undoubtedly, several problems with this version of events. First, due to record company fears about Beatles sounding similar to the German slang word for penis, "My Bonnie" was credited to Tony Sheridan and The Beat Brothers. (The label was not amended until January 1962, and then at Brian Epstein's own instigation.) Bob Wooler would have read this on the record label, and so there would have been no point in him advising people to ask retailers for a record by The Beatles. Secondly, Bill Harry himself has asserted that, since *Mersey Beat*'s launch just four months earlier, NEMS had been one of the paper's main outlets, selling 12 dozen copies of the second issue, which featured the front page headline, "Beatles Sign Recording Contract!" This was accompanied by a photo of the band and an article about their deal with Bert Kaempfert.

Furthermore, starting with the third issue, Brian had actually been reviewing the latest record releases in the paper. So, even though he may not have been overly interested in rock music, the chances of him ignoring the other articles—including one titled "Well Now—Dig This!" by Bob Wooler, in which the knowledgeable disc jockey celebrated The Beatles' talents a good two years before anyone else—have to be slim to none. Besides, NEMS had also been selling concert tickets featuring The Beatles' name.

All of this gives you some idea as to how personal recollections often fly in the face of undeniable facts. Whatever the truth of the matter, there is no doubt that, on November 9, 1961, Brian Epstein's curiosity resulted in his unexpected presence at a Beatles lunchtime Cavern session. When Bob Wooler announced that the manager of NEMS was there, all heads turned to see a suave man in a pinstriped suit holding a briefcase and looking decidedly out of place in the dank atmosphere of this musty cellar. Then The Beatles kicked off their set and Brian was mesmerized.

Now, whether or not this was due to what Brian would later cite as their "personal charm" or what others have asserted was a physical attraction is open to conjecture. What *is* known is that, when Brian made his way to the club's band room after the show, George Harrison's personal charm manifested itself in the form of a sarcastic, "What brings Mr. Epstein here?" Probably blushing, Brian explained that he was searching for the group's recording of "My Bonnie" and, after hearing it courtesy of Bob Wooler, he promptly left. Nevertheless, this man who loved the classical arts and knew very little about pop music was, for reasons best known (or perhaps even unknown) to him, completely smitten with The Beatles, and throughout the rest of November he attended a number of their gigs at The Cavern. Simultaneously, a thought began to germinate inside his head: maybe, just maybe, he could somehow take these scruffy rockers under his wing and give them some professional guidance.

Being for the Benefit of The Beatles

You've just gained some insight into Brian's fascination with The Beatles, but, from their perspective, what was there to see in *him*? Well, quite a lot, actually.

For one thing, even though Brian was clearly from a completely different social class to the circles that they usually mixed in, John, Paul, George, and Pete would have immediately recognized the benefit of being associated with somebody who appeared to be more like the entertainment industry bigwigs who they'd have to impress to obtain a prized recording contract and secure TV appearances. Indeed, Brian could build a much-needed bridge between themselves and those seemingly out-of-reach execs who he looked and sounded like, but who would normally never venture anywhere near Liverpool, let alone a dump like The Cavern. Hence George's inquiry as to what the 27-year-old Mr. Epstein would be doing there.

When it emerged that "Eppy" was actually interested in The Beatles and wanted to help them achieve their goals, their natural cynicism began giving way to curiosity and interest. Brian was professional in his approach, sincere in his attitude, and, unlike many of the small-time opportunists they'd associated with, intent on developing their long-term prospects. What did they have to lose?

Besides, Brian drove a brand-new Ford Zephyr Zodiac—Ringo Starr was the only other guy they knew who owned one and it wasn't in the same immaculate shape as Brian's. Without a doubt, this man was impressive.

The Rookie Manager

Each time Brian visited The Cavern Club to watch The Beatles perform during November 1961, he also hung around to say a few words to them and, in a roundabout way, find out where else they were playing and for how much. Soon, he began asking his record company and retail contacts in London about the artist/manager relationship, and he even visited Allan Williams at the Blue Angel Club to ask what he thought about handling The Beatles. Williams' response was that he "wouldn't touch them with a fucking barge pole," and while others were perhaps not quite so explicit in their advice, they were equally negative. What did Brian know about managing a band or even about the pop biz in general? And why would he want to get involved with a bunch of unreliable layabouts who turned up late for gigs and reneged on professional agreements?

Brian couldn't be dissuaded that easily. He at least wanted to have a formal meeting with John, Paul, George, and Pete to form some opinions of his own. So, he invited them to visit his office during the early afternoon of November 29 and they accepted. Disk jockey Bob Wooler duly accompanied The Beatles as their friend and adviser, and Brian Epstein made his pitch. He would arrange all of their concert bookings and ensure they were better organized, in better venues, and in many more areas of England than just Merseyside. (He probably didn't mention Aldershot.) As a result, from now on their minimum performance fee would be £15 ($37), except for Cavern lunchtime sessions where he would settle for doubling their present payment to £10 ($24). The Beatles listened and were fairly receptive. Brian, however, was saving the best for last: he would work on Bert Kaempfert to have the band released from its West German recording contract and then utilize his contacts within the industry to secure a proper deal with a major British record company.

This was heady stuff coming from a man with no previous pop experience, which is why The Beatles, while not rejecting his proposal, were not yet ready to commit. Another meeting was therefore scheduled for 4:30 p.m. on Sunday, December 3, giving everyone time to think about the situation while Brian traveled to London to gauge interest in the group—and try to arrange some auditions—by playing "My Bonnie" to several of his record company contacts.

Bob Wooler didn't attend the second meeting, and Paul conveyed his uncertainty about Brian's involvement in The Beatles' affairs by being the only one to turn up late. Brian, always punctual, was annoyed by this no-show, and his anger turned to disgust when, at around 5:15, George telephoned the McCartney home and discovered that, having only just gotten out of bed, Paul was in the bath. "How can he be so late for an important thing?" fumed Brian, to which George dryly retorted, "Well, he may be late, but he's very clean..."

Paul eventually arrived about an hour-and-a-half late and proceeded to ask most of the questions. Would being managed interfere with the kind of music The Beatles played? Brian assured him it wouldn't. The interrogation continued, and the meeting that commenced at Brian's office eventually concluded at a local pub where John took charge of the all-important decision by unilaterally declaring, "Right then, Brian, manage us. Where's the contract? I'*ll* sign it."

At this point, Brian didn't actually have a contract. The problem was, when he had looked at the typical agreement artists and managers entered into, he had found it totally weighted in favor of the manager. The artist was a virtual slave to exploitation—sometimes giving up half or more of his or her earnings—and Eppy, whose inherent sense of fairness characterized all of his business dealings until the end of his life, was not about to be a party to that. So, on December 6, he consulted Epstein family attorney and next-door neighbor, E. Rex Makin, asking for advice on the type of contract that should be drawn up. Makin, who had known Harry and Queenie's eldest son all his life, made it clear that, to him at least, this whole pop management idea sounded like another in the long line of fanciful plans that Brian invariably lost interest in. Brian insisted otherwise, and the result was a contract that would secure him a standard 10% of The Beatles' gross weekly income, rising to 20% if the band members' individual yearly earnings exceeded £1,500 ($3,600). Currently, they were raking in about two thirds of that amount, so if Brian did his job, that 20% wouldn't be hard to attain.

John, Paul, George, and Pete eventually signed the agreement at the NEMS office on January 24, 1962, following a lunchtime session at The Cavern. Brian's assistant, Alistair Taylor, witnessed and countersigned all of the signatures, including Brian's, even though the new manager didn't actually put pen to paper. The reason for this isn't altogether clear—perhaps Brian was being canny about tying himself to an agreement with these wayward rock 'n' rollers who hadn't yet proved their reliability. Or maybe he just didn't want to commit them before having proven himself. Whatever his motives, he eventually signed about nine months later. In the meantime, he was, to all intents and purposes, The Beatles' official manager.

Within the space of about two-and-a-half months, Brian Epstein had achieved his initial goal. Now it was a case of whether or not he could achieve what The Beatles wanted. Some of their parents weren't too sure. While Harry and Queenie were disturbed to learn that their young man would once again be distracted from his duties within the family business, Aunt Mimi had other concerns. "It's all right for you," she told

Brian. "If all this group business just turns out to be a flash in the pan, it won't matter. It's just a hobby to you. But what happens to them?"

She needn't have worried.

Chapter 13

Moptop Hair and Mohair Suits—The Road to Success

After years of struggling, of playing to indifferent audiences in unsavory venues, The Beatles finally turn the corner in this chapter.

Within less than a year of taking over as the group's manager, Brian Epstein came through on every single one of his promises. Initially, however, it looked as if he would fall at the vital hurdle: trying to secure the much sought-after recording contract. None of the major London companies were interested in signing the group, and The Beatles themselves began to lose faith in what Eppy could achieve. Yet, he persevered, and the subsequent results were hardly disappointing—except, that is, for Pete Best.

John, Paul, and George made some shifty moves to oust their unwitting drummer when success came knocking on their door, leaving Pete shell-shocked and his fans furious. Nevertheless, Ringo became a Beatle and, amid outrage and controversy, the Fab Four took a bow.

Failed Auditions: Part II

During the early morning hours of New Year's Day, 1962, The Beatles crammed themselves into an old van alongside their equipment and, with Neil Aspinall at the wheel, embarked on the long journey down to London. Their destination was the studio of Decca Records, where they were to perform a recording audition that Brian Epstein had attained for them with the help of a London-based pop journalist named Tony Barrow.

The previous month, thanks to Barrow's efforts, Decca's Head of A&R, Dick Rowe, had sent his young assistant Mike Smith to see and hear The Beatles play in The Cavern. Smith was duly impressed, but he wasn't prepared to sign them to a contract until his boss had the chance to hear them for himself. Hence the band's New Year's Day trip down to London.

The Beatles reached their destination at around 11 a.m. and were met there by Brian, who had traveled down by train. Mike Smith would be supervising the audition, but he had been at an all-night New Year's Eve party and didn't show up on time. Brian was miffed. Then, when Smith finally did appear, he recommended that John, Paul, and George should discard their own battered amplifiers in favor of the studio's better, more up-market equipment. They agreed, but this probably added to the unease that would be audible when The Beatles' recording test began.

In an attempt to display their versatility, they had decided to perform an eclectic collection of songs that encompassed several musical styles: Lennon-McCartney originals such as "Like Dreamers Do," "Hello Little Girl," and "Love of the Loved"; pop ballads such as "Till There Was You"; country & western ditties such as "Sure to Fall (In Love with You)"; R&B numbers such as "Searchin'"; and old standards given the "comic" treatment, such as "Three Cool Cats" and "The Sheik of Araby." In all, there were 15 songs and plenty of variety, yet there was no cohesion.

The Beatles plugged their guitar leads into unfamiliar amps and went for it. Yet, as evidenced on the recording of that session, George's rudimentary guitar solos sounded as if he was playing it safe while the uncharacteristically lackluster lead vocals of both John and Paul betrayed their nervousness. Even all-out rock numbers like "Money (That's What I Want)" came off as surprisingly tame.

After two hours, during which time they hadn't been able to re-record or overdub any extra parts, The Beatles were rushed out of the studio to make way for another band that Mike Smith was auditioning: Brian Poole and the Tremeloes. John, Paul, George, and Pete would have to wait for Decca's decision. Smith, however, had seem impressed, so they were quietly confident when returning to Liverpool for a string of gigs at The Cavern.

On January 4, the band's confidence received a boost when the local pop paper, *Mersey Beat*, published its first-ever popularity poll. The Beatles had been clear winners in the group category, fending off tough competition from other Liverpool bands such as Gerry and the Pacemakers, The Remo Four, Rory Storm and the Hurricanes, and Johnny Sandon and the Searchers.

Capitalizing on that success, Brian sent an application to the BBC six days later for The Beatles to perform a radio audition. This was duly approved, and on February 12 the band was put through its paces by producer Peter Pilbeam at Broadcasting House in Manchester. Pilbeam didn't like Paul's renditions of "Like Dreamers Do" and "Till There Was You," but he was impressed by John's vocalizing on "Memphis, Tennessee" and "Hello Little Girl." Noting that the group leaned more toward country & western than rock 'n' roll, he nevertheless gave The Beatles the thumbs-up and booked them for their first-ever radio appearance. This would be on *Teenager's Turn—Here We Go*, to be recorded on March 7 and broadcast the next day.

In the meantime, there was an unexpected setback: in early February, Decca rejected The Beatles and opted to sign Brian Poole and the Tremeloes instead. Brian was beside himself. How could the company turn down his boys after Mike Smith had seen them play twice and been so enthusiastic? The main reason offered—that "guitar groups are on the way out"—was totally unacceptable. Brian was going to London.

Once there, he met with Decca's A&R chief, Dick Rowe, and the company's sales manager, Sidney Beecher-Stevens. Brian gave them the whole pitch on The Beatles' talents and then some. Still, the executives weren't interested and Brian gave full vent to his frustration. "You must be out of your minds," he exclaimed as his voice rose several octaves. "These boys are going to explode. I am completely confident that one day they will be bigger than Elvis Presley!" The execs probably smiled facetiously and thought, *Yeah, right!* (Or *Hardly, my dear fellow.* After all, they were English.)

The line that the Decca execs fed Brian about guitar groups being "on the way out" was almost certainly just record company malarkey. After all, Brian Poole and the Tremeloes were hardly a jazz combo. They were a beat group like The Beatles, but in Mike Smith's eyes they had one distinct advantage; they were from Barking in Essex, close to London, and a couple hundred miles south of Liverpool. That would make them far easier and— more to the point—cheaper to work with. Dick Rowe had only permitted the inexperienced Smith to sign one of the bands that he auditioned, and Smith therefore went for Brian Poole and the Tremeloes. (Dick Rowe would later sign The Rolling Stones thanks to a tip-off by George Harrison, yet more bad maneuvers by Decca Records would eventually result in the company's demise.)

While still in London, and with the pair of reel-to-reel recordings from the Decca disaster in his briefcase, disillusioned Brian decided to visit the few major British record labels that hadn't yet rejected The Beatles. (In those days, there were few labels to start with.) At both Pye and Oriole he made his pitch and played the tapes, but in both cases he received the same negative response. With The Beatles breathing down his neck and John doing little to disguise his displeasure, Brian knew he had very few cards left in his hand.

Smartening Up for Better Bookings

A few months into 1962, The Beatles appeared to be a very different group from the one Brian had first laid eyes on just several months earlier. No longer were they late for gigs, while onstage they poured everything into the music, related to their audience, and cut out the smoking, eating, and talking among themselves. Brian had made things very clear: if The Beatles wanted a prosperous future, it really was a case of shape up or ship out.

Having always loved the theater, Brian knew a thing or two about presentation. From now on, The Beatles would conform to carefully pre-arranged sets of about an hour's duration. The set lists, the musicianship, and the presentation had to be tight, and those grubby leather outfits had to go, along with the scruffy T-shirts, jeans, and sneakers.

John Lennon would later say that, unlike Paul, he and George hated the idea of wearing suits, but in reality it appears that all four group members were more than happy to go along with Brian's directive. On March 7, 1962, The Beatles walked onto the stage of the Playhouse Theatre in Manchester for their radio debut on *Teenager's Turn—Here We Go* wearing dark gray mohair suits with pencil-thin lapels, button-down shirts, and knitted ties—all obtained from Beno Dorn, "The Master Tailor For Impeccable Hand-Made Clothes," located in the Liverpool suburb of Birkenhead. This was the sharp, early-sixties look for young guys in the West, although hereafter The Beatles would be fashion leaders, not followers.

Meanwhile, around the time "the boys" were changing into more natty clothes, Brian also oversaw another significant switch: the move away from tatty "jive halls" such as the Aintree Institute and Hambleton Hall (where, for some reason, there would be a fight whenever the band played "Hully Gully") to more sedate, respectable, and up-market concert venues. This was a hallmark of the Epstein touch that became evident almost immediately after he took over the managerial reins. Theaters, ballrooms, and colleges were now the norm, not just around Merseyside, but up and down the entire country, and The Beatles soon became used to performing shorter sets for more money.

The Aintree Institute in Walton, where The Beatles played 31 times between January 1961 and January 1962 for concertgoers who, in many cases, enjoyed throwing chairs at the band as well as at each other.

This was even the case with regard to their stints at the Star-Club in Hamburg. Now, if only Brian could deliver on his promise to secure a decent recording contract...

Congratulations Boys: The EMI Signing

Having nearly exhausted the list of major British record companies, Brian turned up at the massive HMV record store on London's Oxford Street on February 8, 1962. He went there to renew his acquaintance with yet another industry contact, Bob Boast, and, of course, to play him some of the Decca audition recordings. Boast was unable to help, but he did advise Brian to utilize the services of the small HMV studio located within the same building and transfer the tapes onto 78 rpm discs. These would look quite professional when presented to whatever record companies were still out there. Brian agreed.

Jim Foy cut the discs that day and, when he remarked that The Beatles demo sounded very good, Brian proudly pointed out that some of the songs were actually written by members of the group. Foy asked if these had been published. They hadn't. So, he put in a call to Sid Colman, the general manager of EMI publishing company Ardmore and Beechwood. (HMV was also a subsidiary of EMI.)

Coming down from the top floor of the HMV building, Colman liked what he heard and, back in his office, offered to publish the Lennon-McCartney songs. However, Brian was more interested in a recording deal, so Colman immediately phoned Judy Lockhart-Smith, the secretary (and future wife) of George Martin, head of A&R for EMI's smallest label, Parlophone. The reason Colman didn't first contact the A&R people at EMI's other, more prestigious labels, HMV and Columbia, was probably because, having listened to "My Bonnie," they had already turned Brian down by mail prior to the Decca audition.

A meeting between George Martin and Brian Epstein subsequently took place in George's office on February 13. Before playing the Decca recordings (on shiny new discs, no less), Brian went into his spiel about how massive the band was on Merseyside. According to George Martin's later recollections, he listened to the recordings and, although a little underwhelmed by what he heard, still felt that there was "something interesting" to the band's sound. That feeling would change many lives, including his own, but in the short term it led him to conclude that maybe he should meet The Beatles face to face. Brian was encouraged, but George Martin turned out to be apathetic. Nearly three months passed before Sid Colman, eager to sign Lennon and McCartney to a publishing deal, pushed him into a second meeting with their manager.

By then, The Beatles had embarked on their third Hamburg jaunt and Brian was back in London, trying to see if he could make any headway with the remaining record companies. One of these was Philips, who Colman was thinking of introducing him to should Parlophone's A&R chief pass up the opportunity. That never happened. At 11:30 on the morning of Wednesday, May 9, George Martin met Brian Epstein at the EMI Studios in Abbey Road, St. John's Wood, and, under pressure from his company bosses to secure Ardmore and Beechwood the publishing rights to the songs of Lennon and McCartney, informed Brian he was signing The Beatles. Their first recording session would take place on June 6.

Brian was ecstatic. He ran around the corner to a post office on Wellington Road, telephoned Harry and Queenie, and then rattled off a couple of telegrams. The first of these was addressed to The Beatles in Hamburg: "Congratulations boys. EMI request recording session. Please rehearse new material." The second, sent to Bill Harry at *Mersey Beat*, stated: "Have secured contract for Beatles to recorded [sic] for EMI on Parlaphone [sic] label. 1st recording date set for June 6th."

Several people, including recording engineer Norman Smith, would subsequently recall the June 6 session as some sort of audition. However, as revealed conclusively in Mark Lewisohn's *The Beatles: All These Years, Volume One—Tune In*, it was, in fact, a proper recording date; to be overseen by George Martin's assistant, Ron Richards, but also to help the A&R chief determine how to best present EMI's new pop group to the general public.

On June 2, 1962, The Beatles returned from Hamburg and four days later found themselves in EMI's Studio 2 for the first time, expecting to record a debut single that would be released that July. Out of the many songs that they performed for George Martin's assistant Ron Richards that day, four were recorded: the old Latin number, "Besame Mucho," and three Lennon-McCartney compositions: "Love Me Do," "P.S. I Love You," and "Ask Me Why." It was only when balance engineer Norman Smith particularly liked the sound of "Love Me Do" that the tape operator, Chris Neal, persuaded George Martin to leave the downstairs canteen and join everyone else in the studio.

Not the Best of Exits... And Ringo Makes Four

According to Paul, he, John, and George had started to become "a little bit dissatisfied" with Pete when comparing him to other drummers in Hamburg. According to George, Pete would sometimes fail to turn up for gigs and the band would have to turn to Ringo. And, according to many of the Liverpudlians who knew and watched The Beatles during 1961 and 1962, John, Paul, and George were basically jealous of the fact that handsome Pete was the most popular member of the group, especially among the female fans. The fact is, Pete Best's modest ability as a drummer and detached personality as a band member sealed his fate.

The same "mean, moody, magnificence" that undeniably excited the girls was also one of the factors that set Pete apart from the other Beatles. All of them, including George, had brash, devil-may-care personalities, but not Pete. He was shy, introverted, and rarely socialized with the others; instead preferring to spend his free time alone or with a girlfriend. He was the only Beatle who didn't take Prellies to stay awake during the long Hamburg nights. He was also the only Beatle to resist having his brushed-back hair re-styled into a moptop. Consequently, one of the group's biggest attractions did little to integrate himself within an otherwise cohesive unit.

Without Pete's knowledge, his colleagues had been thinking of ousting him for quite some time. In early 1962, they began excluding him from the group's affairs—he was the last to discover that The Beatles had failed their Decca audition because the others supposedly "didn't want to upset" him. Then, in mid-June, Joe Flannery, manager of a Liverpool group named Lee Curtis and the All-Stars, asked, "When are you going to join us, Pete?" The drummer didn't know what the manager meant, prompting Flannery to conclude he must have "jumped the gun" while mumbling that what he'd been hearing around town was perhaps just a rumor.

A few days later, Pete questioned Brian Epstein about this "rumor" and was assured there were absolutely no plans to replace him in The Beatles. However, while from Pete's perspective things continued as normal, the ax was about to fall and Brian knew it. Pete Best's lack of ability, evident to fellow professionals for quite some time, had once again been exposed during the June 6 recording session at EMI; the low-light being an awkwardly executed change of tempo on "Love Me Do." George Martin's subsequent comment to Brian that, in future, he would use a session drummer when recording The Beatles had simply added fuel to the flames, and thereafter no one even told Pete that EMI had signed the group.

Personally, John, Paul, and George obviously didn't feel they had much in common with their drummer. Musically, they no longer needed him. They were now Liverpool's hottest band and they would have little difficulty recruiting a more competent replacement. Still, what was lousy was the timing of their decision and the manner in which they chose to have him dismissed; leaving the chore to their hapless manager instead of having the good grace to confront Pete themselves.

After salvaging the band from its drummer-less Silver Beetles days, struggling through all of the disappointments, and even taking care of many of the bookings, Pete Best played with The Beatles for the last time on Wednesday, August 15, 1962. It was a nighttime Cavern gig, and afterwards, when John was leaving, Pete called out that, as usual, he and Neil Aspinall would come to fetch him in the van the following evening before setting off for a concert in Chester. John told him to not bother; he had "other arrangements." Then Brian approached Pete and said he would like to meet him at his NEMS office at 10:00 the next morning.

When Pete arrived at NEMS, Brian appeared nervous. He made a lot of small talk but avoided talking about business. Pete was waiting for him to get to the point. Brian eventually did: "The boys want you out and Ringo in." A bomb exploded inside Pete's head. What was the reason? "They don't think you're a good enough drummer, Pete." It had taken them two years to come to that decision. "And George Martin doesn't think you're a good enough drummer." Right. What about Ringo? Did he know about this yet? As it turned out, the fellow musician who Pete had hung out with in Hamburg and entertained in his own home had agreed to join the day before.

So there it was, signed, sealed, and delivered. Yet Brian, having at last got this worrying issue off his chest, now had the cheek to ask for one last favor: as Ringo couldn't join until Saturday, would Pete mind playing at the two preceding gigs? In his befuddled state of mind, Pete actually agreed. Then, after trying to drown his sorrows in a few pints of beer, he came to his senses and changed his mind.

Brian and The Beatles were surprised and disappointed when Pete never turned up at Chester, but they got by that night and the next by quickly drafting Johnny Hutchinson of The Big Three. "Hutch," you may recall, was the drummer who, just over three years earlier, had fulfilled the same task for The Silver Beetles at the Larry Parnes audition.

On the morning of August 14, in the middle of a summer season with Rory Storm and the Hurricanes at Butlin's holiday camp in Skegness—and just a day before Pete's sacking—Ringo had received a phone call from Brian asking him to join The Beatles. He would be paid a weekly wage of £25 ($62). Ringo immediately accepted but, out of a sense of loyalty to Rory, decided that it would be fair to give him a whole three days to find a replacement. His first official appearance as a Beatle, therefore, took place at a Horticultural Society Dance in Chester on Saturday, August 18, 1962. No doubt, a splendid time was had by all, but the following night it was a very different story down in The Cavern.

Word of Pete Best's sacking had spread like wildfire among The Beatles' followers and many of them now turned up looking for a confrontation. As a result, Brian needed a bodyguard to walk down Mathew Street and his nice new car was vandalized. Protesters shouted, "Pete forever, Ringo never!" "Pete is best!" and "We want Pete!" Meanwhile, Ringo's supporters were having none of it, and fists started to fly both inside and outside the club. It took quite a few weeks before things settled down.

As for Pete Best—well, life carried on, but, as you might imagine, it wasn't easy. Not only did The Beatles manage to pour a ton of salt into his wound by becoming the biggest showbiz phenomenon of the 20th century, but he also had to watch this happen while he himself failed to make any impact whatsoever. It has to be said that, while the way in which The Beatles got rid of Pete was heartless, their reasons were fairly justified—listen to his pedestrian performances on many of the recordings that he made with the band and it's evident that Ringo was a far, far better drummer.

Resounding failure led Pete to quit the music business altogether in 1968 and totally shun the media spotlight. Then, in 1978, he accepted the invitation of TV host and producer, Dick Clark, to talk about his Beatle days on U.S. television, and the following year he also acted as Technical Adviser on Clark's TV movie, *Birth of the Beatles*. Since then, Pete has appeared at numerous Beatle fan conventions, and has even co-written his memoirs (with Patrick Doncaster and then Bill Harry).

Many key players in The Beatles' story died young. Pete Best is a survivor, and in 1995 he at last earned royalties for his work with the band. 10 of the 19 musical tracks on *Anthology 1* consist of recordings that they made together for Bert Kaempfert in Hamburg, as well as for Decca and EMI in London. Accordingly, while the popular perception is that Pete was terribly unlucky to miss out on all the fame and fortune, it can also be argued that such a limited musician was extremely fortunate to have been a member of The Beatles for an extended period, resulting in global recognition ever since as well as a handsome payday when the above-mentioned recordings were finally issued.

Still, some things never change—on the *Anthology 1* album cover, a central portrait of the leather-clad Beatles features Pete's head torn off to reveal Ringo's face underneath...

Cavendish Avenue

"I saw a cool, blurred fan photo of Paul, taken outside his London home in early 1967 as he was breezing past, possibly on his way to the EMI Studios just around the corner on Abbey Road. I thought, 'What a great second in time,' capturing how, if you were in the St. John's Wood neighborhood back then, a Beatle might happen to walk by you. I wanted this painting to convey the feeling of, 'I think that was Paul McCartney with the mustache and sunglasses!' The other guys aren't around, but all four are about to continue their work on Sgt. Pepper. That alone is a pretty neat thought, so I painted it for myself and put it on my wall."

– Eric Cash

Chapter 14

Hitman for Hire—George Martin

George Martin may not have been overly enthused when he first heard The Beatles perform, but he was soon converted. From the time he worked with them on their first EMI single in 1962 to their final recordings in 1970, he was completely dedicated to what the band did in the studio. (Even if, toward the end, he was not always fully involved.)

The producer's role in recording changed quite dramatically during those years. As people, George and The Beatles hit it off, collaborating in the studio alongside engineers Norman Smith and Geoff Emerick. George's contribution to the sounds the band made and the arrangements they played cannot be underestimated.

Niche Recordings

George Martin's assistant, Ron Richards, initially took charge of The Beatles' first EMI recording session on June 6, 1962, largely because he knew a lot more about rock 'n' roll than Parlophone's chief producer and head of A&R.

Having studied piano and learned to play the oboe at the London Guildhall School of Music, George had carved out a career for himself in light orchestral music and comedy records since joining EMI back in 1950. At that time he had been assistant to Parlophone's then head of A&R, Oscar Preuss; when Preuss retired in 1955, George, at 29, became the youngest A&R head of any major British record label. (That same year, EMI bought out the American company Capitol Records.)

Parlophone was not the most prestigious label within the EMI empire. That honor went to Columbia and HMV courtesy of their rosters of major, mainstream pop and classical artists—Columbia's Head of A&R, Norrie Paramour, had discovered and nurtured Britain's biggest popular music discovery to date, Cliff Richard and the Shadows.

In the late 1950s, Cliff was Britain's main "answer to Elvis," and his biggest rival in teen popularity was a cockney singer by the name of Tommy Steele. George Martin had auditioned Tommy but turned him down, opting instead to sign his backing band, The Vipers Skiffle Group. (Decca subsequently signed Steele.) Parlophone did eventually add hit artists Adam Faith and Shane Fenton to its roster, but rock 'n' roll really wasn't George's bag. He left that to Ron Richards while he concentrated on producing the timeless solo comedy records of Goons member Peter Sellers; the classic live recordings of comic team Flanders & Swann; an album of the groundbreaking comedy show, *Beyond the Fringe*, featuring the talents of Cambridge University undergraduates Dudley Moore, Peter Cook, Jonathan Miller, and Alan Bennett; the inventive offerings of comedian Bernard Cribbins; and the middle-of-the-road musical talents of Matt Monro, Rolf Harris, and The Temperance Seven.

So, all in all, even though Parlophone's small budgets were in proportion to its chart successes, George Martin had a busy schedule overseeing numerous highly creative niche recordings. Then along came The Beatles.

George's initial lack of involvement at the June 6 recording session probably indicates that, once again, he was ready to hand over the rock 'n' roll reins to Ron Richards. So, considering that neither George nor Ron were exactly stunned by the band's performance that day, why did the head of A&R then actively take on the producer's role himself? Well, George Martin's intuition could have identified The Beatles as a possible means by which to diversify both his own career and the offerings of his label. More than that, however, it was almost certainly their endearing personalities—at least those of John, Paul, and George—that eventually reeled him in.

When the 7:00–10:00 p.m. session was over, George and recording engineer Norman Smith spoke to The Beatles about the workings of the recording studio and the inadequacies of the band's amplifiers. John, Paul, George, and Pete just sat around in the control room, listening but not reacting. Then, once he had finished lecturing them, the producer said, "Look, I've laid into you for quite a time. You haven't responded. Is there anything you don't like?"

The Beatles looked at each other with blank expressions, until George Harrison finally broke the ice: "Yeah, I don't like your tie."

The deadpan line immediately struck a chord with George Martin, who The Beatles admired for having worked with a couple of their beloved Goons. The joking continued for another 20 minutes or so, and, when they all left Studio 2 that night, there was more than a hint of mutual admiration between the two parties. Now G.M. had to decide—who should he focus on as the group's leader? After all, so many bands had one—Cliff Richard and the Shadows, Shane Fenton and the Fentones, Peter Jay and the Jay Walkers.

As things turned out, none of the four got the nod. The Beatles each had personal traits and abilities that appeared to complement one another, and so George Martin decided they should be presented to the public as a balanced unit.

The man who signed The Beatles to a recording contract and then played such a vital role in helping to shape their music—George Martin in his London office, 1985.

Well, Look Chaps

The Beatles, now with Ringo as their drummer, returned to the EMI Studios on Abbey Road on September 4, 1962, to record their new single. Again, Ron Richards initially took charge, rehearsing the band in the afternoon. George Martin took over for the evening session, recording take after take of a song written by Mitch Murray. Titled "How Do You Do It," George thought it would be ideal as The Beatles' first A-side, and had mailed them the demo, featuring a lead vocal by Barry Mason and backing by an unknown London group named The Dave Clark Five. The Fab Four rearranged the song and committed it to tape, yet they weren't keen about releasing someone else's material and the so-so results reflected that.

Although John and Paul wanted only their own compositions to be released as singles, they came to this session with hardly any studio experience and no chart success. Therefore, on the pointed advice of manager Brian Epstein, they followed the wishes of the man in charge, George Martin. They wouldn't do so again.

The producer soon took heed of their protests and agreed to give their own material a chance. That proved to be a wise decision. Throughout The Beatles' career, all of their singles, both A-sides and B-sides, would feature the compositions of only Lennon, McCartney, and Harrison. They would cover other people's songs on most of their early albums, but "How Do You Do It" wouldn't be among them. Instead, it would be passed on to fellow Merseysiders, Gerry and the Pacemakers, who'd use The Beatles' arrangement and take the single to the top of the British charts. A short while later, impressed by the Lennon-McCartney compositions that he'd already heard, music publisher Dick James set up a meeting with Brian Epstein and eventually signed a deal to publish their songs.

So, round one in the creative-decisions arena went to The Beatles. This would soon become the trend, to the point where George Martin would eventually make suggestions rather than issue directives. For now, however, he still had his hands on the wheel. The Beatles recorded more than 15 takes of "Love Me Do" on September 4 and none of them were deemed satisfactory. Furthermore, the producer and—according to Ron Richards—Paul McCartney were none too impressed with the drumming technique of Ringo who, on discovering that he only had two hands with which to play several percussion instruments, resorted to hitting the hi-hat with a maraca instead of a drumstick.

When The Beatles returned to Abbey Road seven days later they discovered that Ron Richards was taking no chances. He'd booked a session drummer named Andy White. Ringo feared the worst—perhaps they were about to "do a Pete" on him.

While Andy White took care of the beat, Ringo was given a tambourine for "Love Me Do" and some maracas to shake on "P.S. I Love You." Still, when those two tracks were released as The Beatles' first single on October 5, 1962, the cut of "Love Me Do" was one actually featuring Ringo on drums. To add some confusion, the *Please Please Me* LP released in March 1963 included the version of "Love Me Do" with Andy White. This was also used for later pressings of the single, coupled with White's drumming on "P.S. I Love You."

In hindsight, it seems clear that the Andy White episode was really just an insurance measure. In the days when four songs were expected to be recorded within three hours, The Beatles had gone through two three-hour sessions without nailing down their first single. Ron Richards obviously wanted to ensure that the third session would achieve the right results, and so he brought in Andy White because he knew he would be reliable. Now, it isn't clear whether Ron and George Martin were impressed by Ringo's maraca-and-tambourine-shaking, or if they just recognized that White didn't do anything that Ringo couldn't. Either way, Ringo was there to stay as The Beatles' full-time drummer, both onstage and in the studio. Not quite so permanent, however, was the whole studio routine.

When The Beatles first entered the EMI Studios in 1962, they, their producer, and the recording engineers were still expected to wear shirts and ties. The technical staff walked around in white coats, the equipment that they oversaw had to be used according to the strict guidelines that they laid down, and there were just three sessions per day: 10:00 a.m.-1:00 p.m., 2:30–5:30 p.m., and 7:00–10:00 p.m. Within a few years The Beatles changed all that—with the exception of the Abbey Road technicians, who didn't discard their beloved white coats until the early 1970s.

During the *Rubber Soul* sessions in late 1965, the group started booking sessions that lasted well into the morning hours. Given The Beatles' runaway success, EMI wasn't about to stand in the way of more hit records, so the scheduling arrangement became freer and easier, as did the amount of time (and therefore money) allotted to recording. Instead of a few hours, it invariably became days, weeks, and even months.

As The Beatles and other Liverpudlian acts that he signed in their wake began to take off, Parlophone's head of A&R distanced himself from the company's business affairs to concentrate more on studio work. As a result, in the landmark year of 1963, the singles that he was credited with producing spent 37 weeks at the top of the British charts. EMI couldn't believe its luck—and neither could George Martin when he compared his meager salary to the fortune that he was helping the company amass. In 1965, he quit and, together with Ron Richards, their colleague John Burgess, and Decca's Peter Sullivan, formed Associated Independent Recordings. A production deal was subsequently struck between AIR and EMI, and George Martin therefore continued to produce The Beatles.

In a broad sense, producing amounted to arranging the songs, introducing innovative ideas, inciting the right performances, and judging which were best. Yet, this was truly a collaborative effort— almost right from the start, the group had a major say in the creative process, and it therefore wasn't long before George Martin went from being The Beatles' musical director to the man who fleshed out and helped them realize many of their own ideas. It was G.M. who advised them to speed up "Please Please Me" from a Roy Orbison-type ballad to a more commercial up-tempo number; who thought it would be better to commence "Can't Buy Me Love" with the chorus; who orchestrated the pop songs "Yesterday" and "Eleanor Rigby"; who lent that classical touch to "In My Life" by playing the Elizabethan piano solo; and who oversaw the feeding of John Lennon's voice through the rotating speaker of a Hammond organ on "Tomorrow Never Knows" to fulfill the artist's wish to sound like "a Dalai Lama singing from the highest mountain top."

George Martin's contributions to The Beatles' artistic development and end product were immense, and he could quite easily point to each of the songs that he produced and say, "That's what *I* did."

George and Norman

Over the years, several recording engineers worked alongside George Martin on The Beatles' sessions, but only two men assumed that role on a consistent basis: Norman Smith and Geoff Emerick. By pure coincidence, they each worked on roughly the same number of projects, and they did so during the two most easily identifiable periods of The Beatles' career. For Smith it was the Beatlemania years, when the band recorded songs that could be performed in concert; for Emerick it was the studio years, when live performances were no longer a consideration.

Norman Smith, who engineered nearly all of The Beatles' recordings until the end of 1965, was nicknamed "Normal" by John and, having balanced the sound on the band's successful June 6, 1962 audition, he was assigned the task for almost every session thereafter. That was the EMI custom back then, yet the studio equipment that Norman had at his disposal wasn't exactly sophisticated, even by early 1960s standards.

The EMI facility already had four-track tape machines by the time The Beatles entered Abbey Road, yet they weren't able to take advantage of them until they had recorded their first two albums, *Please Please Me* and *With The Beatles*. The October 17, 1963 taping of "I Want to Hold Your Hand" was the first time they made use of the four-track, enabling them to, among other things, record the basic instrumental rhythm and then add vocals later on.

Norman Smith also had a small bag of tricks whenever certain effects were desired or required. Among them were...

- Echo, achieved naturally in a reverberant room or artificially with a vibrating plate.

- Double-tracking, whereby lead vocals were recorded more than once onto the same track to fatten the sound.

- Compression, which narrowed the dynamic range.

- Limiting, which curbed the higher frequencies.

- Equalization, which altered the sound by way of changing the frequency response.

Still, Norman's job was much more straightforward than that of engineers today, when it's not uncommon to make 72-and 96-track recordings utilizing all sorts of sound effects.

During the years when Norman Smith engineered The Beatles' records, the group took no active interest in the mixing sessions that involved the sounds being properly balanced, certain takes being spliced together, and some performances being either faded or edited out. Instead, under George Martin's watchful eyes, Norman would adjust the sound levels and tones at the mixing console while an assistant operated the tape machine. The producer usually also decided on the running order of songs on each album (which, in The Beatles' case, applied to the U.K. releases, not their Capitol-contrived U.S. counterparts).

When that routine eventually changed, "Normal" wasn't around to witness it. Having joined the EMI Studios staff in 1959, he was promoted to producer within the company's A&R department in February 1966. This was largely due to the gap left when George Martin, Ron Richards, and John Burgess had quit EMI the previous August to form their own AIR production setup with Peter Sullivan. In January 1967, Norman Smith got the opportunity to produce an unknown London group named The Pink Floyd and he capitalized on it. Then, in 1972, he crossed over to the other side of the studio and actually enjoyed short-lived popularity as the recording artist Hurricane Smith, topping the *Cashbox* chart in America with the single "Oh, Babe, What Would You Say?" Which all goes to show that, for some people at least, there *was* life after The Beatles.

George and Geoff

When Norman Smith moved up, Geoff Emerick moved in. Just 20-years-old at the time of his recruitment as The Beatles' new recording engineer, Geoff had already operated the tape machine on several of their sessions going back to 1963. Now here he was in April 1966, sitting alongside George Martin and working on a John Lennon composition named "Mark I." This would eventually be retitled "Tomorrow Never Knows" and, with its tape loops, artificial double tracking, processed vocals, and backward guitar solos, emerge as the most revolutionary Beatles track to date.

The Fab Four loved the fact that Geoff was young, bright, talented, eager to experiment, and unconcerned by those white-coated technicians warning, "You can't do that with this piece of equipment," or "That just won't work." Meanwhile, George Martin wasn't exactly slow off the mark either when it came to innovating sounds and transforming the sometimes-offbeat ideas of Lennon, McCartney, Harrison, and Starr into musical reality. Consequently, once the innate musical talents of The Beatles merged with the incomparable team of Martin and Emerick, great things were bound to happen.

Sometimes, George and Geoff would come up with a terrific idea only to be thwarted by a niggling little problem—the piece of equipment they needed hadn't been invented yet. In such instances they could turn to Ken Townsend and his EMI Studios technical staff, who would either tamper with the existing gear or come up with some new device to satisfy the demands of artists, producer, and engineer. Indeed, a number of Ken's innovations have been incorporated into several of today's recording studio devices.

For his part, Geoff Emerick's inventiveness can be heard on The Beatles' post-1965 recordings, not only in the form of the multitude of special effects, but also the differences in the sounds of their own instruments. For example, just listen to the thump of Ringo's bass drum on tracks such as "Tomorrow Never Knows" and "Sgt. Pepper's Lonely Hearts Club Band." Thanks to how Geoff positioned the microphones—up close and inside the drum—and then processed the sound, there is a real boom. Today, this isn't unusual, but it was pretty revolutionary back in the mid-sixties when the bass drum was traditionally just recorded as part of the overall beat. Then again, so were a lot of things that were going on in EMI's Studio 2 at that time.

The live area of EMI's Studio 2, where The Beatles crafted the majority of their recordings.

The tape echo employed on John's voice on "A Day in the Life," the fading up and down of the orchestra on that same track, the intricate recording of Indian instruments on George's "Within You Without You," the up-front sound of Paul's bass guitar—these attributes and more earned Geoff a Grammy Award for his engineering work on *Sgt. Pepper*. Still, even though he was working with the world's most famous and accomplished rock band, Geoff had a mind of his own and a clear idea as to how people should collaborate in the studio. Therefore, when tensions began to flare among The Beatles during the "White Album" sessions, Geoff Emerick walked out.

That was in July 1968, and he didn't return for the troubled *Get Back/Let It Be* sessions the following year. (From early 1968 through early 1970, various other people engineered Beatles recording sessions, including Eddie Kramer, Ken Scott, Phil McDonald, and Glyn Johns.) Then, precisely 12 months after his departure, Geoff rejoined The Beatles, quitting EMI to run the Apple Studios facility that was located in the basement of the group's Central London office building. This was a week before he became the first-ever engineer to work at EMI Studios in a freelance capacity, recording tracks for The Beatles' *Abbey Road* album.

That turned out to be the band's swansong, but not the end of the story as far as either George Martin or Geoff Emerick were concerned. Both have continued to work with Paul McCartney over the years, and Geoff even engineered the two new Beatles recordings that were released respectively in 1995 and 1996: "Free as a Bird" and "Real Love."

Chapter 15

Her Majesty's a Pretty Nice Girl—Changing Audiences

As you've already seen, The Beatles walked a long and sometimes torturous road before they achieved any measure of success. However, once they arrived at their destination, things changed very rapidly, as indicated by the venues where they started playing.

In this chapter the key phrase is *stark contrast*, and never was this more appropriate to a period of The Beatles' career than the 12 months from December 1962 to November 1963. In that time the band went from playing in a Liverpool basement club to the London Palladium, while performing for audiences ranging from late-night beer swillers to the Royal Family.

A quartet of concerts perfectly symbolized the Fab Four's sudden rise to prominence, so let's now join the group in saying some fast hellos and quick goodbyes.

Last of the Long Nights—Auf Wiedersehn, Hamburg

When The Beatles left for their fifth and final trip to Hamburg on December 18, 1962, "Love Me Do" was a Top 20 hit on the British charts and they were in the middle of numerous radio and TV appearances. The last thing the band members wanted to do was face another grueling stint in Germany, but they had already been contracted to do so. Reluctantly, therefore, they took to the Star-Club stage the night they arrived, embarking on yet another 42 hours of performances within two weeks.

One concession that the venue made was to allow The Beatles to have Christmas Day off. Nevertheless, on New Year's Eve they were back onstage for their last Star-Club performance, captured in part by Ted "Kingsize" Taylor's portable Grundig tape recorder. The recording, which lasts just over 70 minutes and has numerous edits, comprises one of the two sets the band performed that night, and its 30 numbers provide a snapshot of The Beatles at the vital turning point in their career.

The songs include just two Lennon-McCartney originals, "I Saw Her Standing There" and "Ask Me Why," both of which they soon recorded for their first album. Interestingly, the two sides of the group's then-current and, thus far, only single, "Love Me Do"/"P.S. I Love You," were not performed. (Perhaps they were in the other set.) Of the remaining numbers, nine were eventually recorded and released on Beatles albums, while the others—an eclectic mixture of rock 'n' roll oldies, rearranged music hall numbers, contemporary pop hits, and past and present romantic ballads—would all disappear from their stage repertoire within a year.

By then, the Fab Four would be headlining package tours in which they only had around half an hour to perform a selection of their own recordings. No longer would they play sets boasting either the variety or duration of those at the Star-Club, and, while that may have been a relief to them, it was certainly a loss to their future fans.

The Best of Cellars—Goodbye, Cavern

When, on February 19, 1963, Cavern Club DJ Bob Wooler informed the audience that The Beatles' second single, "Please Please Me," had just reached the top of the U.K.'s *New Musical Express* chart, there was almost complete silence. Proud yet possessive of "their boys," the hometown fans realized that success would result in John, Paul, George, and Ringo moving out of The Cavern and away from Liverpool. Many of them even resisted buying the record to avert that possibility, yet they were battling the inevitable. (Some of them probably knew this when they stood in line for tickets a whole two days beforehand.)

During the next few months, The Beatles' follow-up single, "From Me to You," would top the U.K. charts for seven weeks; their debut album, *Please Please Me*, would also hit the Number One spot; and a non-stop series of nationwide concert, radio, and TV appearances would turn them into the new sensations of the British pop scene. At the same time, while groups such as Gerry and the Pacemakers, Billy J. Kramer with the Dakotas, and The Searchers joined Liverpool's invasion of the hit parade, The Beatles started to attract blanket coverage in both the local and national press. On August 1 they even became the sole subject of a new magazine titled *The Beatles Monthly Book*, and then a couple of days later the inevitable finally happened: the group gave its last performance at The Cavern Club.

The venue that had helped shape and nurture The Beatles wasn't able to accommodate the number of people who now wanted to see them play. Nor could it pay the kind of appearance fees that Brian Epstein was now commanding for them. Nearly 300 Cavern appearances earlier, they had been paid £5 ($12), whereas in August '63 the club shelled out a record £300 ($720) for what was only the second Beatles Cavern gig in the past five-and-a-half months. The tickets went on sale at precisely 1:30 on July 21 and by 2:00 they were all gone. So, for that matter, were the chances of The Beatles ever returning.

Brian Epstein reportedly assured Bob Wooler that, one day, the Fab Four would be back, yet that day never came. In many ways, it was a shame. The Cavern obviously wasn't as attractive as the venues The Beatles would perform in from now on, but its intimate atmosphere was virtually irreplaceable, and at least people could see and hear them play.

In Everyone's Home—Sunday Night at the London Palladium

On October 13, 1963, more than a quarter of Britain's population got to see what all the fuss was about when The Beatles topped the bill on Val Parnell's *Sunday Night at the London Palladium*. Produced by Associated TeleVision, Britain's top-rated entertainment show was broadcast live across the nation from 8:25 p.m. to 9:25 p.m. and attracted an estimated 15 million viewers—not a record-breaking statistic, but pretty significant nonetheless.

One of many variety shows that were extremely popular during television's earlier years, *Sunday Night at the London Palladium* offered British viewers the same diverse assortment of acts that their American counterparts watched on *The Ed Sullivan Show*: jugglers, dancers, acrobats, ventriloquists, comedians, singers, you name it. The host was all-round entertainer, Bruce Forsyth, and members of the public even took to the stage each week to compete in a game called "Beat the Clock."

On October 13, 1963, it was The Beatles who almost everyone tuned in and—judging by the crowds outside the famous old theater—turned out to see. Pictures of the crowds blocking Argyll Street in Central London were splashed across the next day's newspapers, as were reports of how fab and gorgeous The Beatles were. John, Paul, George, and Ringo had made the most of their big opportunity.

Normally, the headlining act didn't appear until the end of the show, but on this occasion the decision was taken to wind up the screaming teens by providing them with a brief glimpse of their idols right at the start. Bruce Forsyth provided the bait by teasing, "If you want to see them again, they'll be back in 42 minutes..." That allowed the kids to go off and have a Coke while American R&B singer Brook Benton and British singer-comedian Des O'Connor did their thing. Then the big moment arrived. Forsyth strung things out as long as he could, counting down "5-4-3-2-1" while the squealing members of the audience were practically beside themselves with excitement, and their squeals turned into high-pitched screams when The Beatles appeared and launched straight into "From Me to You." Welcome to instant hysteria—not just inside the Palladium, but in living rooms all across Britain. Allan Williams, watching at home, suddenly regretted not patching things up with the band he'd taken to Hamburg just over three years earlier. Later recalling how he threw a cushion at the TV screen out of sheer frustration, he asserted that, if he had a brick, he would have done the same.

The Beatles next stormed their way through "I'll Get You" and their latest chart sensation, "She Loves You," before Paul tried to announce their last number while John shouted at the screaming girls to "Shut up!" No major star behaved like that back then—come to think of it, no major star behaves like that *now*, and the same certainly applied to John's response when Paul encouraged members of the audience to clap their hands and stamp their feet. There stood Lennon with a demented look on his face, clapping and stamping like a cripple. Talk about political incorrectness—these days, such "clowning around" wouldn't elicit the laughter and applause that greeted his antics back in the early-to-mid-sixties.

"Twist and Shout" was The Beatles' final song, after which the performers and their host all engaged in the traditional show-closing routine of standing on a revolving stage and waving to the folks in the theater and at home. 12 minutes was all it had taken to slay the Great British public.

For most artists, this kind of appearance would be an all-time career high. And, to all intents and purposes, that's what many people assumed it would be for The Beatles—including The Beatles themselves. Yet, as things turned out, it was just another step up a ladder stretching toward the stratosphere.

By Royal Command

Just two days after the Palladium appearance, it was announced that The Beatles had accepted an invitation to perform at the 1963 Royal Command Performance. It would take place at Central London's Prince of Wales Theatre on Monday, November 4, and be broadcast on network TV on Sunday, November 10.

A lengthy, upscale variety show, this annual charity gala always boasts an international lineup of stars, as well as the attendance of certain royal household residents. In November 1963, Queen Elizabeth II was five months pregnant with her youngest child, Prince Edward, and as the expectant monarch's bulging belly was deemed inappropriate for public viewing (unlike Lennon's cripple impersonations), she and Prince Philip were replaced in the Royal Box by the Queen Mother and Princess Margaret.

Now, while the royals never have to pay for the best seats in the house, many consider it an honor to perform in their presence. In 1963, The Beatles' fellow honorees included Marlene Dietrich, Buddy Greco, and those singing puppet pigs, Pinky and Perky. In all, there were 19 acts and the Fab Four were the seventh onstage, yet at this point in 1963, with British Beatlemania in high gear, it was a surefire bet they would steal the show.

As at their Palladium gig, The Beatles kicked off with "From Me to You" just before the curtains opened. Their playing was tight, their moptops looked perfect, and Paul's nervousness manifested itself in the form of a blunt "Good evening. How are you? All right?" You would have thought he was at The Cavern rather than the Prince of Wales. Yet, it was just this kind of unpretentious, down-to-earth attitude that personified The Beatles and it quickly disarmed the assembled glitterati.

After a typically vivacious rendition of the band's biggest hit to date, "She Loves You," Paul then amused the audience at another, ample-figured artists's expense by announcing that the next song, "Till There Was You," was from composer Meredith Wilson's show, *The Music Man*, and had been "recorded by our favorite American group, Sophie Tucker." Cue polite audience laughter before a visibly nervous Paul crooned the song, exaggeratedly nodding his head from side to side.

So far, so good. However, John Winston Lennon hadn't yet said his piece, and anyone who knew him was well aware that a little gem could emerge from his mouth at any given moment. Would he have the nerve in this setting to contort his face and body while inviting audience participation? They didn't have to wait long to find out. Peering out at the staid, stuffy Prince of Wales patrons, he ventured, "For our last number I'd like to ask your help. Would the people in the cheaper seats clap your hands..."

There was mild, almost nervous chuckling while the aristocrats—unsure where this was heading—monitored reaction up in the Royal Box.

"...and the rest of you, if you'll just rattle your jewelry."

This pointed yet pleasantly-delivered quip prompted laughter, applause, and probably sighs of relief around the theater, before the usually sedate audience started clapping along when The Beatles launched full-tilt into "Twist and Shout."

Britain's newspapers had a field day, blaring the word "Beatlemania" all over their front and center pages while a *Daily Mirror* headline confirmed the favorable royal reaction: "They Loved Them—Yeah, Yeah, Yeah!" Predictably, the general public could hardly wait to see the cause of all this excitement. When the show aired on TV the following Sunday, nearly 40 percent of the population tuned in to watch, while many of the three million people who still didn't have television sets listened to the BBC Radio highlights.

As for the quartet attracting all of the attention—having rapidly scaled the heights in their home country, The Beatles would soon be looking to conquer foreign shores. The royal show was certainly another notch on their belt, but to them it was more of an experience rather than a real move forward. Every year after 1963, The Fab Four would secretly be invited to make another appearance at the Royal Command Performance. Every year they would secretly decline.

PART 4

TO THE TOPPERMOST OF THE POPPERMOST

"When they were depressed or we were all depressed," John Lennon once recalled with regard to The Beatles, "thinking that the group was going nowhere, and this is a shitty deal and we're in a shitty dressing room, I'd say, 'Where are we going, fellas?' And they'd go, 'To the top, Johnny,' in pseudo-American voices. And I'd say, 'Where is that, fellas?' and they'd say, 'To the toppermost of the poppermost!' And I'd say, 'Right!' Then we'd all sort of cheer up."

In this part of Beatles 101, *that ambition turns into reality. The Fab Four become international superstars of the stage, television, radio, and silver screen before growing sick of all the pressure and deciding to kick back for a while. We'll take a look at their public careers and private lives, and then, just to give you some sense of the incredible decade with which The Beatles will always be associated, I'll run through some of the burning issues of those turbulent years.*

After all, as the saying goes, if you can remember the 1960s you probably weren't there...

Chapter 16

Scene and Heard—Radio Days and TV Times

Several million people attended The Beatles' live concert performances over the years. However, during the 1960s several billion others had to make do with watching the group on TV, listening to them on the radio, and reading about them in the press. Until the end of 1966, John, Paul, George, and Ringo were hardly slackers about touring. But, if it hadn't been for the electronic image and the written word, most people wouldn't have had a clue as to what they were really like.

The Beatles were very much children of the modern media age, and while they took full advantage of every available means to publicize themselves, they were also exploited by the same people who helped promote them. It was, in essence, a truly symbiotic relationship.

The Beatles at the Beeb

In January 1962, Brian Epstein wrote to the Variety Department at the Manchester headquarters of the BBC (a.k.a. the Beeb), asking if The Beatles could audition for *Teenager's Turn—Here We Go*. As previously mentioned, that was one audition they did pass, and from March 1962 until March 1963 they appeared five times on the show (titled just *Here We Go* from October 1962). Unfortunately, while there are lo-fi recordings of The Beatles' 1962 BBC radio broadcasts, none exist of their Luxembourg debut in October of that year on *The Friday Spectacular*.

In 1963, the BBC helped spread the band's name at home and, eventually, abroad. To start with, on January 26, the Fab Four made their first of 10 appearances on *Saturday Club*, the Beeb's premiere pop show. This two-hour transmission could attract an audience of around 10 million people and double that figure during the second half, when the company's General Overseas Service (now known as the World Service) also broadcast the proceedings to Africa, the Middle East, the Far East, Southeast Asia, Australasia, and parts of Europe.

After both "Please Please Me" and "From Me to You" topped the British charts (the latter in the spring of 1963), not only did The Beatles' BBC radio appearances dramatically increase, but so did the number of shows willing to feature them: *The Talent Spot, Here We Go, Saturday Club, Easy Beat, Pop Inn, Parade of the Pops, Non Stop Pop, Side By Side, The Beat Show, The Public Ear, On the Scene, Steppin' Out*, and *Swinging Sound '63*.

Swinging Sound '63 was a live broadcast of the band's April 18 performance at London's Royal Albert Hall. Otherwise, while a few shows were taped at Manchester's Playhouse Theatre, the majority were recorded at London venues: the BBC's own Broadcasting House, Aeolian Hall, Piccadilly Studios, Maida Vale Studios, the Paris Studio, and yet another Playhouse Theatre where, on May 21, *Steppin' Out* host Diz Disley memorably announced, "We have here four young fellas who, since they emerged from the trackless interior of Merseyside a mere matter of months ago, have been laying 'em in the aisles all over the Isles, from Land's End to John O' Groats. So, mind your backs, wacks, for it's the earth-shaking sounds of The Beatles!"

Usually, the band had only a few hours to record several songs on the BBC's mono tape machines, so everything had to be performed live, with no opportunity to overdub any of the voices or instruments. The most strenuous sessions took place on July 16, 1963, when 17 songs were taped for three separate broadcasts of *Pop Go The Beatles*, the band's own half-hour show that ran for 15 weeks throughout the summer, and on September 3, when 18 numbers were recorded for three more of those shows. Since John, Paul, George, and Ringo had so little time to rehearse, it's hardly surprising that many of the songs they performed were culled from their stage repertoire. Indeed, the 15 *Pop Go The Beatles* episodes featured them running through 56 different numbers, 25 of which were never released on any albums or singles. Many were classics by rock pioneers like Chuck Berry, Carl Perkins, Elvis Presley, and Little Richard, as well as unusual numbers such as Marino Marini's "The Honeymoon Song." Lee Peters hosted the first four shows and was promptly renamed "Pee Liters" by John Lennon. Thereafter, Pee was replaced by Rodney Burke.

When the last edition of *Pop Go The Beatles* was broadcast in late September, the band's fourth single, "She Loves You," was in pole position on the British charts and John, Paul, George, and Ringo were on the verge of becoming household names. They no longer needed to rush all over the place to capitalize on radio's publicity value, and Brian

Epstein—perhaps also trying to avoid overexposure—even began canceling BBC contracts. As a result, whereas the first nine months of 1963 saw The Beatles perform on 34 BBC Radio shows, they only played on 15 from October 1963 to June 1965.

The corporation that had, only a short time earlier, auditioned The Beatles, now found itself begging them to make return appearances. Brian agreed to several more performances for *Saturday Club*, as well as on a new late night show named *Top Gear* and for some "holiday specials" titled *From Us to You*. In addition, the Fab Four recorded messages for overseas radio stations and, when they were touring abroad, agreed to incessant interviews as well as occasional broadcasts of their concerts.

The end of radio performing came with a BBC special broadcast on June 7, 1965 ("Whit Monday" in England) and unimaginatively titled *The Beatles (Invite You to Take a Ticket to Ride)*.

Thereafter, the Beeb and other radio networks would have to make do with interviews, usually featuring individual group members. On March 7, 1982, BBC Radio 1 celebrated the 20th anniversary of the Fab Four's first broadcast with a two-hour show titled *The Beatles at the Beeb*. This contained songs and chit-chat that had been unheard since the original 1960s transmissions. Next, stories began to circulate about a legitimate album of those recordings. The problem was, who had the right to authorize such a release? The BBC, who owned the tapes? EMI, who had an exclusive record deal with the group during the years when the BBC sessions took place? Or Apple Corps, The Beatles' own company, which always appears to have first and last say about any such matters? Negotiations among all three parties were long and protracted, but in 1994 a two-CD set on the Apple label, under exclusive license to EMI Records, and by arrangement with BBC Enterprises, was finally released.

Titled *Live at the BBC*, the CD featured 56 songs digitally remastered and compiled by George Martin. Interspersing the songs with chat and banter, this package revived memories of an era when music was the message and innocence still reigned. In 2013, a second two-CD set was released: *On Air—Live at the BBC Volume 2*, featuring 40 songs and 23 spoken segments, including introductions, interviews, and Beeb studio banter.

Love is All You Need

"Another of my personal favorites, adapted from a photo taken at the rehearsal for the Our World *TV broadcast. It's a John moment: John singing a John song live in front of billions of people and nailing it.*

"Although I moved his hand slightly, having it in there provided me with an opportunity to show some good detail, such as the tendons and the fingernails. Next to the face, someone's hands are often the most expressive thing in a painting—John might have been nervous on this occasion, but the way he's barely holding the headphone with his fingertips shows him to be in a relaxed mood. Then again, having his hand near the center of the painting might distract the viewer, so I balanced that by spending extra time working on the glasses in order to shift people's focus.

"As the photo that I used had a blank background, I added some of the elements that are present in the video—the balloons, flowers, and 'All You Need is Love' sign—to give it a really cool, colorful '67 look. That said, the biggest challenge was the hippie shirt. I've seen photos of John wearing it, but the shirt in the image I was working from didn't have a distinct pattern. So, I had to make it up, and I also wanted it to look like silk instead of cotton. The folds on a cotton shirt are a little bit more billowy, a little bit thicker, whereas the wrinkles on this shirt had to be flatter and more dense to give it that silk look. It also had to have the appropriate shine without looking like plastic.

"Originally, my idea was to subtly paint the song's lyrics over the whole image—not clear enough to read all of them, but enough to pick up a word here and there. So, that's what I did, until about halfway through that experiment I realized it wasn't going to work. The words were obscuring John's face along with other things that I wanted to highlight in the painting, and I therefore trashed the idea in favor of a more straightforward approach."

— Eric Cash

Beatles on the Box

TV sets were already in most Western homes by the early 1960s and, in many cases, were almost a member of the family. Television's cultural impact was enormous, so it was only natural that The Beatles quickly developed a close relationship with "the box." Let's take a look at The Beatles' TV exploits—both live and animated—and see how, as with radio, they used the medium to advance their career.

Early Fabs in the Flesh

Although The Beatles performed in front of TV cameras for the first time during a Cavern lunchtime gig on August 22, 1962, this didn't turn out to be their first TV appearance. The cameras were there as a result of fans writing to Manchester-based Granada Television, and the results were supposed to end up on a local show called *Know the North*. John, Paul, George, and the recently installed Ringo performed two numbers, "Some Other Guy" and "Kansas City"/"Hey-Hey-Hey-Hey!" but, for various reasons, the planned broadcast was canceled. The footage didn't turn up on TV until November 6, 1963, when Granada aired "Some Other Guy" on *Scene At 6.30*. The film has been widely shown ever since, complete with silent "cutaway" shots which are all that remain of the band's performance of "Kansas City." (The audio snippet of "Kansas City" that appears in the first installment of the *Beatles Anthology* documentary comes from further Granada sound recordings of the group performing that number and "Some Other Guy" at the Cavern on September 5, 1962. Five seven-inch acetate discs of those recordings were pressed and, in 1993, Apple bought one of them at auction for £15,000/$22,000.)

Regardless, The Beatles *did* appear on TV in 1962, on a variety of local networks spanning several parts of Britain. The very first show was *People and Places*, broadcast live on October 17 from Granada's Manchester studios to the north and northwest of England. Once again, they performed "Some Other Guy" (the Ritchie Barrett band favorite that, in the wake of its March 1963 release by The Big Three, would never be recorded by The Beatles at EMI Studios) and "Love Me Do." Then, on October 29, they taped a return appearance for broadcast on November 2, singing "Love Me Do" and "A Taste of Honey."

The Beatles next appeared on *Discs a Gogo*, set in "the gayest coffee bar in town" and broadcast in Wales and the west of England. This was followed by *Tuesday Rendezvous* in the London area, *Roundup* in Scotland, and then the top-rated *Thank Your Lucky Stars* across the nation. Independent Television was responsible for all of these broadcasts, but BBC TV soon got in on the act and, between them, the two networks ensured that 1963 was a hectic year for the Fab Four.

Among the many shows to feature The Beatles during this period were *At Large*, *The 625 Show*, *Scene at 6.30*, *Pops and Lenny*, *Juke Box Jury*, *Day by Day*, *Big Night Out*, *This Week*, *South Today*, *Ready, Steady, Go!*, *Late Scene Extra*, and the ludicrously titled *Move Over, Dad*. On October 9, John's 23rd birthday, the BBC broadcast *The Mersey Sound*, a documentary that included performances by The Beatles, as well as interviews with them and Brian Epstein. This was followed four days later by the landmark *Sunday Night at the London Palladium* appearance on ITV and, in early November, the Beeb's transmission of the Royal Command Show. Not for nothing were people increasingly joking that BBC stood for the "Beatles Broadcasting Corporation."

Small Screens, Big Screams

The British were no longer the only people who could turn their TV dials to a Beatle broadcast. In October, when John, Paul, George, and Ringo undertook their first foreign tour—a week-long jaunt around Sweden—they taped a performance on the pop show *Drop In* (broadcast on November 3). Then, on October 31, they returned to the U.K. and wild scenes of Beatlemania at London Airport—witnessed by, of all people, a certain Ed Sullivan. This was the man whose Sunday night variety show on CBS had become a TV institution in the U.S., promoting the talents of too many stars to mention and, in 1956 and 1957, helping the young Elvis Presley to take the nation by storm. Now here Ed was in 1963, watching normally sedate British teens screaming themselves into a frenzy. It set him thinking...

In early November, while Brian Epstein and Billy J. Kramer (one of several artists Brian was by now managing) were in New York on a promotional visit, Ed met with the young manager and talked terms. Brian demanded that The Beatles, then unknown in the U.S., be given prominent billing on Sullivan's Sunday night extravaganza. That sounded completely ridiculous to the stone-faced host—until Brian accepted his offer of $10,000 for three headlining appearances. Being that a top act would normally command around $7,500 for a single performance on his show, Ed was delighted to strike such a bargain-basement deal and even offered to pay for the group's air fare and hotel stay. Brian, on the other hand, had ensured that his charges would be *top of the bill for three consecutive weeks* on America's top-rated TV variety show, providing them with the best possible opportunity to do what no other British pop act had previously done: conquer the all-important U.S. market.

Before The Beatles ever made it to New York, a clip of them singing "She Loves You" from the BBC's *Mersey Sound* documentary was aired on NBC's *Jack Paar Program* on January 4, 1964. The next morning, *New York Times* critic Jack Gould commented, "It would not seem quite so likely that the accompanying fever known as Beatlemania will also be successfully exported. On this side of the Atlantic it is dated stuff."

Fast-forward to February 7 and The Beatles' arrival on U.S. soil, prompting a media frenzy unlike anything ever seen in America. Then, a couple of days later, the Fab Four appeared live on *The Ed Sullivan Show* and all hell broke loose.

During the afternoon of that historic day, The Beatles actually taped what would be their third Sullivan appearance, to be broadcast a couple of weeks later after they had returned to the U.K. The group performed "Twist and Shout," "Please Please Me," and "I Want to Hold Your Hand," after Ed stated, with the utmost feeling, "All of us on the show are so darned sorry, and sincerely sorry, that this is the third—and thus our last—current show with The Beatles, because these youngsters from Liverpool, England, and their conduct over here, not only as fine professional singers but as a group of fine youngsters, will leave an imprint on everyone over here who's met them..."

The "third audience," so to speak, was shipped out of CBS' Studio 50 in midtown Manhattan and replaced by the "first audience," comprising the lucky 728 people who had somehow managed to get tickets. The show went on air live at 8:00 that night, and an estimated 73 million people in more than 23 million homes tuned in to see The Beatles live up to all of the publicity hype. This smashed the U.S. TV viewing record along with another one relating to local crime statistics—purportedly, throughout the entire hour of the show's broadcast, not one car hubcap was reported stolen in New York City.

If the October 13, 1963 broadcast of Val Parnell's *Sunday Night at the London Palladium* helped spread Beatlemania across Britain, the February 9, 1964 edition of *The Ed Sullivan Show* rewrote the history books.

At the same time, American film producers Albert and David Maysles, with funding from Britain's Granada Television, were filming much of what The Beatles said and did on their first U.S. visit. This included scenes at Kennedy Airport, inside their Plaza Hotel suite, at a Central Park photo shoot, inside their limo, out on the town, on the train to Washington, D.C., and in Miami where, on February 16, they made their second live *Ed Sullivan Show* appearance, watched this time by 70 million people. The resulting 36-minute documentary was screened in the U.K. on February 12, 1964, while a 45-minute version aired in America on November 13. (In 1991, an 83-minute video was released. Titled *The Beatles: The First U.S. Visit*, this also included footage from the Sullivan shows and the band's first American concert, in Washington, D.C.)

The Beatles performed on *The Ed Sullivan Show* for a fourth and final time on August 14, 1965. The next evening, they played their legendary concert at Shea Stadium in New York. To tie in with that momentous occasion, the group was filmed behind the scenes and onstage, as 55,600 delirious fans went wild. *The Beatles at Shea Stadium* captured Beatlemania at its peak, and it was given its world premiere on BBC1 on March 1, 1966. British TV broadcasts were still only black-and-white, but American viewers were able to view the documentary in glorious color on ABC... 10 months later, on January 10, 1967.

Between 1964 and 1966, TV viewers in Australia, Britain, France, Germany, and Japan all saw local concert performances by the Fab Four. However, at around the same time that the touring stopped, so did the live television appearances. The next-to-last of these took place on BBC1's *Top of the Pops* on June 16, 1966, with The Beatles miming to "Paperback Writer" and "Rain." It was the group's only live contribution to the Beeb's premiere pop show. However, in 1971, as part of the corporation's ridiculous "waste not, want not" policy, this film was recorded over and an irreplaceable piece of history was destroyed, all for the price of a reel of tape.

Fortunately, more respect has been accorded to The Beatles' very last live television appearance. It wasn't announced as such at the time—no one, including The Beatles, perceived it that way—but, since it did turn out to be an end of sorts, the size of the audience was certainly fitting. People in North and Central America, Britain, Europe, North Africa, Australia, and Japan all watched a live broadcast of the BBC's *Our World* show on June 25 and 26, 1967 (depending on their location). In Britain, the 25th was a Sunday evening and The Beatles, George Martin, a 13-piece orchestra, and assorted family and friends were all assembled inside EMI's Studio One on Abbey Road.

Selected as Britain's representatives for this first-ever TV link across five continents, The Beatles were asked to compose and perform a song especially for the occasion. Their only instruction was to keep the lyrics simple, so people from all nations could understand them. John's response was "All You Need is Love," an anthem for the "Summer of Love." Decked out in beads and bells, and assisted by musician friends such as Mick Jagger, Keith Richard, Marianne Faithfull, Keith Moon, Graham Nash, and Eric Clapton, the Fab Four relayed their message to the world and this time it wasn't lost to future generations. A 16mm black-and-white print of the full *Our World* broadcast was deposited with the United Nations, and in 1995 the *Beatles Anthology* TV series unveiled a computer colorized version of the "All You Need is Love" performance.

Cartoon Characters

In September 1965, while The Beatles were taking a well-earned rest after their second U.S. concert tour, their dwindling live performances on American television were suddenly supplemented by the appearance of some cartoon doubles.

Titled simply *The Beatles*, the 52-part series had been in the works since late 1964, when King Features Syndicate secured the TV animation rights to the Fab Four. Half of the episodes were made in Britain and the others were put together by independent teams of Canadian and Australian animators, working from Peter Sander's specifications as to how the characters should look, move, and behave. Taking a month to create, each half-hour episode contained at least two songs by the real-life Beatles. Their speaking voices, however, were not quite as original, with American actor Paul Frees supplying those of John and George, and British actor-comedian Lance Percival filling in for Paul and Ringo.

Sophisticated it wasn't, but this was 1965, Beatlemania was still at its peak, and the fans couldn't get enough of their fab idols. The Beatles cartoon shot straight to the top of the U.S. television ratings and remained there throughout its first season... aside, that is, from a brief period of shame, when the basebal World Series pushed it into second place.

Fab Video Promos (Pre-MTV)

While they were taping the Granada TV special *The Music of Lennon & McCartney* in November 1965, The Beatles first thought of producing and videotaping their own promotional clips to accompany the release of their songs.

The Granada show featured a variety of artists performing some of John and Paul's compositions while The Beatles themselves plugged their new double A-sided single by miming to "Day Tripper" and "We Can Work it Out." Before the show aired in Britain in mid-December, the group decided to do more of the same in the form of some formally conceived pop videos that could be distributed to TV stations, thus saving them the hassle of filming separate appearances for the U.K., U.S., and other overseas markets.

On November 24 and 25, 1965, The Beatles mimed their way through 10 separate black-and-white clips for five songs: three versions of "We Can Work it Out," three for "Day Tripper," one each for "Help!" and "Ticket to Ride," and two for the year-old "I Feel Fine." Then, on May 19, 1966, they went before the cameras once again to promote a new single, "Paperback Writer"/"Rain." There were mimed performances in color for exclusive broadcast on *The Ed Sullivan Show*, as well as separate black-and-white versions—two of "Paperback Writer," one of

"Rain"—for the U.K. and elsewhere. The following day, John, Paul, George, and Ringo were also filmed in the 18th-century gardens of Chiswick (pronounced "Chizick") House in West London, for color promos of both songs.

The Chiswick House clips differed in that The Beatles broke with the tradition of "performing" the numbers by only miming to certain parts while the cameras also filmed them walking, relaxing, and just being themselves as the music continued. These paved the way for the color "Strawberry Fields Forever" and "Penny Lane" promotional films that were shot in late January and early February 1967 at outdoor locations in London and nearby Kent. The most inventive promos that The Beatles themselves ever made, they interpreted the music with abstract visual images and pioneered the rock videos that would be seen by subsequent generations on MTV.

Thereafter, things regressed when a promo for "A Day in the Life" never made it onto TV screens after the song itself was banned. In November 1967, Paul directed a number of clips featuring The Beatles once again just miming to a song—in this case, "Hello Goodbye." However, as Britain's Musician's Union had already instigated a miming ban on all TV appearances by singers and musicians, those clips couldn't be screened in the U.K. either.

In March 1968, the "Lady Madonna" promo comprised footage of The Beatles recording in the studio. This, however, was actually filmed at the session for "Hey Bulldog," and it would be more than 30 years before it would be re-edited and synchronized to the correct song. Meanwhile, on September 4, 1968, John, Paul, George, and Ringo shot their most enduring promos for the group's landmark single, "Hey Jude"/"Revolution," doing full justice to the magnificent songs they were publicizing.

Two color clips shot for each number captured The Beatles "in performance," and what performances they were: for "Revolution" they were onstage at Twickenham Film Studios, where John belted out the lead vocal while George and Paul supported him with well-rehearsed *shooby-doo-wops*. For "Hey Jude," on the other hand, the seated band members were backed by a 36-piece orchestra and surrounded by an audience of 300. To fool Britain's Musician's Union into thinking that no miming had taken place, The Beatles did sing live for these promos, but the music had been pre-recorded. Still, the ruse worked, and the "Hey Jude" clip had its world premiere on British TV's *Frost on Sunday* on September 8, 1968.

In 1969 and 1970, clips of The Beatles performing during the *Let It Be* sessions were utilized for the "Let It Be" single and, in part, "The Ballad of John and Yoko." However, the group's November 1969 promo, shot to coincide with the release of "Something," clearly spelled the end. The Beatles and their wives were all captured strolling around outdoors, yet at no time were John, Paul, George, and Ringo ever in the same shot. Instead, John and Yoko were filmed outside their home in Ascot, Paul and Linda were on their Scottish farm, George and Pattie were outside their house in Esher, and Ringo and Maureen were in the garden of their Elstead home.

No longer could—or would—The Beatles make a joint effort to promote their work.

Have You Heard the News?

In the beginning, The Beatles could do almost no wrong according to the British press. I say *almost* because their first national headline—"Beatle in brawl"— happened to be about John getting drunk and beating up Cavern DJ, Bob Wooler, at Paul's 21st birthday party in Liverpool. That made the back page of the June 21, 1963 edition of *The Daily Mirror.* Soon afterwards, however, the popular paper began employing the term "Beatlemania" and became one of the group's chief advocates.

Throughout 1963, there were nonstop newspaper reports about screaming, sobbing, fainting fans all over the British Isles. Intellectuals wrote about The Beatles' artistic endeavors, psychologists gave their opinions regarding the fans' behavior, and every two-bit reporter attempted to drum up a new piece of Fab Four gossip. No publication, it seemed, considered itself above discussing anything relating to John, Paul, George, and Ringo.

"An examination of the heart of the nation at this moment would find the name 'Beatles' upon it," concluded London's *Evening Standard* in an article headlined "Why Do We Love Them So Much?" Meanwhile, in *The Times*, music critic William Mann referred to the "chains of pandiatonic clusters" in "This Boy," and "an Aeolian cadence—the chord progression which ends Mahler's 'Song of the Earth'" in "Not a Second Time." Lennon and McCartney, according to Mann, were "the outstanding English composers of 1963."

Daily papers, weekly papers, monthly magazines—almost everything the Fab Four said and did was reported in the press during the Beatlemania years. When John's entire acceptance speech at an April, 1964 Foyle's literary luncheon honoring *In His Own Write* amounted to, "Er, thank you all very much, God bless you. You've got a lucky face," the *Daily Mirror* ran the headline, "I Wanna Hold My Tongue!" And when, in August 1964, an irascible George threw his drink at a photographer during a visit to the Whisky-A-Go-Go nightclub on L.A.'s Sunset Strip, the victim's picture of this incident was published in newspapers across America. Some of them even ran a doctored version of the shot, featuring hand-drawn droplets of George's drink to enhance the effect.

Still, perhaps the most amusing articles were those in which certain so-called "experts" attempted to analyze the effect The Beatles had on their teenage fans. In British weekly newspaper the *News of the World*, a psychologist asserted that, "The girls are subconsciously preparing for motherhood. Their frenzied screams are a rehearsal for that moment." In America, the *Seattle Daily News* had a Dr. Bernard Saibel blaming adults for "allowing the children a mad, erotic world of their own," while the *New York Post* described an episode in which two "teenage blondes" perched themselves on the 22nd floor ledge of New York City's Americana Hotel and demanded to see Paul McCartney. After the police grabbed them, doctors at the nearby Roosevelt Hospital diagnosed their behavior as "acute situation reaction." According to the *Post*, the entire incident had simply been a case of attempted "Beatlecide"...

To press editors (including the *Philadelphia Daily News*' very own "Beatle Editor") the message was clear—Beatle-related stories and photos helped sell papers. Accordingly, while they ran in-depth reports about such earth-shattering issues as George's influenza and Ringo's tonsillectomy, they initially avoided criticizing the source of all their extra sales-related profit. That would come later, once John, Paul, George, and Ringo had been placed on a pedestal and the only thing left to do was knock them back off.

Chapter 17

Beatlemania—You Make Me Wanna Shout!

The Beatles weren't the first 20th century icons to generate widespread hysteria and enjoy mass adulation. Others ranging from Adolf Hitler to Frank Sinatra and Elvis Presley had already experienced that. However, the phenomenon that came to be known as Beatlemania was truly special because it was global. In recent history, no one person or group of individuals has been adored on the scale that John, Paul, George, and Ringo were in the mid-sixties.

John later likened the whole experience to standing in the eye of a hurricane while the rest of the world went completely crazy—Beatle-crazy. Indeed, for the masses, Beatlemania was an almost entirely positive experience, but for the men themselves the fun soon turned into something of a nightmare. Privacy was almost non-existent, safety was a major concern, and freedom was a thing of the past. With wealth and success under their belts, the Fab Four once again yearned for the simpler things in life.

1963—That Was the Year That Was

It seems fairly appropriate that the suffix "mania" is used to indicate an extreme enthusiasm for something or even a form of madness. After all, in 1963, the year before The Beatles hit America, the Reverend Ronald Gibbons of the Trinity Methodist Church in Basildon, Essex, publicly asked the group to record "Oh Come All Ye Faithful, Yeah, Yeah, Yeah" to help boost his Christmas congregation. Then there was the bakery in northern England that sold "Beatle cakes" for the very generous "party price" of five shillings (then equivalent to about 12 cents). And, if those didn't keep people happy, they could instead chew on some "Ringo Roll" or book tickets for a ballet titled *Mods and Rockers* that featured the music of Lennon and McCartney.

This was Beatlemania in its original British form, as reported by the national newspapers after the craze began to pick up speed in the late spring of '63, when The Beatles undertook their third nationwide tour of the year. The first, in early February, had the band at the bottom of a six-act bill topped by 16-year-old singer Helen Shapiro. Five days after that tour ended, a second one commenced. American artists Tommy Roe and Chris Montez were supposed to top the bill, but fan reaction during the first concert convinced the promoter to have the Fab Four close the show.

Much the same happened during the third tour, which ran from May 18 to June 9. Roy Orbison was the original headliner, but he couldn't compete with the exploding popularity of John, Paul, George, and Ringo. Every time they walked onstage and launched into their 25-minute set, the girls would become hysterical, alternately screaming and stuffing handkerchiefs into their mouths while sobbing, wetting themselves, clawing at themselves, and throwing jelly babies at the band (thanks to an interview in which George had divulged that he liked them). Meanwhile, the numerous guys in the audience would just watch the manic proceedings and try, often in vain, to actually listen to the music.

In the wake of The Beatles' success, numerous other Merseyside acts managed to crash onto the British pop charts, including Gerry and the Pacemakers, Billy J. Kramer with the Dakotas, Cilla Black, The Searchers, The Fourmost, The Swinging Blue Jeans, and The Merseybeats. Some of them recorded Lennon-McCartney compositions, many of them were managed by Brian Epstein, and during 1963 three of them spent a combined 45 weeks in the Top 10. For their part, The Beatles enjoyed their own 40 weeks in the Top 10. At the end of 1963, *Record Retailer* estimated that, during the preceding 12 months, Brits had spent £6.25 million (about $15 million) on Beatles records alone.

After the Fab Four's televised October appearance on *Sunday Night at the London Palladium*, the media really caught on. Then, following a highly successful trip to Sweden, the group returned to London Airport on October 31 and a reception they didn't expect. Braving heavy rain, several thousand enthusiastic fans showed up and screamed so loud, they drowned out the noise of the jet engines. Completely astonished, The Beatles initially assumed this welcome was intended for a dignitary or head of state, only to discover otherwise when news reporters surrounded them the moment they descended the aircraft steps. Thus began the tradition of the airport receptions, characterized by fan-related pandemonium and Beatles songs being broadcast over London

Airport's public address system whenever the band departed for—and returned from—foreign shores.

Britain's bobbies, assigned the unenviable task of keeping matters under control—at the airport as well as at concert venues and wherever else The Beatles appeared—didn't always succeed. In Carlisle, for instance, 600 fans waited 36 hours for a theater box office to open. When it did, the sudden surge of bodies propelled some people through store windows and nine of them ended up in hospital. In Newcastle-upon-Tyne, according to the *Daily Mirror*, an estimated 10,000 Beatlemaniacs who lined up to buy tickets "went wild in a fantastic stampede." Apparently, one girl lost her jeans amid all the excitement (or at least that's what she told her parents), while 120 others had to receive first aid and seven were treated for shock. Similar scenes took place all over the U.K.

The next Beatles concert tour, kicking off on November 1, consisted of two shows per night in 34 towns across Britain. For John, Paul, George, and Ringo—who now sometimes resorted to wearing disguises when venturing out in public, and whose family homes were constantly under siege—concert work presented a mind numbing routine: arriving in a town; being smuggled into a theater; performing a show (or often two) where the screaming was so loud, they could hardly hear themselves play; and then being hustled back out of the theater and into a waiting van or limousine for a high-speed escape to a nearby hotel.

This was "normality" for The Beatles during those frantic final months of 1963. So, imagine how they must have felt when a Labour Party Member of Parliament stood up in Britain's House of Commons and demanded that, to save on unnecessary public costs, there should be no further police protection for The Beatles.

1964—12 Months That Shook the World

If 1963 was the year of Beatlemania in Britain, 1964 was the year it went global. While the French took their time making up their minds about The Beatles, every other place the Fab Four visited took them to their hearts in a big way. This was great news not only for Liverpool's suddenly-favorite sons, but also for the host of other British artists who suddenly found themselves in demand; first at home, then overseas. Here's how those foreign visits panned out in 1964...

Les Français? Pouf!

Two weeks into 1964, after completing the 16-night, 30-performance run of *The Beatles' Christmas Show* at the Astoria Cinema in North London and making a return appearance on Val Parnell's *Sunday Night at the London Palladium,* The Beatles set off for a three-week engagement in Paris. John, Paul, and George arrived on January 14; Ringo, trapped by fog in Liverpool, followed with Neil Aspinall the next day. This initial delay turned out to be an ominous sign, as did the fact that The Beatles could walk down Paris's main thoroughfare, Les Champs Elysées, without being crowded.

After giving what they considered to be a below-par warm-up performance at the Cinéma Cyrano in Versailles, the Fab Four embarked on 18 days at Paris's famed Olympia Theatre, during which they played two—and sometimes three—shows a night. However, the premiere, on January 16, again proved to be a profound disappointment. For one thing, the audience comprised not teenage fans, but mostly Parisian socialites in full evening dress. It was like being back at the Royal Command performance, except this crowd wasn't nearly as friendly. The French appeared to be largely unimpressed by Les Beatles and, for their part, Les Beatles were less than impressed with the Olympia's facilities.

Before the show, attempts by the group's press officer, Brian Sommerville, to keep reporters and photographers out of the band's dressing room resulted in a violent scuffle. Then, when The Beatles' amplification equipment broke down on three separate occasions during their performance, George Harrison openly complained of sabotage. The traditionally fragile Anglo-French relationship was teetering on the brink. The next day, the critic for the popular evening paper, *France-Soir*, dismissed the moptops as "delinquents" and "has-beens," while the famous Parisian department store, Les Galaries Lafayette, canceled plans to fill one of its main windows with Beatles merchandise. Not that the main men really cared—after returning to their suite at the George V Hotel the previous night, they had been informed that "I Want to

Hold Your Hand" was topping the *Cashbox* singles chart in America.

John, Paul, George, and Ringo played the remainder of their three-week Paris engagement to audiences that often appeared far less interested in what The Beatles had to offer than in the sexy pouting of local chanteuse Sylvie Vartan and the singing of "If I Had a Hammer" by Texas-born Trini Lopez. The French would get a second chance about 18 months later, at which point they'd fall in line with the rest of the Beatle-mad planet. Yet, for now, the Fab Four weren't holding their collective breath. Instead, they were focused on bigger things in the U.S.

The Beatles are Coming!

Due to coincidence of the very best kind, The Beatles' 1963 albums and singles were storming the American charts when the group arrived in New York on February 7, 1964. Part of the reason was that, by the time Brian Epstein arranged the trip the previous November, Capitol Records had at last been persuaded by its parent company, EMI, to release "I Want to Hold Your Hand." Couple this with the small, independent Tollie, Swan, and Vee Jay labels pushing the group's other discs, and there was no shortage of Beatles material for Americans to purchase.

At first there was little interest, but when "I Want to Hold Your Hand" started getting airplay on U.S. radio stations, the single sold by the bucket load—remember, 10,000 copies per hour in New York City alone. The sound was so fresh, so different, so exciting, American kids couldn't wait to see who was responsible. Capitol Records therefore embarked on a massive publicity campaign, distributing five million posters and car bumper stickers announcing "The Beatles Are Coming!" Meanwhile, this same message was broadcast repeatedly by disc jockeys who, as the big day approached, also informed their listeners that "The Beatles will be touching down this Friday at 1:20 Beatle-time!"

In classrooms across the country on that memorable day, Beatles-obsessed students started counting down as the magic moment finally arrived. Others cut class to listen to the up-to-the-minute radio reports concerning the band's visit, and in New York about 3,000 screaming Beatlemaniacs appeared at Kennedy Airport to greet Pan Am flight 101.

Predictably, John, Paul, George, and Ringo were all over the nation's TV screens that evening.

From that moment on, America was totally besotted with The Beatles. Everything they said or did seemed to be of major importance, as was anything or anyone connected to them, or in fact anyone with a British accent. Today The Beatles, tomorrow The Dave Clark Five, Gerry and the Pacemakers, The Kinks, The Animals, The Rolling Stones, Dusty Springfield, Petula Clark, and Herman's Hermits. The charts were swamped and the sudden tidal wave was quickly dubbed "the British Invasion."

Of course, none of those bands had the same initial impact as The Beatles. Half a ton of Beatle wigs and 24,000 rolls of Beatle wallpaper were flown in from Britain to meet the huge demand for all things Fab. Back in the U.K., George Harrison received 52 sacks of mail containing around 15,000 cards on his 21st birthday, together with four large hampers packed with gifts. In March, the release of the single "Can't Buy Me Love" was preceded by advance orders of 2.1 million copies in the U.S. (with another million in Britain). And on *Billboard* magazine's "Hot 100" singles chart of April 4, Beatles records stood at numbers 1, 2, 3, 4, 5, 31, 41, 46, 58, 65, 68, and 79.

Now, aside from this being the only occasion when one act has held the first five positions, those records were also on four different labels:

1. "Can't Buy Me Love" (Capitol)

2. "Twist and Shout" (Tollie)

3. "She Loves You" (Swan)

4. "I Want to Hold Your Hand" (Capitol)

5. "Please Please Me" (Vee Jay)

Can you imagine anyone matching that achievement today? In short, what took place in the U.S. (as well as in Britain and elsewhere) during 1964 was a musical and cultural revolution, not just a quick craze that would fizzle and fade. The Beatles were clearly going to be a major force for some time to come and, if this needed confirming, the proof would be evident when the band undertook its first full-fledged American tour during August and September. But first there were other territories to conquer.

All Around the World

1964 was quite a year. After their initial, brief, triumphant America trip, the longest rest The Beatles had during those 12 incredibly hectic months was a four-week break in May. This preceded a 25-day world tour that commenced in Denmark, yet only three of the Fab Four were there for the opening show on June 4. The day before, Ringo collapsed during a photo session and was rushed to a hospital suffering from tonsillitis and pharyngitis. Although George wanted to cancel the tour, Brian Epstein and George Martin persuaded him this couldn't be done, meaning a temporary replacement for Ringo had to be found.

Enter Jimmy Nicol, a relatively unknown session drummer who, it was correctly assumed, wouldn't be perceived by anyone as a permanent fixture within The Beatles. Nicol played with his own group, The Shubdubs, and he had also backed artists such as Georgie Fame and Epstein protégé Tommy Quickly. Now, just hours after Ringo's collapse, 24-year-old Jimmy found himself at EMI's Abbey Road studios, rehearsing six numbers with the world's greatest supergroup. Then he went home to pack his bags in preparation for the following day's flight to Denmark and instant megastardom.

Thereafter, Beatlemania was rampant not only at the concert venues in Denmark, the Netherlands, and Hong Kong, but also wherever the Refabricated Four's plane touched down for refueling. At all hours, in even the remotest of places, hordes of screaming fans would try to catch a glimpse of their idols. And that was fine, except for those inconvenient occasions when The Beatles were expected to reciprocate. Take their arrival at Mascot International Airport in Sydney, Australia, on June 11, when they were cajoled into parading in an open-top truck in a torrential rainstorm while the crowd was packed safely into the sheltered airport enclosures. John, Paul, George, and Jimmy got absolutely drenched.

After Ringo finally rejoined his bandmates in Melbourne on June 14 and Jimmy Nicol returned to almost immediate obscurity, The Beatles were greeted by crowds that were even larger than those in America the preceding February. The crowd outside their Melbourne hotel numbered 250,000 people, while the one in Adelaide topped 300,000. Unfortunately, however, this fan worship coincided with an increasing number of death threats against the band members. Prior to their flight in New Zealand from Auckland to nearby Dunedin, someone anonymously—and, as it turned out, falsely—claimed to have planted a germ bomb on board the plane. Similar instances occured during the subsequent American tour, and while no one was hurt, the collective feelings of anxiety were becoming unbearable.

America, America

The Beatles first full U.S. concert tour consisted of 32 shows in 24 cities within 34 days, with the limo/concert/limo/hotel routine evolving into one that regularly comprised airplane/limo/press conference/meeting with dignitaries/concert/limo/hotel. John, Paul, George, and Ringo saw so little of the cities they were in, they sometimes didn't even know *which* cities they were in. All they knew was that they were making plenty of money and somehow provoking fan hysteria wherever they went. Aside from traveling to and from the concert venues, and to and from the airports, they certainly couldn't leave their hotels. What's more, their check-out from those hotels wasn't always the end of the story.

In Kansas City, for instance, the manager of the Muehlebach sold the 16 sheets and 8 pillow cases from The Beatles' suite to a pair of Chicago businessmen for $750. Of course, in order to remain authentic, the linen couldn't be washed; it was cut into three-inch squares, mounted on a card, and sold at a bargain $10 a piece. Much the same fate was accorded the towels with which The Beatles wiped their faces after leaving the stage of the Hollywood Bowl. By the summer of 1964, no commodity was too outrageous for eagle-eyed American entrepreneurs: bottled "Beatle Breath," "Beatle Bathwater," and even used shaving foam were among the many items that exploited fans were lured into purchasing. Beatlemania had gone over the top.

Just under three weeks after arriving back from America, the Fab Four embarked on their first U.K. tour of 1964, comprising 54 shows in 25 cities within 33 days. What's more, they also found time to make studio recordings in addition to TV and radio appearances before undertaking *Another Beatles Christmas Show* at London's Hammersmith Odeon—38 shows over the course of 20 nights during December and January. Never again would The Beatles attempt this kind of schedule.

1965—"Like Monkeys in a Zoo"

In 1965, the Fab Four's concert tours basically comprised more of the same, save for the unprecedented 1965 Shea Stadium gig in New York that saw them perform for a then-record breaking 55,600 people. They were still the biggest showbiz attraction on the planet, yet whereas only a few concert venues didn't sell out in 1964, this now became more common as Beatlemania started to lose steam.

At the same time, the hoax death threats increased, as did the unintentional terrorization by fans. A notable example of this took place in Houston, Texas, on August 19, 1965. It was 2:00 a.m., yet 5,000 screaming kids were present for The Beatles' arrival. As the plane taxied to a halt, the hysterical crowd broke through the airport barriers and police cordons. Within seconds people were thronging around the plane, underneath it, and even on top of the wings, looking through the windows at the Fab Four who were trapped inside with their small entourage. 40 minutes passed before they were able to jump into a service truck from a nine-foot-high emergency exit at the rear of the plane. Representatives for Lloyd's of London, who had insured each Beatle for $5.5 million against personal injury, would have been apoplectic if they'd witnessed scenes like this. However, imagine what it must have been like to be a Beatle.

One person who certainly could was Elvis Presley. The Beatles finally met him at his Beverly Hills home on August 27, 1965, yet even though they spent the evening chatting, listening to records, and, according to John, jamming, the Fab Four were undeniably disappointed that their idol had *gone Hollywood*. Indeed, with ample money and more fame than they'd ever dreamed of, John, Paul, George, and Ringo were fast becoming fed up with not only the incessant tours and trappings of Beatlemania, but also the phony people they met along the way.

At this point, they had no privacy and no freedom, they feared for their own safety, and, what with all of the screaming at their concerts, they were also regressing as musicians. No wonder their main enjoyment was now only found at home, in the nightclubs, or in the recording studio.

"Your own space, man, it's so important," George Harrison asserted in his 1980 autobiography, *I Me Mine*. "That's why we were doomed, because we didn't have any. It is like monkeys in a zoo. They die. You know, everything needs to be left alone."

Mother Nature's Son

"I really liked the main photo that I used for this because it allowed me to get in tight on Paul's face. I then used a combination of other photos to paint his sweater vest—one with him wearing it and another of me posing for a shot of the body—to create a colorful companion piece to the 'Love is All You Need' portrait of John. For the setting, I placed Paul inside the geodesic dome behind his Cavendish Avenue home—the one used as the final location for Don McCullin's July '68 'Mad Day Out' photo session with The Beatles—painting a view through the windows that represents Paul's love of nature and the great outdoors."

– Eric Cash

Chapter 18

Act Naturally—The Celluloid Beatles

The Beatles not only revolutionized the twin worlds of rock music and pop culture in the 1960s, but also—thanks to their own personalities and the combined talents of some of the people with whom they worked—changed the whole nature of rock movies.

Make no mistake about it: The Fab Four were musicians, not actors. Yet, given the opportunity to deliver their lines onscreen, they certainly didn't fluff them. Let's catch up on those efforts, as well as the other celluloid projects that they were—or intended to be—involved with.

A Hard Day's Night: "The Citizen Kane of Juke Box Musicals"

To state it plainly, *A Hard Day's Night* is a classic film and one of the great screen musicals. However, The Beatles' big screen debut was originally envisioned as a cheapo-quickie project to exploit the band's image. In the summer of 1963, United Artists signed a three-picture deal with Brian Epstein and, since The Beatles' recording contract with EMI didn't cover movie soundtracks, they figured this would be lucrative. UA's head, Bud Ornstein, allocated the black-and-white film a £200,000 ($500,000) budget and commissioned independent producer Walter Shenson to put everything together by mid-1964, when the Fabs might also be big news in America.

Shenson hired British-based American Richard Lester to direct the picture, and that was his first good move. Like George Martin, Dick had a Goons connection: he had directed a number of British TV shows featuring their talents, as well as an 11-minute, Oscar-nominated Peter Sellers/Spike Milligan home movie, *The Running, Jumping and Standing Still Film*. This, together with the fact that Lester had also helmed a 1961 teen pic named *It's Trad, Dad!* (*Ring-a-Ding Rhythm* in the U.S.) featuring a performance by Gene Vincent, immediately enhanced his standing with The Beatles.

At the end of October 1963, Liverpudlian playwright Alun Owen, best known in Britain for insightful TV productions such as *No Trams on Lime Street*, was brought aboard to write the Fab Four's screenplay. His directive from Walter Shenson was to clearly delineate each of their personalities, while also capturing their youthful energy and anarchic humor. On November 7—9, 1963, Owen hung out with the group in Ireland and in London to observe their characters, their mannerisms, the way they interacted with one another, and, just as importantly, their hectic lifestyle. Then he went to work, and the result was a fictionalized, documentary-style account of a day in The Beatles' life.

Centering around the adventures of John, Paul, George, and Ringo traveling down to London to film a TV show, Alun Owen's screenplay managed to capture The Beatles' claustrophobic, goldfish-bowl existence while also conveying the general feeling of good fun and mayhem that surrounded them. Indeed, the finished picture often gives the impression that they are just improvising in front of the cameras, whereas every line was, in fact, tightly scripted.

With a Royal Premiere scheduled for July 6, 1964, John and Paul wrote many of the film's new songs during The Beatles' January and February trips to France and the United States. On their return from America, the band members then had just four days to record nine tracks: "Can't Buy Me Love," "You Can't Do That," "And I Love Her," "I Should Have Known Better," "Tell Me Why," "If I Fell," "I'm Happy Just to Dance With You," "I Call Your Name," and Little Richard's "Long Tall Sally." Dick Lester declined the last two, while a segment featuring "You Can't Do That" was filmed and then cut from the finished picture. The title track wasn't written and recorded until the movie was near completion, and after the non-soundtrack songs were recorded in early June, *A Hard Day's Night* ended up being the first and only Beatles album to consist 100% of Lennon-McCartney originals.

The Beatles saw the shooting script for the first time on February 29, filming began two days later, and by the time it ended on April 24 they had really enjoyed their first excursion into the movies. This is evident onscreen. John, Paul, George, and Ringo are each immensely likable, delivering their lines with a mixture of charm and innocence, and they also manage to shine in their solo scenes. (The sole exception is Paul, who shot a lengthy scene in which he chatted to an actress, only for it to be discarded because the director thought it was awkwardly scripted.)

Although John later dismissed Alun Owen's characterizations of The Beatles as phony and superficial, the band members would be forever identified with their onscreen characters. Indeed, Dick Lester's quickfire pacing enhanced their performances and infused the picture with an infectious energy. This found maximum expression in the madcap visual style of some of the musical sequences, as well as in surreal, anarchic segments such as that where The Beatles, seated inside a train, are suddenly seen running and cycling alongside it.

The inspirational film's world premiere, attended by The Beatles' biggest Royal fan, Princess Margaret, took place on July 6, 1964 at the London Pavilion in Piccadilly Circus, where 200 policeman tried to contend with 20,000 hysterical fans. Then, for the picture's "Northern Premiere," which took place in Liverpool four days later, more than 200,000 people lined the Fab Four's 10-mile route from the airport to the city center, where they were honored with a civic reception at the Town Hall. By now, film critics everywhere were nearly falling over themselves in their efforts to praise the movie and its stars. In America, alluding to Orson Welles' cinematic masterpiece, the *Village Voice* proclaimed *A Hard Day's Night* to be "the *Citizen Kane* of jukebox musicals," while England's *Daily Express* described it as "gorgeous fun! It's a mad, mad, mad, mad film, man. Nothing like it since the Goons on radio and the Marx Brothers in the thirties. Delightfully loony. Palpitating cinema."

A Hard Day's Night wasn't nominated for an Academy Award, and neither were its actors or its director. Scriptwriter Alun Owen was, but lost out to the authors of *Father Goose*. In the music category, *Mary Poppins* scooped the honors, with "Chim-Chim Cher-ee" voted "Best Song." Still, the world's Beatlemaniacs didn't seem to mind. In fact, many of them screamed so loudly when their heroes appeared onscreen that they couldn't hear the music anyway.

Earning $5.8 million during the first six weeks of its release, *A Hard Day's Night* provided United Artists with a pretty good return on its original £200,000 ($500,000) investment. And it also ensured that The Beatles' next movie would be allotted a far bigger budget, although that was no guarantee of greater or even commensurate success.

Help!

Whereas *A Hard Day's Night* is an all-time classic, The Fab Four's second movie, *Help!*, utilizes artful direction, flashy camerawork, and some typically great Beatles music to compensate for a mediocre screenplay that tries to force the laughs instead of allowing its stars to just be themselves.

Like its predecessor, *Help!* was produced by Walter Shenson, directed by Richard Lester, and featured Victor Spinetti in one of the supporting roles. John, Paul, and this time George again wrote the songs without reading the script, and the film again had no title. Originally, it was simply referred to as *Beatles 2*, before being renamed *Eight Arms to Hold You*. That, however, didn't make for an easy song title, so Lester then came up with *Help!*

Now that the Fab Four had proven their box office allure, UA was prepared to more than double the budget to £500,000 ($1.2 million), assign an 11-week shooting schedule (February 23 to May 12, 1965), and have the proceedings filmed in glorious Technicolor. With a directive to create a comedy adventure rather than a comic "rockumentary," Marc Behm—whose previous credits included the original storyline for the 1963 Cary Grant/Audrey Hepburn movie, *Charade*—began work on the script. Then Charles Wood, who that year also co-wrote the screenplay for Dick Lester's film *The Knack, and How to Get It* was brought in to revise Behm's efforts.

The result was a lightweight, comic strip adventure about the bungled attempts of followers of a Far Eastern sect to get hold of a sacred, sacrificial ring that has attached itself to one of Ringo's fingers—if the sad-eyed drummer can't remove it, he'll become the cult's next sacrifice. As The Beatles fancied filming in some foreign locales, scenes taking place in the Bahamas and Austria were promptly incorporated into the flimsy storyline. However, they were no longer as enamored with the whole process of moviemaking as they had been the previous year. Instead of waiting around on the set for hours at a time in order for the crew to set up a single shot, they could be elsewhere—writing songs, recording in the studio, or even just relaxing. They had fun making *Help!*, but smoking pot to alleviate the boredom resulted in a discernible lack of focus and far more laid-back demeanor than their alert, fully engaged appearances in *A Hard Day's Night*.

As such, *Help!* was something of a disappointment when compared to its predecessor. Yet, it was still an amusing film with terrific songs and moments of Beatles-inspired magic that generated good business at the box office and mostly positive reviews by critics.

Magical Mystery Tour

On September 1, 1967, just five days after Brian Epstein's death, The Beatles all met at Paul's house on Cavendish Avenue in St. John's Wood, around the corner from the EMI Studios on Abbey Road, to discuss their future. Among their immediate decisions: press ahead with the *Magical Mystery Tour* TV film which had been formulated several months earlier but then put on hold during the summer.

Paul had come up with the film's basic concept back on April 11, during a flight from Los Angeles to London. The inspiration was *The Electric Kool-Aid Acid Test*, writer Tom Wolfe's account of an LSD-drenched bus journey that a hippie troupe called Ken Kesey's Merry Pranksters had made through California in 1965. Macca devised a plan for The Beatles to hire their own bus for a good old-fashioned mystery tour around the English countryside and have a film crew capture whatever magic occurred along the way. After all, there was bound to be plenty of magic, wasn't there?

Drawing a circle on a piece of paper, Paul divided it into segments containing some of the main plot devices: "midgets," a "fat lady," a "lunch" scene, and so on. "He came and showed me what his idea was," John later recalled. "He said, 'Well, here's the segment, you write a little piece for that.' And I thought, *Fuckin' Ada, I've never made a film! What's he mean, write a script?*"

With the benefit of 20/20 hindsight, it's easy to see where things went wrong. Having succeeded at practically everything they'd attempted— and basking in the glory of their *Sgt. Pepper* album and latest smash-hit single, "All You Need is Love"—The Beatles appeared to believe they were infallible. Consequently, they didn't see the need to act in a slickly produced movie that was devised for them by a bunch of professionals.

No, they would approach *Magical Mystery Tour* as they now did everything else, flying by the seat of their pants. To that end, they would write, produce, direct, and supervise the editing of the movie, in addition to starring in it and composing all of the songs.

Unfortunately, John, Paul, George, and Ringo overlooked several key things. To start with, while they had performed admirably in *Help!* and, especially, *A Hard Day's Night*, much of the credit belonged to Walter Shenson for the production values, Alun Owen for the *AHDN* screenplay, and Dick Lester for his direction while also overseeing the camerawork and editing. None of the Fabs were exactly accomplished actors, yet their experience in that regard was gargantuan compared to what they knew about scriptwriting, directing, and editing.

Then there was the job of production. In The Beatles' case this amounted to hiring a small film crew, a tour bus, and a cast of actors, relatives, and friends, while assigning one week to shooting around Devon and Cornwall in southwest England, another for interior scenes at Shepperton Studios, and a third week for the editing. After that they could all go off to India and spend some time with the Maharishi. That, at least, was the theory. However, after The Beatles set the enterprise in motion on Monday, September 11, the result was an administrative and artistic nightmare.

The multi-colored *Magical Mystery Tour* bus was still being hastily decorated when most of its passengers gathered at the starting point in Central London, and it eventually arrived two hours late. Then, on the first full day of filming, the driver decided to take an unconventional route to avoid traffic and managed to get the large vehicle wedged on a narrow bridge, blocking cars in both directions. While the cameras rolled, tempers flared—especially John's—and the driver had to reverse the bus for half a mile before the situation was resolved. Little magic was to be found anywhere on the trip, and as hotel bookings were only made at the last minute, Neil Aspinall was handed the unenviable task of finding accommodation for 43 people who were often choosy about who they wanted to room with.

The disjointed, confusing, often shoddy 53-minute movie received such a mauling from the British press and public following its December

26 "Boxing Day" screening on BBC1—in black-and-white, although it had been shot in color—that American TV networks shied away from acquiring the transmission rights and, aside from a couple of screenings at New York rock venue the Fillmore East in August 1968, *Magical Mystery Tour* wasn't seen in the U.S. until its theatrical release in 1974.

The day after its BBC debut, Paul responded to the critical barbs by conceding that *MMT* probably wasn't ideal Christmas entertainment. The passing years, however, have seen him drastically revise that opinion, asserting, "it's quite a little classic for its time," while citing its approval by "people like Spielberg." Certainly the film—with its sporadic moments of inspirational, Monty Pythonesque humor—comes off somewhat better today than it did all those years ago; a sometimes-charming slice of British eccentricity that taps into many of the holiday and showbiz traditions that The Beatles and their generation grew up with. However, it also still stands as little more than what it always was: a muddled, self-satisfied home movie with several moments of Beatles magic.

Yellow Submarine ("The Best Film The Beatles Never Made")

In 1966, Al Brodax, who had produced 39 episodes of the King Features TV cartoon *The Beatles*, began pitching Brian Epstein about the possibility of making a full-length animated Fabs feature for cinema release. When it became clear that, if released by UA, this would fulfill the group's three-picture deal with the company, Brian agreed, and Lee Minoff was subsequently commissioned to write an original story based upon one of The Beatles' hit songs. He chose "Yellow Submarine."

Brodax and Minoff, together with Erich Segal and Jack Mendelsohn, wrote the screenplay in which those enemies of happiness, color, and music, the Blue Meanies, launch a merciless attack on the fun-loving but defenseless inhabitants of Pepperland. Eventually, The Beatles come to the rescue after making a long and harrowing journey from Liverpool in a yellow submarine, and everyone lives happily, colorfully, and musically ever after.

German graphic artist, Heinz Edelmann, created the varied and imaginative cast of characters, including Max the Blue Meanie, the Snapping Turtle Turks, the Apple Bonkers, the Flying Glove, the

Count Down Clown, orchestra leader Old Fred, and Jeremy the Boob (the "Nowhere Man"). A team of 40 animators and 140 technical artists then adapted Edelmann's original sketches into around half a million cells (the individual animated frames that together made up an animated work), following the directives of George Dunning—who had previously directed the Beatles TV cartoons—to create a collage of 1960s pop art and hallucinogen-based psychedelia.

Disney this was not, even though, when they were first consulted about the project, The Beatles themselves envisioned a far-out yet Disneyesque picture. The King Features team didn't agree and, thereafter, the Fab Four had absolutely no involvement in the conception and production processes. Indeed, courtesy of professional actors, the UA execs even got the mid-Atlantic "Beatle" voices that they had always desired, yet the deluge of one-liners they had to speak rarely matched the sharp and witty humor of *A Hard Day's Night*.

Visually, the film was a treat, crammed with splendidly bizarre sight gags that, in those days at least, only animation could achieve. And then, of course, there was the music, combining four new or previously unissued songs—"Hey Bulldog," "Only a Northern Song," "It's All Too Much," and "All Together Now"—with numerous other Beatles hits, many from their psychedelic period. These four originals, together with the title track and "All You Need is Love," made up side one of the *Yellow Submarine* album (released in January 1969), while the second side consisted of George Martin's orchestral film score.

In January 1968, possibly to fulfill contractual obligations or perhaps just to give the impression that they were actually involved with the project, The Beatles filmed a short cameo appearance that was inserted just before the end of *Yellow Submarine*. All four attended the film's world premiere at the London Pavilion on July 17 of that year, where there were Beatlemania-type scenes reminiscent of 1964 and 1965, with a massive crowd bringing Central London's traffic to a standstill.

Yellow Submarine initially did disappointing business in the U.K. and didn't even get a general release, yet it was applauded by the critics, and today, as an encapsulation of late-sixties sensibilities, it's loved by old and young alike. Described by Alexander Walker as "the key film of the

Beatles era… a pop voyage that sails under the psychedelic colours of Carnaby Street to the turned-on music of *Sgt. Pepper's Lonely Hearts Club Band*," the cartoon was also, according to Ian Christie, "an absolute joy" and "the best film The Beatles never made."

Let It Be

The *Yellow Submarine* premiere was the last occasion on which all four Beatles attended an opening night together. None of them turned up for *Let It Be*. They were past caring.

We'll soon examine the problems that plagued the recording sessions, but suffice it to say that the finished movie barely disguises them. Aside from one notable instance in which George famously tells Paul, "I'll play whatever you want me to play, or I won't play at all if you don't want me to play," we don't actually see The Beatles arguing. Nevertheless, their collectively listless appearance, disengaged attitude, and generally lackluster standard of musicianship underscores that this is a band disintegrating before our very eyes.

Throughout much of 1968, enthusiasm had been waning among the members of the world's greatest supergroup. Only Paul still seemed motivated to keep moving the band forward, and this, he suggested, should take the form of actually getting back to what they once did best: a live performance. The other three, especially George and John, weren't overly keen about this, but they half-heartedly went along with an idea to perform an eight-song, one-hour show in front of an audience for a live or videotaped television broadcast. The big question was where to stage it. After all, this was the late-sixties, so the setting just had to be exotic or, at the very least, unusual.

After a few ideas—a disused flour mill, a ship, a stage in the middle of the Sahara Desert, a Roman amphitheater in North Africa—were tossed out, film producer Denis O'Dell advised the band to kick things off by rehearsing for the big occasion… whatever that might be.

As O'Dell was also producing the Peter Sellers/Ringo Starr movie *The Magic Christian* that would commence filming at Twickenham Film Studios in early February 1969, The Beatles went along with his suggestion of rehearsing there, and they also allowed themselves to be filmed for a possible at-work TV documentary that could tie in with the live performance. Michael Lindsay-Hogg was hired to direct, but as soon as John, Paul, George, and Ringo assembled at Twickenham on January 2 and the cameras started to roll, there was trouble in the air and everything was captured on 16mm film: George and Paul bickering; Ringo looking totally bored; and John, under the influence of heroin, in the constant presence of girlfriend Yoko Ono, frequently tuning out and showing his mind was elsewhere.

On January 10, fed up with what he considered to be a condescending attitude on the part of John and Paul toward his musicianship, George quit the band. When he returned several days later, it was on the understanding that a live performance be abandoned in favor of The Beatles just recording an album. Accordingly, the TV show idea went out the window and the not-feeling-Fab Four relocated to their new Apple recording studio for the purpose of producing an at-work feature film. The title? *Get Back*.

At George's invitation, keyboard player Billy Preston sat in with The Beatles during the Apple-based recording sessions and the atmosphere lightened a little. Then, toward the end of January, someone came up with the idea of the group giving an unannounced live performance on the Apple rooftop during the lunch hour, thus providing free entertainment for the people working in Central London. This garnered general approval and, despite some last minute hesitations, the performance went ahead as planned on Thursday, January 30. It was The Beatles' last ever live appearance together, and it provided a fitting end to the motion picture that would eventually be more wistfully titled *Let It Be*.

After much intra-group wrangling and heavy editing of the film, *Let It Be* eventually appeared on the big screen in May 1970, and at the following year's Academy Awards ceremony The Beatles finally got their Oscar; winning for Best Original Song Score. By then, however, the band was history.

Today, *Let It Be* serves as an invaluable document of The Beatles falling out of love with one another. The original concept was to show them at work and at play, yet their purposes would have been better served had the cameras started rolling about 18 months earlier. By 1969 the game was basically over. The work was haphazard and even the "play" was largely strained. Nevertheless, the movie still contains some fine moments, most notably toward the end of the film when, having rehearsed numerous songs half to death, The Beatles perform a few of them properly both in the studio and up on the roof.

The inevitable conclusion: when they put their personal problems to one side and got on with the job of making music, the Fab Four were still unbeatable.

Aborted Projects

So much for the films that The Beatles made, but what about the ones they didn't make? Here's a rundown of the aborted projects, as well as scripts that they turned down...

The Yellow Teddybears

In 1963, before *A Hard Day's Night*, The Beatles were offered a cameo role in a low-budget British exploitation flick called *The Yellow Teddybears* (a.k.a. *Gutter Girls* and *The Thrill Seekers*). Richard Hartford-Davis was the producer-director of this turkey which featured teenage girls wearing teddy bear pins on their blouses to show the world they had lost their virginity. Fortunately, The Beatles declined because they were told they'd either have to perform songs written by someone else or have their own songs copyrighted by the film's production company. In the end, the music was written and performed by a singer-guitarist named Malcolm Mitchell.

A Talent for Loving

In early 1965, around the time when *Help!* was going into production, it was announced that The Beatles' third movie would be a gun-totin' Western titled *A Talent for Loving*. Scheduled to start shooting the following year, this would be based on a true-life 1,400-mile horse race that took place between the Rio Grande and Mexico City in 1871. The winner's prize: a wealthy and glamorous girl.

Richard Condon, who was adapting the script from his own novel, envisioned The Beatles as a bunch of pioneering Liverpudlians who had traveled West. As unlikely as that sounds, it never came to fruition because, for reasons that were never made perfectly clear, the Fab Four withdrew from the project. *A Talent for Loving* was eventually released in 1969, starring Richard Widmark, Topol, Cesar Romero, and Genevieve Page.

Lord of the Rings

During the acid-drenched mid-sixties, John Lennon thought it would be a good idea for The Beatles to purchase the rights to J.R.R. Tolkien's epic fantasy novel *The Lord of the Rings* and cast himself in the most attention-getting role. For those familiar with the book, John wanted the part of Gollum while Paul would play Frodo Baggins, George would portray Gandalf, and Ringo would be Sam Merryweather.

As it turned out, John's colleagues weren't turned on by his suggestion, the rights to the book weren't even attainable, and the project was therefore conveniently forgotten.

The Three Musketeers

Alexander Dumas' classic novel had already been filmed in 1935, 1939, and 1948 when The Beatles considered starring in another remake. Done properly, this could have been a good vehicle for them, yet the Fabs ultimately decided they just weren't suited to the characters of the Musketeers and D'Artagnan.

It isn't clear who suggested this idea or who would have directed the film, yet it's interesting to note that when *The Three Musketeers* next reached the big screen in 1974, Dick Lester was at the helm, and thereafter he also directed *The Four Musketeers* (1974) and *Return of the Musketeers* (1989).

Shades of a Personality

By 1966, producer Walter Shenson was desperately searching for a Beatles movie vehicle that would mark a significant departure from *A Hard Day's Night* and *Help!*, and at year's end he announced that Owen Holder was working on a script for "*Beatles 3.*" By June 1967, this had evolved into *Shades of a Personality*, to be shot in Malaga, Spain, and directed by the award-winning maker of *Blow-Up*, Michelangelo Antonioni.

The story would concern a man (John) who suffers from a three-way split personality, with each of these personalities (portrayed by Paul, George, and Ringo) emerging in separate sub-plots. An interesting idea, but the universal acclaim that greeted the release of the *Sgt. Pepper* album prompted The Beatles to consider other projects and *Shades of a Personality* was quickly dropped from the schedule.

Up Against It

In January 1967, while the script for *Shades of a Personality* was still in development, Walter Shenson also approached cutting-edge English playwright Joe Orton (the author of *Loot*) about writing a screenplay for The Beatles. Orton's darkly humorous writing style appealed to the band members, and so Walter Shenson paid him a £5,000 ($12,000) advance to come up with something.

Unbeknown to Shenson and the Fab Four, Orton simply embellished one of his early novels, *The Silver Bucket*, with elements of another that would later be published as *Head to Toe*. The result was *Up Against It* and, to quote an entry in Orton's own diary, "with its political assassination, guerrilla warfare, and transvestitism, it might have been designed with The Beatles in mind!"

Orton completed the script for *Up Against It* in late February and it was returned by Brian Epstein's office in early April without even an explanation. Then, on August 9, 1967, just 18 days before Brian's death, Joe Orton was murdered at home by his lover, Kenneth Halliwell. He was just 34.

In the final analysis, the most notable film projects The Beatles rejected ranged from the inane to the insane, the enticing to the unexciting. Beyond that there's no way of knowing how any of them would have turned out, but one thing's for sure: they would have been hard-pressed to match or improve on *A Hard Day's Night*.

Chapter 19

Hop off the Bus—An End to Touring

As the saying goes, all good things must come to an end, and after giving more than 1,400 live performances in just nine years The Beatles finally quit the concert scene in 1966. What had once been fun-filled events in which the band and the fans shared in a mutual love for the music had by now turned into what John Lennon described as "bloody tribal rites."

Often playing in huge outdoor stadiums, John, Paul, George, and Ringo were no longer in close contact with teens who had come to scream at their idols instead of listen to them sing and play. Sometimes the noise was so loud, The Beatles would stop playing and just mime. Nobody noticed anyway. Not surprisingly, the Fab Four's performances began to sound tired and lackluster, and their obvious boredom was increased by concert equipment that, primitive by today's standards, made it virtually impossible for them to reproduce onstage the revolutionary new sounds that they were creating in the studio. That's why, in 1966, they didn't perform—and therefore didn't promote—any of the numbers from their latest album, *Revolver.*

Still, if The Beatles were now seriously thinking about withdrawing from the live scene, their minds were made up by several unsavory incidents that took place during their final concert tours. Here are some of the highlights—and lowlights—of that tumultuous year…

May Day in the U.K.

At the start of 1966, The Beatles enjoyed their longest period of relaxation since their Quarry Men days—a full three months. In early April, they entered the studio to commence work on what would become their *Revolver* album, after which they were scheduled to tour West Germany, Japan, and the Philippines in late June and early July; North America in August; and then Britain toward the end of the year. At least, that was the plan announced in February. But then, after assorted events that occurred during the summer of '66, the British tour was shelved and their homeland fans had to make do with their memories, including that year's solitary live Beatles performance in the U.K.

On Sunday, May 1, the *New Musical Express* Annual Poll-Winners' All-

Star Concert was staged in front of 10,000 fans at London's Empire Pool (later renamed Wembley Arena). And what a lineup it featured: The Beatles, The Rolling Stones, The Spencer Davis Group, The Who, The Yardbirds, Herman's Hermits, Roy Orbison, Cliff Richard, The Small Faces, Sounds Incorporated, Dusty Springfield, and The Walker Brothers—some of the most popular acts of the time. Beforehand, however, the executives of Britain's ABC Television network—which was videotaping the event—failed to agree with the managers of The Beatles and The Rolling Stones on the terms of the broadcast contract. This resulted in the cameras being switched off during both bands' performances—one of them The Beatles' final paid British concert, comprising just five songs in 15 minutes: "I Feel Fine," "Nowhere Man," "Day Tripper," "If I Needed Someone," and "I'm Down." Then the cameras were switched back on to capture the Fab Four receiving their *NME* poll prizes, as well as John being handed an individual award.

Known as May Day, the first day of the fifth month is celebrated as an international holiday in honor of workers. Accordingly, it's a pity that The Beatles' work wasn't properly celebrated by ABC Television on this notable occasion.

Hamburg: Sentimental Journey

Although Hamburg had been so vital to the development of The Beatles as concert artists, they never actually performed there—or anywhere in West Germany— during 1963, 1964, and 1965. Perhaps they figured that, having spent about 800 hours on Hamburg club stages, the people there had already been given more than enough opportunities to see them. Nevertheless, by 1966 it seemed only fair that they should return to the country where they had enjoyed early success.

After concert appearances in Munich and Essen on June 24 and 25 of '66, The Beatles arrived by train in Hamburg on the morning of the 26th. There to greet them at the city's central station—as well as backstage before the group's two shows—were a number of familiar faces from the past, including their good friend Astrid Kirchherr, who had taken some of their most iconic photos; Bert Kaempfert, who had produced the group's first professional recordings; and Bettina Derlien, the well-upholstered Star-Club barmaid who had been a particular favorite of John's.

The 5,600 capacity Ernst Merck Halle was the chosen venue for The Beatles' latest—and, as it turned out, last—Hamburg concerts, and this time around there would be no all-night performances, no cries of "mach shau," no crates of beer being passed onto the stage, and no insulting Nazi-related comments by Herr Lennon. Instead, at each show the all-seated, all-screaming audience was treated to a straightforward 30-minute performance consisting of just 11 songs and a few pre-rehearsed comments.

Afterwards, for old times' sake, John and Paul managed to take a late night stroll down the Reeperbahn to visit some of the clubs and bars that they had once frequented, as well as to look up former friends and acquaintances. Some were still there, others weren't, yet Hamburg hadn't changed nearly as much as The Beatles had since they'd last set foot in the city on January 1, 1963.

Sayonara Japan

It was during The Beatles' only visit to Japan that things started to go wrong, initiating a cycle of events that would soon persuade them to give up concert tours for good. The group left London for Tokyo on June 27, but when a typhoon was forecast to be approaching, their plane had to touch down in Anchorage, Alaska. Needless to say, several hundred Alaskan Beatlemaniacs immediately crawled out of the woodwork and surrounded the group's hotel until the Fab Four resumed their flight to Tokyo. Then, when John, Paul, George, and Ringo arrived there at 3:40 a.m. on June 29, they encountered a storm that had been brewing in Japan for several days—a storm of protest.

Tokyo promoter Tatsuji Nagashima had booked The Beatles to perform five shows in three days at the city's Nippon Budokan Hall, an octagonal venue that catered to traditional martial arts events. As some people considered it far too sacred to host Western rock 'n' roll concerts, there were violent demonstrations outside the building both before and after The Beatles' appearances. (The Budokan has since been used to host rock concerts by numerous artists, but The Beatles were the first.)

No less than 35,000 security men were on hand to control the rioters, while at each concert the 10,000 fans were closely watched by 3,000 policemen who ordered anyone who stood up to sit down. Consequently, while there was enthusiastic applause in between numbers, Tokyo's Beatlemaniacs sat quietly and listened while the band played, which perhaps wasn't all that wise considering the level to which the Fab Four's live musicianship had now sunk. Their inability to hear themselves sing or play during the usual scream fests resulted in some off-key, out-of-time performances, and that's how things remained throughout their time in Japan, even if nobody appeared to notice or care.

Meanwhile, when they weren't at the Budokan, The Beatles were compelled by the local security force to remain inside their 18th floor suites at the Tokyo Hilton Hotel. There, heavily protected by armed guards, John, Paul, George, and Ringo were visited by assorted sales people with all kinds of goods to offer: cameras, radios, clothes, you name it. This proved to be profitable for the merchandisers, but The Beatles were basically being held captive, and any attempts to escape were thwarted by the police who briskly returned them to their rooms. Indeed, when John *did* manage to slip by them, the security force threatened to withdraw its protection of the group. Among other things, this would have meant no more 70 mph escorted motorcades to and from the Budokan. (And, as anyone in traffic-congested Tokyo will tell you, a 70 mph car trip is a treat to be savored...)

Still, if our heroes thought their Japanese visit was less than fun, they would soon look upon it as a lighthearted pleasure trip compared to the nightmare that awaited them in the Philippines.

The Thrilla in Manila

For two decades, Filipino dictator Ferdinand Marcos presided over a brutal regime to rule his country before being chased out of the presidential palace in 1986. Alongside him was his wife, Imelda, the notoriously extravagant owner of several thousand pairs of shoes who, 20 years earlier, had played a central role in a domestic drama involving The Beatles.

Ferdinand and Imelda were at the height of their power when John, Paul, George, and Ringo arrived in Manila on July 3, 1966, prior to giving two concerts there the next day. The *Manila Sunday Times* ran an article stating that the President, his wife, and their three children had been invited as guests of honor at the concerts, and that beforehand—at 11:00 the next morning—The Beatles would be paying a courtesy call on the First Lady at Malacañang Palace. At least, that's what Imelda had apparently been told.

In fact, on the agenda drawn up by local promoter Ramon Ramos Jr., the palace visit was originally scheduled for 3:00 p.m. but, as the first show was due to start at 4:00, The Beatles had rejected that idea. Ramos, however, had committed himself, and the last thing he wanted to do was offend Mrs. Marcos. Therefore, when an 11:00 a.m. visit was suggested as an alternative, he left matters there, assuming the Fab Four would do what was expected of them. The problem was, The Beatles had no idea about this new arrangement. So, when a palace official came to collect them the following morning, they were fast asleep and Brian Epstein refused to wake them.

As it turned out, Brian would have been better off putting up with The Beatles' irate reactions than trying to deal with the national outrage that ensued. For, the morning after the band performed its two concerts, all hell broke loose. Alongside a photo showing the First Lady "waiting in vain," the *Manila Times* ran an article headlined "Imelda Stood Up" that reported how The Beatles had "snubbed" Mrs. Marcos, her three children, and 400 family friends. At the same time, Ramon Ramos expressed his own outrage by refusing to hand over the group's substantial share of the concert receipts, while the British Embassy and The Beatles themselves received bomb and death threats.

Brian intervened by having a camera crew visit The Beatles' hotel so they could videotape a statement that he had written with press officer Tony Barrow, asserting they had no knowledge of the rearranged rendezvous with Imelda. This was transmitted later that evening but, wouldn't you know it, at the precise moment the statement commenced, a surge of static just happened to obliterate the message on TV sets nationwide. Broadcast technicians did eventually manage to correct the problem... but only after the statement had finished.

The following day, a Filipino tax commissioner insisted that The Beatles couldn't leave the country unless they paid income tax on the concert revenue that Ramon Ramos had withheld. (Not even the IRS has come up with that little scheme.) The inevitable row ensued, but Brian quickly realized it would be worth biting the bullet just to make a safe getaway.

So, he filed a bond for just under £7,000 (about $17,000), even though it in no way guaranteed the safety of either him or his clients because the security forces who'd been protecting The Beatles had now been withdrawn.

The band members and their entourage were subsequently kicked and punched as they departed the hotel and much the same happened when they arrived at Manila International Airport. There, the terminal manager got in on the act by demanding that the power to the escalators be shut off, forcing The Beatles and their associates to haul their luggage up several flights of stairs. Then, when they reached the second floor, a mob of 200 Filipinos set upon them. Remarkably, John, Paul, George, and Ringo emerged unscathed—"I was very delicate and moved every time they touched me," John later quipped—but Brian was injured, Mal Evans was knocked to the floor and kicked in the ribs, and the group's chauffeur, Alf Bicknell, suffered a fractured rib and damage to his spine.

As if that wasn't enough, The Beatles and their party next had to sprint, bags in hand, across the tarmac to their airplane, only to then be told that Mal Evans and Tony Barrow must return to the terminal. Big Mal, fearing the worst, was almost in tears and asked his fellow travelers to tell his wife that he loved her. However, back inside the airport, he and Barrow were simply informed that The Beatles' plane still wasn't permitted to take off—because, somehow, there was no record of the band members' arrival in the country, they were now deemed to be "illegal immigrants" and therefore couldn't leave.

It took 45 minutes to sort out the necessary paperwork before the plane—with all of its passengers aboard—finally took off, at which point President Marcos issued a press statement acknowledging that The Beatles had in no way intended to slight Imelda or his government. At London Airport on July 8, following a two-day stop-off in India, John assured a press interviewer that he and his bandmates would "never go to any nuthouses again." However, it wouldn't be long long before he'd find himself unintentionally breaking that vow.

Half an Hour in the Park

The Beatles' troubles on their final U.S. tour began before they'd even arrived in America. I'll soon describe how John Lennon caused an uproar in parts of the United States when, in a London newspaper interview, he predicted Christianity's demise and asserted that, in 1966, The Beatles attracted more attention than Jesus Christ. Suffice it to say, the ensuing bad publicity cast a shadow over the first part of the tour, culminating in an anonymous phone call on August 19 promising that one or more of the band members would be assassinated during either of their two shows in Memphis later that day. When a firecracker subsequently exploded midway through the evening concert, The Beatles immediately looked at each other to see who had been shot.

None of them had, but the following night the Fab Four were equally scared when they were due to take to the open-air stage of Cincinnati's Crosley Field during a torrential rainstorm. The promoter had failed to cover said stage with a canopy, and so, while 35,000 fans sat inside the stadium waiting to see their idols, the musicians feared almost certain electrocution if they were to plug in their instruments or touch the microphones. Petrified, Paul threw up backstage, but at the last minute the show was canceled and re-scheduled for the following day.

This set the tone for the rest of the tour which culminated on the cold and windy night of Monday, August 29, 1966, when, at 9:27, The Beatles took to a concert stage for the very last time. The setting was San Francisco's Candlestick Park and the stage—positioned at second base, far away from the 25,000 fans—was elevated five feet above the ground inside a six-foot metal fence that was surrounded by 200 policemen. The Cavern Club this was not.

The Beatles played until precisely 10:00 p.m., closing the show nostalgically for the only time on the tour with "Long Tall Sally" instead of "I'm Down." Then they departed in an armored car, fully aware that this was the end. John had taken a camera onstage to snap photos of himself (at arm's length) and the other group members between songs, and Paul had asked press officer Tony Barrow to make a cassette recording of their performance. Barrow had obliged, but since auto-reverse wasn't yet available, the 30-minute-per-side-tape didn't capture "Long Tall Sally."

"Well, that's it," George Harrison dryly remarked as The Beatles' plane left San Francisco that night. "I'm not a Beatle anymore."

An Inner Light

"I was watching the 'Hey Bulldog' video and immediately loved this image of George. I'm fascinated by interesting picture compositions, and the angle of this shot—probably achieved by a cameraman lying on his back—grabbed my attention. There are a lot of really cool studio photos of the guys taken from interesting angles, and quite honestly I'd be happy to do paintings like this all the time, but I guess that would diminish the effect."

– Eric Cash

Chapter 20

When I Get Home—Life Away from the Road

For more years than they cared to remember, The Beatles had worked their butts off. The packed schedule and incessant globetrotting meant they'd hardly had time to stop, think, and take stock of their situation, but that all changed once they quit touring. Money was no longer a concern and neither was publicity, so the Fab Four could now devote their creative energies to working in the recording studio. The only challenge was figuring out what to do in their spare time. Major changes loomed.

John: Floating Downstream

The Beatles returned to the U.K. from their last concert tour in the U.S. on August 31, 1966, and five days later John was off to Celle in West Germany to appear opposite Michael Crawford in the Dick Lester-directed movie *How I Won the War*.

This anti-war black comedy, adapted from Patrick Ryan's novel and set during World War II, featured John as Private Gripweed; a role that required him to wear circular National Health "granny glasses" and have his hair cut into a "short-back-and-sides." After two weeks of filming in Celle, the entire company then relocated to Carboneras in Spain, where John was joined by his British chauffeur who drove him to the set each morning in his Rolls-Royce. Each evening, John would then be driven to the villa in Almeria that he and wife Cynthia were sharing with Michael Crawford and his family.

By November 7, the filming was completed and the Lennons returned to England (where the movie would subsequently garner hostile reviews and do mediocre business). Then, on November 9, John attended a private preview of a London art exhibition titled *Unfinished Paintings and Objects* by avant-garde Japanese artist Yoko Ono. Indeed, during the last months of 1966, John visited a number of art events while being chased by publishers to write a follow-up to his bestselling books, *In His Own Write* and *A Spaniard in the Works*.

The Lennon home, "Kenwood," was located in Weybridge, Surrey, southwest of London, and, prior to The Beatles' return to the recording studio on November 24, John just drifted there for days on end—reading, watching TV, and staring out of windows while hardly uttering a word to Cynthia or their three-year-old son, Julian. At other times, he would disappear into his small home studio and write songs or make private recordings. Consumed with introspective thoughts, John was also consuming increasing amounts of the hallucinogenic drug LSD, which he and George had been introduced to the previous year. Subconsciously waiting for "the next big thing" to happen, he didn't have a clue what that would be.

On November 27, shortly after The Beatles began recording "Strawberry Fields Forever," John filmed a brief appearance in an episode of the BBC2 TV comedy series *Not Only... But Also*, starring Peter Cooke and Dudley Moore. In the sketch he played the part of Dan, a doorman at a trendy London nightclub, garbed in fancy clothes and granny glasses. Although people didn't realize it at the time, the new image was here to stay.

Paul: Semi-Attached in Swinging London

Of all The Beatles, Paul enjoyed live performances the most. However, as the final, grueling American tour wore on, even he became convinced that the time had come to quit the road.

While John, George, and Ringo were all pursuing the married life—or their interpretations of it—in cozy suburbia, Paul used his luxurious, recently-purchased property in London's upscale St. John's Wood neighborhood as the base for his bachelor existence in and around the capital. Having always been interested in the theater, he now attended more productions than ever, accompanied by his actress-girlfriend, Jane Asher, and also watching her on the stage. However, those activities—and Jane herself—comprised only a small part of his social calendar.

"People are saying things and painting things and writing things that are great," Paul told London's *Evening Standard* newspaper with regard to the city's thriving cultural scene. "I must know what people are doing."

Accordingly, much of his time was now spent mingling with actors, musicians, artists, journalists, film directors, and the various young movers and shakers of "Swinging London." In later years, John Lennon and Yoko Ono would become synonymous with the avant-garde art scene in both London and New York. However, in 1966, while John was still living the seemingly sedate—if stoned—life in Weybridge, Paul was immersing himself in avant-garde activities. This included making the home movies that would help shape the look of *Magical Mystery Tour*, and also having his fellow Beatles contribute to a recording of experimental noises that, in January 1967, would be utilized in the *Carnival of Light* at London's Roundhouse Theatre.

Still, don't get the idea that everything Paul did when The Beatles quit touring was geared toward the unconventional. He composed the music for a British film starring Hayley Mills and Hywell Bennett titled *The Family Way*, and during November of '66 he spent a couple of weeks on a Kenyan safari vacation with Jane Asher. Life was exciting and, for the first time in years, refreshingly unfocused.

George: In Search of Eastern Promise

While Paul was the Beatle most in love with live performances and fan contact, George was the one who particularly hated intrusions on his private life and made the strongest case for putting a stop to touring. What's more, at the age of 23 he was also the one with the strongest sense of which direction he wanted to pursue: eastward, toward India. This provided George with the music, culture, and philosophy that he was now increasingly embracing in an effort to escape from the stifling pressures of Beatlemania, as well as from the oppressive dominance of John and Paul in the recording studio.

George, like John, was taking LSD to "expand the consciousness," and he'd at last hit on a way to carve out his own artistic niche by introducing entirely new instruments and arrangements to Beatles recordings. George's fascination with the sitar had originated during the 1965 filming of *Help!*, when he heard it being utilized for an Indian-flavored rendition of the song "A Hard Day's Night." Although this was performed for comedic effect, the sound of the long-necked stringed instrument grabbed his attention, so George purchased one for himself and introduced it to Western pop music via John's song, "Norwegian Wood (This Bird Has Flown)."

The following year, George met Ravi Shankar at a London dinner party and immediately accepted the Indian sitar virtuoso's offer to visit the Harrison home in Esher, Surrey, and teach him how to really play the instrument. That July, during a brief stop-off in India after The Beatles' horrific trip to the Philippines, George bought a more expensive sitar, and in September 1966 he and Pattie traveled to Bombay, checking into the Taj Mahal Hotel under the aliases of Mr. and Mrs. Sam Wells. Their cover was soon blown, however. So, after holding a press conference to cite relaxation, studying yoga, and learning to play the sitar as the main reasons for their Indian visit, they moved on to Kashmir where, for the next four-and-a-half weeks, George studied the sitar under Ravi Shankar's guidance while also conversing with assorted students and holy men.

A few days after arriving back in Britain, George returned to London Airport to greet Ravi Shankar. This time, however, the Indian was wearing Western clothes while George was garbed in Eastern attire. The cultural intermingling of popular music was well underway.

Ringo: The Suburban Squire

Of all The Beatles' post-touring schedules in 1966, Ringo's was by far the most straightforward. He opted to stay with wife Maureen and son Zak at "Sunny Heights," their home in Weybridge, Surrey, located close to the Lennons' "Kenwood." Backing onto beautiful, landscaped gardens, the spacious house boasted a billiard table, a slot machine, six TV sets, and its own movie projector—state-of-the-art for the mid-sixties and quite a contrast to the tiny terraced home where Ringo had grown up in Liverpool's rough Dingle neighborhood. Having worked hard for his success, he was now enjoying the associated lifestyle.

In early October, Ringo and Maureen flew to Spain to spend a few days with John and Cynthia during the filming of *How I Won the War*. John never really took to the painfully slow process of moviemaking, but during the next few years The Beatles' drummer would make a concerted effort to become a Starr of the silver screen.

Brian: Nowhere Man

At the age of 31, Brian Epstein was one of the world's most successful showbiz impresarios. His company, NEMS Enterprises, had made the transition from the Merseybeat boom to managing acts such as Cream, The Bee Gees, and The Moody Blues while also retaining clients such as Cilla Black and, of course, The Beatles. In 1965, Brian had purchased the lease on the Saville Theatre in London's West End in order to stage ballet, opera, and rock concerts that he himself promoted, and recently he'd also indulged his artistic aspirations by directing a play, producing a record, and part-funding a few feature films. The *Financial Times* estimated his personal wealth to be in the region of £7 million ($17 million). Yet, none of this made Brian happy.

The Beatles were the sole reason he wasn't still running a record store back in Liverpool, and they remained the chief love of his life. While his other acts and activities were worthy distractions, only John, Paul, George, and Ringo could truly inspire him, fulfill at least some of his dreams, and make him feel special. Between November 1961 and August 1966, Brian had negotiated The Beatles' recording contract, remodeled their look, arranged their concert, TV, and radio appearances, fielded suggestions for prospective movie projects, and generally dealt with any problems that came their way. However, after the Fab Four quit the road and ceased their nonstop cycle of joint press interviews as well as TV and radio engagements, Brian's Beatles-related workload was drastically reduced. Ditto his influence on the band members as they began to take more control of their own lives. A growing awareness that they no longer needed him like they once did, coupled with his own steady stream of doomed love affairs, led to severe depression and, in late 1966, an overdose of sleeping pills in what appeared to be a failed suicide attempt.

That November, Brian dismissed a newspaper report that two of The Beatles had approached Allen Klein about managing the band after their contract with Eppy expired in October 1967. Klein, a tough, no-nonsense New Yorker with a reputation for profitably renegotiating record deals on behalf of artists such as The Rolling Stones, had recently been quoted as saying that, if he were to handle The Beatles, he could turn them into "modern Marx Brothers." Brian asserted the Klein takeover rumor was "ridiculous," but perhaps he knew or suspected otherwise.

Although The Beatles still regarded Brian with affection, they were excluding him more and more from their professional decision-making process, and they'd cut him little slack when his attempts to reassert some influence didn't conform to established guidelines. Previously, he'd let them and their producer take care of all musical considerations, but one night in 1966, during a recording session at the EMI Studios on Abbey Road, Brian crossed this line and suffered the consequences. Standing alongside George Martin in the control room, he switched on the talkback mic after John Lennon finished singing a particular song and commented that he didn't think the vocal was "quite right." John's response was immediate and devastating: "You stick to your percentages, Brian, we'll look after the music."

For Brian Epstein, the writing was on the wall.

Chapter 21

Those Swinging Sixties

The 1960s are often looked back upon as some of the best years of the twentieth century; years of fun, excitement, hope, prosperity, discovery, liberation, and advancement. And this may have been true for those who weren't fighting in a war, living in a ghetto, suffering racial or sexual discrimination, or experiencing the downside of the burgeoning sex, drugs, and political-protest counterculture. It's all a matter of perspective, which is why people who lived through the "swinging sixties" have mixed memories (so long as those memories weren't obliterated by all of the halucinogens).

The multi-faceted nature of this undeniably action-packed decade—joyous and miserable, peaceful and violent—provided a backdrop to The Beatles' success and influence. So, it's important to have a basic knowledge of the major social and political events.

Cold War Blues

Given that 70 percent of Americans thought the Soviet Union was trying to rule the world—and a similar number of Soviets thought the same about America—Cold War fever was rampant during the early 1960s. The previous decade's rush on bomb shelters had subsided a little but, as tensions mounted between East and West, American citizens were still being instructed that, in the event of a nuclear attack, they should assume the duck-and-cover position. That's right; your city, town, or village might be razed to the ground, but by crouching down, shutting your eyes, and putting your arms over your head you should be perfectly safe...

During John F. Kennedy's brief presidency, two notable incidents placed the world on the brink of a nuclear showdown and gave everyone—including the politicians involved in the drama—good cause to panic. The first was the 1961 Bay of Pigs fiasco, in which a force of 1,400 Cuban exiles, trained and equipped by the CIA, attempted to overthrow Fidel Castro's communist regime. President Kennedy denied American involvement in the force's landing at the Bay of Pigs, but the Soviets knew better and vowed to back Castro militarily. In the end it didn't matter. The invasion failed within three days and American pride took a severe hit.

The following year, there was a second and more serious contretemps between the U.S.A. and U.S.S.R. On October 22, 1962, JFK informed the American public—and the world—that the Soviet Union was constructing nuclear missile bases in Cuba for rockets that could easily reach not only the United States, but also many other countries in the Western hemisphere. American air, land, and sea forces were therefore deployed to block the transportation of arms from the Soviet Union to Cuba, while the President warned that the firing of any missiles would be viewed as a declaration of war. For nearly a week the Soviet buildup continued and the world held its breath until Russia's leader, Nikita Khrushchev, blinked first; agreeing to halt construction, dismantle the rockets, and remove them in return for an American guarantee to stay out of Cuba.

Today, the Bay of Pigs fiasco and the Cuban Missile Crisis have been consigned to history. At the time, however, people in both East and West really did fear that the world might be coming to an end, and this concern was reflected in movies such as *Dr. Strangelove (or How I Learned to Stop Worrying and Love the Bomb)*, *Fail Safe*, and *Seven Days in May*. Meanwhile, having stared into the abyss and contemplated the consequences, the two superpowers now withdrew their fingers from the nuclear buttons and started to shadowbox with each other in altogether different ways.

One of these was the taking of opposing sides in other nations' conflicts without actually fighting face to face. The Vietnam War and the 1967 "Six Day War" between the Arabs and Israelis were prime examples of this. And then there was the space race, in which the quest to put a human being on the moon turned into a battle for supremacy between the U.S.A. and U.S.S.R.

Without a doubt, the whole Cold War conflict was costly, unnecessary, and pointless, claiming many lives during the 1960s and casting a pall over countless others. It's therefore little wonder that those fun-loving moptops and later peace-preaching Beatles were so widely embraced as a welcome relief from all the doom, gloom, and misery.

Fly Me to the Moon: A Time of Hope

For many, the 1960s represented a period of tremendous optimism; a time when, thanks to scientific and technological advances, anything seemed possible. People got excited about daredevils attempting to set land, sea, and air speed records, computers pointed the way to the future, great things were promised, and not too much was taken for granted. Only by the end of the decade, when America managed to land a manned spacecraft on the moon, did people start to grow blasé.

Another reason for optimism was the general rise in living standards, even in countries that had been ravaged by the Second World War. Britain was enjoying almost full employment, West Germany and Japan were on the road to full economic recovery, France was attempting to lead the way in Europe, and, at the start of the decade, the real income of the average American was more than a third higher than just 15 years earlier. With this extra money came a greater choice of goods to buy and, for some people, unsurpassed material comfort in the form of modernly-equipped homes and two cars parked on the driveway.

Welcome to the "affluent society," where improved mobility coincided with a rapid exodus of families and industries from city centers out to the suburbs—so long as you were white and middle class. For African Americans, it was a different story, resulting in an even greater division of the so-called "two nations"—one white and one black—that had taken root in America long before. Consequently, a decade that opened so brightly wound down on a bitter note, with the hopeful image of nearly half a million youngsters congregating at the Woodstock music festival being canceled out by the violence of anti-war, anti-establishment riots; a series of key political assassinations; and the senseless Tate/La Bianco murders by the Charles Manson gang.

To many it seemed to be a case of abusing too much of a good thing.

Riots, Protests, and the Youth Revolution

The 1960s were a time of considerable social reform, violent unrest, and relaxed standards of behavior. The push for equal racial and gender-based rights, the louder collective voice of youth, new forms of music and chemical stimulation, and a war that provoked widespread protests all converged to create a climate of chaos, experimentation, and upheaval.

Desegregation was a hot topic in America during the early 1960s, with the Universities of Mississippi and Alabama both attracting international attention for their steadfast refusal to admit black students. In the case of Mississippi, the U.S. Justice Department and U.S. Marshals had to be called in to enforce federal law, while the National Guard was required in Alabama to prevent Governor George Wallace from personally blocking the path of two black students who were trying to register.

At the head of the Civil Rights movement, Dr. Martin Luther King, Jr. led those who sought to attain racial equality by way of peaceful protests. On August 28, 1963, more than 200,000 people gathered in front of the Lincoln Memorial in Washington, D.C. to hear him deliver his now-historic "I Have a Dream" speech that demanded equality not only for black Americans, but for "all of God's children." Nevertheless, the inferior housing, education, and employment opportunities that black Americans were still experiencing by the mid-sixties resulted in some eventually placing less faith in Dr. King's pacifist approach than in the black-power remonstrations of Stokely Carmichael and radical organizations such as the Nation of Islam and the Black Panther Party.

The Panthers demanded the release of all black prisoners, together with the redistribution of property and wealth from whites to blacks. They also urged the black community to arm itself in order to "off the pigs" (kill white cops), and this added fuel to the fires that were already raging in ghettos across America. A case in point was the Watts area of Los Angeles where, in August 1965, 35 deaths and $200 million worth of damage resulted from an uprising among the residents.

For the most part, the black power movement had more of a cultural impact than a political one, with "black is beautiful" becoming a popular catchphrase during the second half of the 1960s among people who were no longer interested in trying to "act white" to be accepted. Instead of straightening their hair, many black people now opted for a more natural look while wearing African-style clothing, promoting their own forms of popular music, and watching actors such as Bill Cosby and Diahann Carroll portray TV characters that were far less stereotypical than the shuffling, smiling servants of years past.

By the Time We Got to Woodstock

As the 1960s progressed, moral attitudes changed, long-held values were questioned, and the old order was challenged by the voice of youth, with popular music evolving from simple boy-loves-girl, boy-loses-girl ditties into songs with a message... whatever that message might be.

At the decade's midway mark, Bob Dylan took the revolutionary step of plugging his folk guitar into an electric amplifier in order to reach a wider youth audience. Despite heavy criticism from his old "folky" fans, Dylan's protest songs—dealing with issues such as social injustice and a counterculture populated by drug peddlers and homeless youngsters—burst onto the pop charts. Music was now the trendy form of mass communication and others jumped on board, ranging from The Beatles telling everyone "All You Need is Love" to Country Joe and the Fish attacking America's involvement in the Vietnam War with the "I Feel Like I'm Fixin' to Die Rag."

Huge pop music festivals such as Monterey (1967) and Woodstock (1969) were the natural outcome of a youth movement that was pushing for peace, love, and unity. However, the chaos of The Rolling Stones' Altamont Speedway Free Festival on December 6, 1969, culminating in the fatal Hell's Angel stabbing of a gun-toting 18-year-old black spectator named Meredith Hunter during the Stones' performance of "Sympathy for the Devil," was also symbolic of pacifist naiveté gone badly awry.

This had already been evident in the violent protests that had exploded on university campuses around the United States and western Europe. In May 1968, students across France took to the streets to vent their anger against what they considered to be an archaic, inadequate university system and the national government that was doing nothing to improve it. Pitched battles were fought with the police, cars were burned, gasoline bombs were thrown, and when teachers and workers decided to join in the action, the country was brought to a virtual standstill. For a time it looked as if there would be a civil war, until the usual promises of reform managed to calm everyone down.

In America, where students were largely against their nation's involvement in the Vietnam War, 1965 protests on the Berkeley campus of the University of California and that year's Vietnam Day march through the streets of Oakland paved the way for 100,000 people marching on the Pentagon on October 21, 1967. Still, the war continued, both in Southeast Asia and on U.S. university campuses, leading to the May 4, 1970 Kent State massacre in which members of the Ohio National Guard fatally shot four students and wounded nine others (one of whom was permanently paralyzed). Meanwhile, across the pond, on March 17, 1968, blood was also spilled in front of the American Embassy in London's Grosvenor Square when anti-Vietnam protestors clashed with police, resulting in 86 injuries and 200 arrests.

Not only had the young rebels of the 1950s and early-sixties been superseded by political radicals, but rockers and beatniks had given way to flower children, college politicos, and a counterculture of freaks, hippies, and yippies who were into psychedelic music, mind-bending drugs, and conflicting messages of peace, love, and bloody insurrection.

The Beatles were at the forefront of all these intertwining movements and activities that saw youthful challenges to traditional law and order coincide with more liberal attitudes toward sexual freedom. Courtesy of John Lennon, "All You Need is Love" and "Give Peace a Chance" were anthems for a generation at the same time as the "make love, not war" slogan was made possible by a contraceptive pill that had a far greater social impact than the LSD tablets that some folks took to "turn on, tune in, and drop out."

Indeed, perhaps the biggest threat to the long-established status quo was the onset of the women's liberation movement. No longer content just to stay at home and raise babies, many more females went out and got jobs. And, while men grew their hair long, wore bright clothes, and some of them openly proclaimed they were gay, radical women put on pants and burned their bras. It was a mass case of trading places.

The killing of President John F. Kennedy on November 22, 1963 had a devastating effect on America and was a profound shock to the rest of the world. A youthful man who promised reform had been snatched away from millions of people who'd been instilled with hope and who, after his slaying, had to grow up and face some harsh realities.

The Assassins' Bullets: Robert, Martin, and John

Still, JFK's death wasn't the end of the dream as far as those involved in the Civil Rights movement were concerned. While militant organizations such as the Black Panthers advocated the use of force to achieve their ends, those who sought a more peaceful solution to the racial strife and Vietnam conflict were still able to look toward luminaries such as Dr. Martin Luther King and, for a brief time, Senator Robert Kennedy.

Having served as a tough-as-nails Attorney General during his older brother's presidency, Robert Kennedy reemerged with a greater social conscience and represented renewed hope to millions the world over when he entered the presidential race in 1968. Within just a few months, however, that hope would be extinguished. On April 4, Dr. King was gunned down on a balcony at the Lorraine Motel in Memphis, Tennessee. Riots immediately exploded in black neighborhoods across America, and one of the leading figures to make a well-heard plea for calmness was Bobby Kennedy. Then, on June 5, Kennedy himself was fatally shot while campaigning in Los Angeles.

In London the previous day, John Lennon had recorded the vocal to "Revolution 1," in which he expressed doubt about whether he should be counted "out/in" when talking about destruction. It was about time people made up their minds.

PART 5

UPSETTING THE APPLE CART

Clearly, this book isn't just full of good vibes and happy anecdotes, and in this part of Beatles 101 *there really isn't that much to celebrate—unless you love controversy—because what we're dealing with here are the episodes that earned The Beatles fewer plaudits than brickbats.*

Also included are the personal and professional setbacks they experienced, before we get to the point in the story that shall live in infamy for Beatle People everywhere: the group's split and the acrimony that followed. Lastly, even though this book's main focus is on the band you've known for all these years, I'll also give you a brief rundown on the solo careers of John, Paul, George, and Ringo.

Chapter 22

Bad Boys (You Can't Do That)

During the early years of Beatlemania, our Fab heroes enjoyed plenty of positive media coverage. However, when the tide turned, those waves of bad press came crashing down on more than one occasion.

Not that Messrs. Lennon, McCartney, Harrison, and Starr didn't also court controversy via their sometimes-unconventional words and actions. They did as they pleased and faced the consequences, even if there were times when those consequences were both unjustified and unexpected. The fact is, every good story needs its fair share of ups and downs, so let's get down and dirty…

Rocking the Royals

When Beatlemania was at its height, no one, including members of Britain's royal household, considered themselves above being associated with the world's most famous musical quartet. However, when the Queen rewarded the Beatles' "services to British industry" with Membership of the Most Excellent Order of the British Empire, some people decided things had gone too far. So, they protested, and four years later they would feel that their stance had been justified.

It was on the night of June 11, 1965, that the world learned about The Beatles being awarded MBEs by Queen Elizabeth II. John, Paul, George, and Ringo had known about the honor for some time, and although they had to remain silent until the news embargo was lifted, their own reaction had been mixed. John, for one, didn't have much regard for the whole concept of royalty, and he would later admit to having had reservations about accepting the honor in the first place. Nevertheless, in 1965 Brian Epstein was still able to exert some measure of influence over the band, and so John was soon persuaded to toe the line and "do the right thing."

Others weren't so agreeable. Certain military figures and heroes objected to The Beatles receiving MBEs, asserting that this cheapened the honor, and several even returned their medals to Buckingham Palace as a protest. One such character was Hector Dupuis, a member of the Canadian House of Commons, who complained that he'd been placed on the "same level as vulgar nincompoops!" George's response: "If Dupuis doesn't want the medal, he had better give it to us. Then we can give it to our manager, Brian Epstein. MBE really stands for 'Mr. Brian Epstein.'"

After the investiture took place in the Great Throne Room of Buckingham Palace on October 26, 1965, Paul asserted that the Queen had been "just like a mum to us." As for what to do with the awards, he said this would be "what you normally do with medals. Put them in a box." John, meanwhile, gave his to Aunt Mimi, who placed it proudly on top of her television set. It wouldn't remain there for very long.

Fast-forward to late 1969: Brian Epstein was no longer around, The Beatles had all but officially disbanded, and John and Yoko had been attracting widespread attention, notoriety, and ridicule for many—if not all—of the wrong reasons. A prime example came on November 25, when John returned his MBE to the Queen by having his chauffeur, Les Anthony, hand-deliver it to Buckingham Palace with a letter from his boss: "Your Majesty, I am returning this MBE in protest against Britain's involvement in the Nigeria-Biafra thing, against our support of America in Vietnam, and against 'Cold Turkey' slipping down the charts. With love, John Lennon of Bag."

A copy was also sent to Prime Minister Harold Wilson and the reaction was predictably hostile. The same people who had condemned The Beatles being awarded MBEs in the first place were now pointing out how right they had been all along. Such an honor should never have been bestowed on a bunch of irresponsible young upstarts. Still, they would say that, wouldn't they?

Butchers Undercover

On March 25, 1966, The Beatles had their photos taken at a London studio by Robert Whittaker. For some of that year's official publicity shots, they wore light turtleneck sweaters and dark jackets; for others, they donned white butchers' smocks and posed gleefully with decapitated dolls and chunks of raw, bloody meat. Bored with doing the same old same old, they were happy to try one of Whittaker's more offbeat ideas, but when they then used one of those joyfully macabre photos for the cover of their new *Yesterday and Today* album in the U.S.—while also employing it to advertise their "Paperback Writer" single in the U.K.—public reaction was swift and largely negative.

It was in early June that promotional copies of the record were sent out to deejays and reviewers. At the same time, billboards and posters adorned with the "Butcher" photo started appearing all over America, before around 750,000 copies of the album were issued to stores. Many retailers complained and Capitol Records, obeying orders from EMI chairman Sir Joseph Lockwood, announced that it was immediately withdrawing and replacing the original album sleeve.

Yesterday and Today, under the slightly revised title of *"Yesterday"...and Today*, was subsequently released to the American public with a bland and nonsensical cover photo of the bored-looking Beatles posing in and around an empty trunk. In some cases, the record had been placed inside a brand new sleeve, but there were also countless others that just had the new photo pasted over the old one. Capitol, which had been raking in millions during the past couple of years thanks to The Beatles, wanted to save a few thousand dollars. However, it didn't take the sharp-eyed fans long to spot the sleeves with the pasted-on covers, or to work out that, by carefully applying a little steam, those covers could be peeled off to reveal the *real* ones underneath. The Capitol execs could have saved themselves a lot of time and effort... as well as several thousand more dollars.

In the summer of 1966, The Beatles had to contend with not only the horrors of their final concert tours and the flak over their "Butcher" cover, but also the furor in the United States caused by an innocent remark that John had made regarding religion.

Bigger Than Jesus

On March 4, John gave an in-depth interview to journalist and friend Maureen Cleave for publication in London's *Evening Standard* newspaper. This featured him describing his domestic life and interests in art and reading while also expressing some opinions on money, politics, and religion. Having read extensively about the latter subject, John noted the dwindling role of the church within modern society, as well as people's increased preference for material rather than spiritual possessions.

"Christianity will go," he predicted. "It will vanish and shrink. I needn't argue about that; I'm right and I will be proved right. We're more popular than Jesus now; I don't know which will go first—rock 'n' roll or Christianity. Jesus was all right but his disciples were thick and ordinary. It's them twisting it that ruins it for me."

Rather than being sacrilegious, John was condemning the fact that more people were flocking to Beatles concerts than to their local churches. However, when the American teen magazine *Datebook* picked up on the quote on July 29, it totally distorted his statement. A banner headline paraphrased him as having said that The Beatles were *greater* than Jesus, not bigger, and the result was John Lennon's near-immediate denouncement by a number of holier-than-thou conservatives in America's south-eastern and south-central Bible Belt regions.

Led by Birmingham, Alabama's WAQY, 22 radio stations banned the broadcasting of Beatles music on the airwaves (some of them conveniently ignoring the fact that they hadn't ever played them in the first place). At the same time, for the benefit of the press and TV cameras, public "Beatles bonfires" were organized to burn records, books, and merchandise relating to the group, while the Ku Klux Klan boasted it would somehow disrupt the band's upcoming American tour.

Brian Epstein could see things were getting out of hand, and so on August 6, 1966, he held a press conference in New York to explain the true meaning of John's remarks. Still, the zealots weren't satisfied; they wanted to hear what that "devil worshipping Beatle" now had to say for himself. On August 11 they found out, when John and his bandmates faced the press at Chicago's Astor Towers Hotel, prior to kicking off their North American tour: "You know, I'm not saying that we're better or greater, or comparing us with Jesus Christ as a person or God as a thing, or whatever it is. I just said what I said and it was wrong, or was taken wrong, and now it's all this..."

Thus sayeth the beleaguered Beatle—as well as "sorry," which was almost certainly what he felt for himself rather than a heartfelt apology. Still, it largely did the trick and the tour proceeded pretty much as planned.

Day Trippers

Lysergic acid diethylamide is a powerful hallucinogenic drug that had a significant impact on the rock generation of the mid-to-late 1960s. The music community actually started to experiment with it seriously back in 1965, when non-medical use of LSD was still legal, and even after it was banned in both the U.S. and U.K. the following year, many acts "dropped acid" as a means of artistic experimentation and "expanding the consciousness." These ranged from The Byrds to The Beach Boys, The Jefferson Airplane to The Rolling Stones.

The Beatles' first experience with LSD took place when someone covertly dropped it into the drinks of John and George at a London dinner party. Previously, the Fab Four had all taken uppers such as Preludin and smoked pot, but LSD was initially too much of a step into the unknown for either Paul or Ringo. So, they resisted while John and George swallowed the little pills willingly and frequently, and this in turn had a marked influence on the group's music, especially John's songwriting.

For instance, "She Said, She Said" evolved out of the second acid trip—and first intentional one—experienced by John and George, during an August 1965 Hollywood party alongside actor Peter Fonda and members of The Byrds. When Fonda kept approaching John and murmuring, "Hey, man, I know what it's like to be dead," the stoned Beatle urged him to stop in case he raised suspicions among attending press reporters. Later, however, John adapted that line into one of the song's refrains, and the following year he then invited the world to trip along with him via "Tomorrow Never Knows," the first track recorded for—and last one featured on—The Beatles' magnificent *Revolver* album.

While the song's quasi-religious, acid-laced lyrics encouraged the listener to "listen to the colour of your dreams," it's backward guitar solo and surreal sound effects brilliantly conveyed the mind-swirling sensation of taking the drug, and this continued with the majestic orchestral crescendos on "A Day in the Life," which similarly concluded the landmark *Sgt. Pepper's Lonely Hearts Club Band* album. On May 20, 1967, just under a week before *Pepper*'s release, the BBC imposed a TV and radio ban on "A Day in the Life," explaining that it could encourage drug taking, and several U.S. broadcasters followed suit. By then, Paul and Ringo had finally experimented with LSD, and it didn't take long for Paul to reveal in a *Life* magazine interview that LSD had "opened my eyes" and remark that "we only use one-tenth of our brains. Just think what we'd accomplish if we could tap that hidden part."

Britain's *Daily Mail* responded by calling Paul "an irresponsible idiot," and much the same was implied by a TV reporter when Paul admitted to his use of LSD during an interview intended for a U.K. news broadcast. Since The Beatles' young fans imitated their idols in oh-so-many ways, didn't the band have a moral duty to act responsibly and set the right example? Paul immediately pointed out that the interview needn't be broadcast. "It's you who've got responsibility not to spread this," he said. "If you'll shut up about it, I will."

That was never going to happen. The interview was broadcast on June 19, 1967, and was seen around the world shortly thereafter. The inevitable uproar and condemnation ensued before, on July 24, all four Beatles and Brian Epstein signed a petition that appeared in *The Times*, calling for the legalization of marijuana. This actually gave John, Paul, George, and Ringo added credibility as the unofficial "leaders of a generation" in the eyes of many of their fans, and it also helped them dispense with the glossy image that they considered to be outdated and out of sync with who they truly were. However, for numerous other people in their teens and early twenties, as well as for the majority of parents, things could never be the same again.

Busted—It's Pilcher of the Yard!

Sgt. Pilcher had been building up to this moment for quite some time. Donovan had been the first British pop star to be busted for drugs, and he'd been followed by a number of other rock artists, including Mick Jagger, Keith Richard, and Brian Jones of The Rolling Stones. At the top of the pecking order, however, were The Beatles, and so on October 18, 1968, Pilcher made his move.

Just a few months after having separated from his wife, Cynthia, John was staying with his girlfriend Yoko Ono at 34 Montagu Square in Central London, in an apartment loaned to them by Ringo. The couple were in bed when Pilcher arrived with his men and a posse of sniffer dogs, threatening to break the door down if they weren't permitted immediate entry to search the premises. So, John stalled while he contacted his lawyer, and he and Yoko were consequently charged with obstructing the police in execution of a search warrant.

Having received a tip-off from *Daily Mirror* journalist Don Short that Scotland Yard might pay him a visit, John had already tidied up the apartment. But that still didn't prevent the police from "finding" some cannabis stored in a trunk, and this was cause for concern because Yoko, who wasn't a British citizen, might face deportation. Therefore, when the case came to court on November 28, John took it upon himself to plead guilty to possession of cannabis resin, ensuring that he and Yoko were acquitted of the obstruction charge. The punishment was a £150 fine with 20 guineas' costs; equivalent to about $410 dollars. (A guinea, in old currency, was worth 21 shillings while a pound equalled 20 shillings.) However, the overall cost to John would prove to be far greater a few years later when the U.S. Government would cite his drug conviction as just cause to have him deported from America.

In the meantime, having successfully nailed one Beatle, Sgt. Pilcher decided to go after another. On March 12, 1969, the day that Paul married Linda Eastman, George was sitting in one of the Apple Corps offices when he received a phone call from his wife, Pattie, informing him that Pilcher and his men were swarming all over the Harrison home in Esher, Surrey. After talking things over with Apple's chief executive, Neil Aspinall, George decided it would best to reveal where he kept his drugs, and so he told Pattie to inform the cops that there was a small amount of marijuana in a box on top of the mantelpiece in the living room.

It was too late. Pilcher and his colleagues had already managed to "find" a much larger stash of the drug inside a boot in George's closet. On March 31, George and Pattie were found guilty of cannabis possession and each was fined £250 with 10 guineas' costs (about $625). Ringo never fell foul of the law in the same way, but Paul and Linda would certainly do so—several times—after The Beatles split.

Bare Assets—Yoko and the Walrus

It was on November 29, 1968, the day after John had been convicted and fined for possessing cannabis, that his and Yoko's album, *Two Virgins*, hit the stores. And what an album it was. First, however, let's revisit how the couple's relationship took off.

As you may recall, they first set eyes on one another in November 1966, when John attended a preview of Yoko's avant-garde art exhibition, *Unfinished Paintings and Objects*, at London's Indica Gallery. John, who had thought he was heading to an "artsy-fartsy orgy," instead discovered an offbeat concept of art that had him mesmerized. The focal piece for him was "Hammer a Nail," comprising a wooden board into which patrons were supposed to, yes, hammer a nail and thus contribute to the artwork's creation. Yoko initially refused to let John do this before the exhibition opened, prompting the Indica's owner, John Dunbar, to exclaim, "Don't you know who this *is*? He's a millionaire! He might *buy* it!" Yoko would later claim she had never heard of The Beatles— which is hard to believe—so her compromise was to permit John to pay five shillings for the privilege of hammering a nail. His self-described smartass response: "I'll give you an imaginary five shillings and hammer an imaginary nail in."

"That's when we locked eyes and she got it and I got it," he'd later recall.

Seven years older than John, Yoko Ono was in the middle of her second marriage and had a daughter named Kyoko when the two of them met. Yoko's dad had been the president of the Bank of Tokyo in New York, yet she had rejected her family's wealthy lifestyle in favor of becoming an avant-garde artist, gaining notoriety during the mid-sixties with her *Bottoms* film that focused on 365 naked rear ends, as well as for covering a Trafalgar Square lion statue with huge white sheets following her relocation from New York to London.

Still, for all of the apparent excitement, John wouldn't hook up with Yoko until 18 months after they first met. During that time, Yoko kept pursuing him, turning up at places where John and Cyn visited, and inching her way into his thoughts by mailing him cryptically humorous messages such as "Breathe," "Dance," or "Watch all the lights until dawn." These appealed to John's sense of the absurd, and eventually her persistence paid off. When Cynthia went with friends on a vacation to Greece in May 1968, John invited Yoko over to his Weybridge home.

There they retired to his small studio, where the Beatle played the progressive artist some experimental tapes that he'd recorded, consisting of various sound effects and electronic noises. Yoko was impressed. Why not make some joint recordings? This they immediately did, squawking, screeching, and farting in both directions to the occasional accompaniment of a piano and slowed-down tape effects. To quote John: "It was midnight when we started *Two Virgins*, it was dawn when we finished, and then we made love at dawn. It was very beautiful."

For John and Yoko, certainly, but not for Cynthia, who returned from Greece to find the virgins playing house together in her marital home. She and Julian promptly moved out and the Lennons' divorce became final on November 8, a couple of weeks before Yoko suffered a miscarriage.

If Cynthia tried to come to terms with what had happened, the press wasn't yet prepared to. There was outrage when John and Yoko started appearing together; planting acorns for peace, attending the first night of the National Theatre's staging of part of John's book, *In His Own Write*, and hosting their first joint art exhibition, *You Are Here*. In addition to newspapers and magazines making fun of them, often by way of crude racial slurs aimed at Yoko, people who saw them out in public would shout "Where's your wife?" at John and "Chink!" at his new partner. Never mind that Ms. Ono wasn't Chinese.

Still, the appearances that John and Yoko made in public were nothing compared to the ones that they made on the album sleeve of *Unfinished Music No.1: Two Virgins* (to give the record its full title). There they stood, on the front cover, facing a remote-controlled camera in all of their naked glory, while on the back they could be seen equally bare from behind. Now, this would be pretty outrageous even by today's standards, so try to imagine the reaction back in 1968.

Meanwhile, what did the other Beatles think of all this? "When two great saints meet it is a humbling experience," Paul was quoted as saying on the cover of *Two Virgins*, underneath the full-frontal nudie of John and Yoko. In private, however, there wasn't such a rich endorsement, George reportedly complaining to John, "You realize that, when you show your cock, it's like *all* of us showing our cocks."

EMI pressed *Two Virgins* but refused to distribute it, with company Chairman Sir Joseph Lockwood informing John and Yoko that a naked Paul would have made a prettier sight on the cover. Consequently, Track Records took care of distribution in the U.K., enveloping the album in a plain brown wrapper, while a label named Tetragrammaton did the same in the U.S.A. Still, 30,000 copies never made it out of a Newark warehouse, having been confiscated by police in New Jersey.

And all for what? Simply because John and Yoko wanted to make a statement or, more like it, test the boundaries of public tolerance. If the reaction was anything to go by, they'd certainly managed to achieve their aim, yet this was by no means the end of what many perceived as their buffoonery.

260

Paul on Mic

"*Like* An Inner Light, *this was adapted from a screen-grab off the 'Hey Bulldog' video. While I was watching it to get the George image, I saw this one of Paul and just loved the shadows. So, I took a chance with it. Shadows create more shadows, and although they tend to distort an image they can also make it really interesting. That's why I actually did this painting before the one of George—I couldn't wait to get to it.*"

– Eric Cash

Chapter 23

Something to Get Hung About—Breaking Up

Artistically, The Beatles were without equal right until the end, producing what many believe are some of their finest recordings during the latter part of their career. In numerous other ways, however, the years 1967 to 1969 represented troubled times for the band, both personally and professionally.

The seeds of their downfall were sown with the tragic early death of Brian Epstein, their adoring, dedicated manager who had done so much to establish The Beatles as the world's foremost supergroup. Things started to go awry from that point on and, with none of the band members willing or able to take hold of the wheel, they really couldn't find their way back home.

A Death in the Family: Brian Epstein

At the age of 32, Brian Epstein was, along with Elvis Presley's manager Colonel Tom Parker, the world's most successful pop impresario. In 1967, he was also the most envied, with a client roster that included The Beatles, a theater on Central London's Shaftesbury Avenue, a Georgian house in the capital's exclusive Belgravia neighborhood, and a spacious country home at Kingsley Hill in Sussex. Yet, he still wasn't a happy man.

Devoid of nonstop work relating to The Beatles, Brian's days now seemed empty while his nights were often consumed with trips around the London casinos, drinking brandy, and suffering muggings and extortion threats as a result of his frequently dangerous sexual liaisons. Sleeping pills were necessary to help him rest from the early morning until late afternoon, and Brian also used them in a second suicide attempt at the beginning of 1967. He visited clinics several times to dry out, but the thought that The Beatles might look to someone else when their management contract expired in October kept coming back to haunt him.

In mid-August, following the death of Harry Epstein at age 63 from a heart attack, Brian's mother Queenie came to stay with him for 10 days at his Belgravia home. During that visit Brian got his act together and conformed to a healthy routine. Queenie returned to Liverpool on Thursday, August 24, and that night The Beatles, together with Cyn, Pattie, Maureen, Jane, and Paul's brother Mike, attended a lecture on Transcendental Meditation that was being given by the Maharishi Mahesh Yogi at the Hilton Hotel on London's Park Lane. Enticed by a philosophy that promised them inner peace and spiritual regeneration, The Beatles immediately agreed to follow the Maharishi to Bangor, North Wales, the next day, where he would be conducting a weekend seminar on TM. Brian was invited to go along but, this being the start of a holiday weekend in Britain, he'd already made plans to entertain some people at Kingsley Hill in Sussex. He said he might join The Beatles later in Wales, but when several of the guests he'd invited couldn't make it, he ended up spending Friday night eating dinner with just a couple of old business friends, Peter Brown and Geoffrey Ellis.

At around 10:00 p.m., Brian announced that he was driving to London and would return the next morning, but he didn't actually phone Peter Brown until around 5:00 on Saturday afternoon. Having slept all day at his Chapel Street home, he still felt drowsy and therefore agreed to travel back to Sussex by train and to call just before he left. That call, however, never came. When Brian still hadn't emerged from his bedroom by the late morning of Sunday, August 27, the butler and his wife became concerned. Brian's assistant, Joanne Newfield, was alerted, as was a doctor, and both rushed to the house where, at around 2:00 in the afternoon, the butler and the doctor broke down the bedroom door and discovered Brian lying on his side in bed. He was dead.

In Bangor, Paul McCartney answered the telephone to hear the shocking news and, after fielding news reporters' questions, he and his colleagues immediately returned to London. None of them attended Brian's funeral in Liverpool on August 29—that was strictly a family affair—but they did go to a memorial service at the New London Synagogue, around the corner from the recording studios on Abbey Road where, thanks to Brian, The Beatles had auditioned for EMI just over five years earlier.

An inquest into Brian's death concluded that he had died accidentally due to the cumulative effects of alcohol and the sedative Carbitrol. There have since been countless rumors about his death being a suicide, while

Beatles biographer Philip Norman has ludicrously suggested that Brian may have been murdered by enemies in the business world. Regardless, John Lennon understood full well the state The Beatles were in without a manager. "I knew that we were in trouble then," he told *Rolling Stone*'s Jann Wenner in 1970. "I didn't really have any misconceptions about our ability to do anything other than play music, and I was scared. I thought, *We've fuckin' had it.*"

Who Buried Paul?

It's one thing to mourn the death of someone near, dear, or just admired and beloved. However, it's also advisable to ensure that the person is actually deceased before breaking out the Kleenex and delivering the eulogy.

Take James Paul McCartney. In October 1969, the release of *Abbey Road* and Paul's foray out of the public spotlight for several weeks fueled an idiotic rumor that he'd been killed and replaced by a lookalike. The instigator was one Russ Gibbs, program coordinator for radio station WKNR-FM in Detroit, who claimed to have received a phone call informing him of Paul's death, while stating that there were vital "clues" on the *Abbey Road* album cover to prove it:

- On the front, as they walk along a zebra-crossing, George is supposedly dressed as a gravedigger; Ringo like an undertaker; and John like a minister. Paul, meanwhile, is garbed in a burial suit, walking out of step with the other Beatles, and barefoot— he is, after all, a corpse.

- On the left-hand side of the road, a Volkswagen Beetle bears the license plate "LMW 281F," relating to the supposed fact that Paul would have been *28 if* he had still been alive. (In reality, he would have been 27, but never mind.)

- On the back cover, a crack in the word *Beatles* signifies a fracture in the band itself.

Politically, of course, this was right on the money, but is it really likely that The Beatles, having concealed the fact that Paul had died, would then reveal the truth by way of daft hints? Clearly, some people thought so, especially in America, where the rumor spread like wildfire and half-baked "investigators" were soon finding a whole host of other "clues" that had supposedly been dropped during the previous three years:

- The real Paul had been replaced by an actor named either William Campbell or Billy Shears who had undergone plastic surgery in order to effect a perfect likeness. Thus the introduction of Billy Shears at the end of the opening track on *Sgt. Pepper*.

- The cause of death ("he blew his mind out in a car") is revealed in a line from the song "A Day in the Life." (In reality, it refers to the fatal road accident of Guinness heir, Tara Browne, in December 1966.)

- At the end of "Strawberry Fields Forever," John mutters, "I buried Paul." (A closer listen reveals that he actually said, "cranberry sauce.")

- On the "White Album" song, "Glass Onion," the line "the walrus was Paul" again symbolizes death, just as the character of the Walrus does in the Lewis Carroll poem, "The Walrus and the Carpenter."

- On the run-out groove to the vinyl *Sgt. Pepper* album, there's a quick burst of randomly spoken gibberish that, when played backwards, sounds like "Turn me on, dead man." (At least, that's what some people insisted. A more likely interpretation is "We'll fuck you like Superman.")

- If you hold the British *Magical Mystery Tour* EP cover up to a mirror, you can see a telephone number which, when dialed, will connect you to Paul in the Hereafter. (As it turned out, the number belonged to a journalist from Britain's *Guardian* newspaper who was none too pleased when a glut of early morning calls started coming his way from across the Atlantic.)

There are also supposed clues on the *Sgt. Pepper* album cover itself:

- Four dark-suited wax dummies of The Beatles look mournfully at a grave bearing a flower wreath shaped like a left-handed bass guitar.

- The raised hand above the head of Paul/William Campbell/ Billy Shears signifies death.

- On the back cover, a group photo features only Campbell/ Shears facing away from the camera, as his facial cosmetic surgery has not yet been perfected.

- The gatefold sleeve's central picture shows Campbell/Shears sporting an arm patch bearing the letters "OPD," standing for "Officially Pronounced Dead." (The letters were, in fact, "OPP," as it was the badge of the Ontario Provincial Police.)

As for the man himself? When tracked down by representatives of *Life* magazine to his farm on the Mull of Kintyre in northwest Scotland, Paul McCartney (or his impostor) asserted, "The rumors of my death have been greatly exaggerated. However, if I was dead I'm sure I'd be the last to know."

In the Court of Sexy Sadie

Although much delayed, The Beatles' Indian summer came early in 1968. John, Cynthia, George, and Pattie arrived there on February 16th, with Paul, Jane, Ringo, and Maureen following four days later.

The twin objectives were peace and meditation, and Rishikesh was the destination where, high amid the Himalayas, the Maharishi Mahesh Yogi had his private compound. Among its many amenities, this boasted a number of fully furnished guest bungalows, offering modern comforts to The Beatles and their companions. Unsure about a vegetarian curry diet, Ringo and Maureen had brought a suitcase full of canned Heinz baked beans with them from London, yet these didn't do the trick for them and neither did the daily regimen of chanting mantras, meditating, and mass prayer. On March 1, just 12 days after arriving, the couple departed Rishikesh, with Ringo likening the compound to Butlin's, the holiday camp where he had once played summer seasons with Rory Storm and the Hurricanes.

The other Beatles, meanwhile, decided to stick it out, at one point engaging in a private competition to see who could meditate the longest. Still, no one could quite compete with actress Mia Farrow's younger sister, Prudence. According to John, "she seemed to go slightly balmy, meditating too long, and couldn't come out of the little hut that we were livin' in..." The result was John's composition, "Dear Prudence," which was one of many songs that The Beatles wrote for the "White Album" when they were in India.

Meanwhile, not content with just a search for internal peace, John and Paul were also looking to the Maharishi for an answer to life, the universe, everything. Nothing was forthcoming in that regard, even when John managed to charm his way onto the Yogi's helicopter and survey the ashram from the air.

On March 26, Paul and Jane decided that they'd had enough and returned to England. John and George stayed on, but then a nasty rumor started to form around their teacher. The word on the compound grapevine was that the Holy Man had attempted to grab hold of Mia Farrow and enlighten more than just her spirit. Now, whether or not that was true, the damage had been done. When even George started to have doubts about the Yogi's credibility, John became convinced, telling Cynthia they should pack their bags and get ready to leave. Next, he led the way into the principal bungalow and informed the Maharishi about this. The pint-sized guru, no longer giggling, asked John why they wanted to depart so suddenly. "Well, if you're so cosmic, you'll know why," came the Lennonish response. Reportedly, the Maharishi couldn't figure that one out. From John and George's viewpoint, however, the game was now up and they were on their way, although not before John quickly penned "Sexy Sadie," a barely disguised attack on the Yogi.

On April 12, 1968, John, Cynthia, George, and Pattie arrived back in London. On May 14, John then publicly denounced "Sadie" on NBC-TV's *The Tonight Show*. George would continue to pursue his interest in Indian culture and the Hindu faith but, as far as The Beatles and the Maharishi Mahesh Yogi were concerned, all bets were off.

White Mischief and Trouble Getting Back

Although it's clear that The Beatles started to lose their sense of direction after Brian Epstein's death, it was during recording sessions for the "White Album" that all-out disharmony between the group members first reared its ugly head.

The failure of the *Magical Mystery Tour* movie had been a definite career low point; a sign to the public that the Fab Four couldn't actually walk on water, as well as an undermining of The Beatles' normally rock solid confidence in each other's artistic judgment. Their convictions were further called into question when the Maharishi, who they'd originally looked upon as some sort of personal messiah, turned out to be—in their eyes, at least—little more than a charlatan. Bitterness began to set in, and then, just at the moment when band unity was of paramount importance, a divisive influence entered onto the scene and, more importantly, into the studio.

Up until now, The Beatles' recording sessions had largely been the domain of John, Paul, George, and Ringo, together with George Martin and the technical staff. Wives and girlfriends might very occasionally drop in for a visit, but nothing more. Well, from May 31, 1968 onward, Yoko Ono attended virtually every Beatles recording session that John participated in, sitting by his side, whispering secretively in his ear, openly making suggestions and criticisms with regard to the music, and generally making her presence known.

Paul, George, and Ringo were, to say the least, ill at ease. They resented the fact that the couple were totally inseparable—with John even insisting Yoko follow him into the bathroom in case Paul tried to hit on her if she remained behind in the studio—and that they could no longer glean an opinion from John without his new partner adding her 10 cents' worth. Yoko, meanwhile, was encouraging John to explore his most wayward and avant-garde artistic ideas, and when it became clear that the other Beatles were not receptive to them or to Yoko's participation in group affairs, this meant the beginning of the end.

Although John had started the band (and, in the early days, been its leader), his colleagues had since invested far too much of their own time and talents to be coerced into activities that didn't interest them. Realizing this, John began to dedicate more of his energy to pursuits with Yoko, and the self-absorption soon proved to be catching. Many but not all of the basic rhythm tracks for the 30 numbers on the "White Album" involved the participation of all four band members. However, the overdubbing of extra instrumental and vocal parts would usually be carried out by the composer of each song. Therefore, instead of pooling their talents in the creative process, The Beatles—especially John and Paul—were now only taking an interest in their own work and simply utilizing the other Beatles as backing musicians. In many cases this attitude caused resentment, leading to friction within the once-cohesive group unit, frayed tempers, and, ultimately, high tension and heated arguments.

Feeling unappreciated for his own steadfast contributions, the normally easygoing Ringo actually quit The Beatles on August 22, 1968. News of this was kept from the press and public while John, Paul, and George continued with the troubled "White Album" sessions. After a couple of weeks, Ringo was cajoled into returning and by mid-October the recordings were finally completed. However, the damage had been done. The double-set *The Beatles* was yet another magnificent body of work, complemented by the concurrent single "Hey Jude," but the group itself was in trouble and all four men knew it.

Paul remained the only one who appeared to have the will to try to keep things moving along. Aside from Yoko's presence and Brian's absence, Paul noted that the two main differences from the good old days were that the band was no longer performing live, and that it was also taking an eternity to record its songs. He therefore reasoned that it might benefit him and his fellow Fabs to dispense with the over-complicated approach to recording—spending weeks and months adding extra parts—and instead just rehearse their numbers together before then recording them in a few takes without overdubs. Furthermore, while touring was out, they should at least return to live public performances.

The result was the *Get Back* project which, when eventually unveiled in the form of a film, an album, and even a book, was renamed *Let It Be*. (A text-and-photo book originally accompanied the album in an over-priced boxed set.) However, the tensions that had characterized the "White Album" sessions immediately resurfaced and, this time around, their disruptive influence was clearly evident in the end products. As captured on film, The Beatles were no longer able to click consistently as a band and, with George Martin wiping his hands of the project, producer-engineer Glyn Johns was handed the tough task of compiling the *Get Back* album.

Glyn made two attempts. However, by sticking to the directive of not adding any extra instrumentation or sound effects to the recordings, he produced results that caused The Beatles to lose their nerve and withhold the album's release. Instead, they went back into the studio with George Martin at the helm, got their collective act together, and recorded one final, polished, and absolutely classic album, *Abbey Road*.

Still, with too much money tied up in *Get Back* to shelve it, legendary producer Phil Spector was called in to try to tidy up the recordings. He did so by editing the material and, in the notorious case of "The Long and Winding Road," adding an orchestra and female choir. This last act was too much for Paul McCartney to bear, and he attempted to have the strings and voices removed just prior to the now-retitled *Let It Be* album's release. This ultimately proved impossible, and Paul therefore went public in expressing his annoyance at Spector's intrusive over-production of his material.

The fact is, if The Beatles had applied themselves with more discipline in the first place, none of this would have come to pass.

Chapter 24

Coming Down Fast—The Curtain Falls

Considering how much John, Paul, George, and Ringo had achieved together during the previous seven years, not to mention their undeniable love and admiration for one another, the manner in which they ended their collaboration was both sad and unfortunate. Then again, given the strength of their personalities as well as their diverging interests, this was also probably inevitable. As such, The Beatles' breakup was like a bad divorce, with all of the accompanying pain and bitterness.

Life with the Ono-Lennons

In 1969, after several months of high-profile antics that had many people thinking John had lost his mind, he and Yoko truly gave free rein to their artistic ideas and political beliefs, involving themselves in all forms of activities that attracted admiration and ridicule on a global scale.

Toward the end of the January *Get Back* sessions, Yoko's divorce from her second husband, Anthony Cox, became final, paving the way for her and John to marry. They did so on the British-governed isle of Gibraltar on March 20 before flying to Paris and then on to Amsterdam where, on March 25, they commenced a seven day "bed-in" for peace in Room 902 of the Hilton Hotel. Reasoning quite rightly that whatever they did on their honeymoon would make the news, Mr. and Mrs. Lennon decided to stage what amounted to a commercial promoting peace and love. After all, doing so from their honeymoon bed ensured they would generate the maximum amount of pacifism-related publicity.

Sitting in or on top of their large double bed, John and Yoko were subsequently surrounded by reporters, friends, flowers, gifts, and a number of hand-drawn posters proclaiming "Bagism," "Remember Love," "Peace," "Bed Peace," and, reflecting John's well known love for word-play, "Hair Peace." So it was that the world's most famous newlyweds managed to capture the world's attention. Yet, instead of having their well-intentioned peace campaign taken seriously, they were treated by many as a laughing stock.

After adopting the middle name of Ono in a formal ceremony on the roof of The Beatles' Apple building in April 1969, John attempted to stage a second bed-in with Yoko in America that May. Due to his drug bust the previous year, however, the U.S. authorities refused to grant him a visa, so the couple then took their road show to Room 1742 of the Queen Elizabeth Hotel in Montreal. There, on June 1, they— together with various friends and acquaintances—recorded "Give Peace a Chance." A timeless anthem, this was the first single to be released by The Plastic Ono Band; the name given to a number of different musicians who would hereafter back John and Yoko on record and in concert.

Later that year, The Plastic Ono Band, featuring John on guitar and vocals, Eric Clapton on lead guitar, Klaus Voormann on bass, and Ringo on drums, recorded the single "Cold Turkey," a brilliant, chilling account of the Ono-Lennons' struggles with heroin withdrawal. This addiction also played a part in John's emotional withdrawal from The Beatles, yet it was by no means his only problem during an action-packed year. At the start of July, he and Yoko were involved in a car crash in Scotland while vacationing with their respective children Julian and Kyoko. In October, Yoko then suffered a second miscarriage, and in November there was John's infamous returning of his MBE.

In the middle of all this activity, John somehow still found time to work on The Beatles' *Abbey Road* album as well as his and Yoko's avant-garde recordings. On September 13, The Plastic Ono Band made a live appearance in the *Toronto Rock and Roll Revival* concert, while on December 15 the temporarily renamed Plastic Ono Supergroup performed in the *Peace for Christmas Prom-Pop Concert* at London's Lyceum Ballroom. As this lineup also included George Harrison, it was the first time that two Beatles had appeared together on a concert stage since August 1966, and also the final such occasion for John and George. In the future, other combinations of former Fabs would perform live together, but the chances of all four doing so—or of Paul appearing with either John or George—would prove to be a forlorn hope.

Paul: Carrying That Weight

If 1969 was a highly adventurous year for John and Yoko, in a professional sense it was a pretty tough one for Paul as he had to deal with the hard fact that The Beatles were basically finished. Still, he did give things his best shot.

Following the traumatic *Get Back* sessions which had seen most of his best-laid plans for the band fall apart, Paul continued to compose, produce, and play on records by a number of other artists. He also dashed the hopes of girls the world over by marrying Linda Louise Eastman in London on March 12, but soon thereafter his domestic bliss was disrupted by legal disputes with his fellow Beatles.

Amid all this unrest, the group recorded *Abbey Road*, an album that Paul largely instigated as another means to get The Beatles to do what they did best: make music. However, while all four band members did themselves magnificent credit on the record, and while Lennon and McCartney contributed roughly the same number of songs, it was undeniably Paul who carried the album's most stunning sequence on Side Two, where tracks merge into one another to produce one of The Beatles' finest recorded achievements. And it was also Paul who came up with the concept for the album's iconic cover photo. The production polish of *Abbey Road* stands in stark contrast to the inconsistent quality of *Let It Be*, and this was largely due to the fact that John, Paul, George, and Ringo managed to collaborate in a more congenial way during the July-August 1969 *Abbey Road* sessions..

Almost inevitably, there were still flare-ups between the band members, but during the fall of '69 Paul still stuck to his belief that, despite all of their differences, The Beatles might get back on track if they resumed live performances. He therefore continued to come up with suggestions until a final rebuff convinced him that The Beatles were no more, after which he started working on his own solo album; a project that proved to be the straw that broke the camel's back.

George: Not a Beatle Anymore

As you might recall, immediately after the Fab Four performed their last ever paid concert, George Harrison commented that he was "not a Beatle anymore." Well, throughout 1969 he said the same thing on several occasions until, wouldn't you know it, he was absolutely right.

As previously mentioned, George quit the band during the *Get Back* sessions, and although he returned soon afterwards, things didn't get much better from that point on. Artistically he continued to feel that Paul adopted a condescending attitude toward him and that John really wasn't interested in recording any "Harrisongs." Certainly, there are two sides to every story—in The Beatles' case there were often four—but there does appear to have been some justification for George feeling short-changed. John was noticeably absent from many of the latter sessions involving the youngest Beatle's compositions.

In early December 1969, George joined the short British and Danish tours of American white-soul husband and wife act, Delaney and Bonnie Bramlett, playing in their backing band alongside Eric Clapton under the billing of Delaney & Bonnie and Friends. The "Quiet Beatle" enjoyed being able to perform two shows a night just as in the old days, as well as the opportunity to do so virtually unnoticed in his long hair and mustache, without any audience screaming to obliterate the music.

Still, he did get together with Paul and Ringo on January 3 and 4, 1970, to record "I Me Mine" and overdub a new guitar solo, harmony vocals, drums, and percussion onto "Let It Be." John was in Denmark, and so at one point during the January 3 session, referring to then-popular British band Dave Dee, Dozy, Beaky, Mick and Tich, George made an announcement over his microphone: "You all will have read that Dave Dee is no longer with us, but Micky and Tich and I would just like to carry on the good work that's always gone down in number two." (You can hear this immediately prior to "I Me Mine" on *Anthology 3*.)

The irony of this show of unity in the face of John's withdrawal from the group is that hereafter it would be Paul who George would steadfastly refuse to work with.

Ringo: Celluloid Satisfaction

Shortly after the band stopped touring, and encouraged by the reviews that he had received for his acting in *A Hard Day's Night* and *Help!*, Ringo asked Brian Epstein's NEMS organization to scout for a solo movie role. Several were probably found, but the one that Ringo agreed to was, quite wisely, a small part in a star-studded film: *Candy*, based on the book by Terry Southern. Marlon Brando, Richard Burton, John Huston, James Coburn, and Walter Matthau headed the international cast that also included Swedish beauty queen Ewa Aulin in the title role of a nymphette who shares her talents at the drop of her panties. For his cameo as Emmanuel, a Mexican gardener, Ringo had his hair dyed jet-black and, in December 1967, flew out to Rome for two weeks of shooting. Unfortunately, he would have been better off staying at home, because the reviews ranged from lukewarm to hostile.

Unfazed, Ringo tried again in 1969, although this time he was provided with a co-starring role alongside Peter Sellers in *The Magic Christian*, which featured guest appearances by the likes of Raquel Welch, Richard Attenborough, John Cleese, Christopher Lee, Yul Brynner, and Roman Polanski. Like *Candy*, *The Magic Christian* was based on a novel by Terry Southern. Unlike *Candy*, it managed to be funny... in part. Centering around the exploits of the world's richest man, Sir Guy Grand (Sellers), and his adopted son, Youngman (Ringo), the film utilized a series of episodes to demonstrate the lengths to which people will go for money. Apple artists Badfinger scored a hit with one of the movie's featured songs, the Paul McCartney composition "Come and Get It," yet *The Magic Christian* still didn't do so well at the box office.

If nothing else, the movie did provide The Beatles' drummer with some welcome respite from the miserable *Get Back* sessions. He would continue to appear in films throughout the 1970s and early-eighties, the most memorable of which—from the public viewpoint—was *That'll Be the Day* (1973) and—from his own viewpoint, since it brought him together with future wife Barbara Bach—*Caveman* (1981).

Apple in De-Klein

On December 7, 1967, the same day that Ringo started filming *Candy* in Rome, The Beatles' Apple Boutique opened at 94 Baker Street in the heart of Central London. Earlier that year, the group had formed a legal business partnership, The Beatles & Co, and now here it was, moving into the retail business.

The Apple Boutique—with its psychedelic exterior mural designed by artists calling themselves The Fool, as well as its stock of "way out" clothes—didn't last long. Evidently, the public had no interest in the fashionable garb... until it was announced at short notice that the store would be closing down and that the remaining clothes were being given away. The night before the closure, The Beatles, their wives, and friends helped themselves to the choice items, and the next day half of London appeared to be standing in line to pick up the remnants. It would prove to be a scary omen of things to come for The Beatles' other business ventures.

94 Baker Street, site of the Apple shop long before the advent of computer stores using that same name. Opening amid much fanfare on December 7, 1967, the boutique that Paul McCartney described as "a beautiful place where beautiful people can buy beautiful things" only lasted until July 30 of the following year, succumbing to the disorganization and rampant pilfering that would undermine much of The Beatles' Apple Corps enterprises. By then, a psychedelic mural adorning the building's exterior had been replaced by whitewashed walls due to complaints by local traders, before the brickwork was eventually returned to its original condition.

As announced by Paul in May 1968, the aim of the umbrella company, Apple Corps Ltd., was "a controlled weirdness... a kind of Western Communism." There would be an Apple Foundation for the Arts, a record division, a film division, an electronics division, a music publishing division, and so on. The possibilities were endless.

In essence, The Beatles wanted to provide creative yet needy young people with initiative and the necessary funds to realize their dreams. A fine objective, this would have been okay had the various divisions been able to simply recoup their costs, let alone produce anything of worth. For the most part, however, they didn't. Only Apple Records initially turned a profit, thanks to division head Ron Kass; Jane's brother (and future record producer) Peter Asher, who was in charge of A&R; and a client roster that included James Taylor, Mary Hopkin, Badfinger, Billy Preston, and... The Beatles and The Plastic Ono Band. Otherwise, it was a dismal tale.

Another retail store, Apple Tailoring (Civil And Theatrical), did about as well as the boutique; the Arts Foundation quickly became a black hole into which money disappeared, along with the "artists" and "innovators" who regularly turned up on the company's doorstep looking for handouts; and as for the Electronics division— well, that was put in the trustworthy hands of Fab friend Alexis Mardas.

Walking around his laboratory in a white coat, busily scrawling notes and diagrams, "Magic Alex" was so called due to the array of incredible inventions he'd promised to come up with for the new Apple recording studio. After all, what a joke EMI's eight-track facility would be when compared to Apple's 72-track studio. And as for those cumbersome screens that normally had to be erected around Ringo's drum kit in order to separate it from the sound of the other instruments—Alex was inventing an invisible force shield to take care of that.

As it turned out, when The Beatles transferred from Twickenham Film Studios to their own studio during the course of the already-troubled *Get Back* project, they discovered to their horror that Alex hadn't quite managed to work his magic. His recording console, hand-carved and featuring an old oscilloscope in the center, was likened by studio engineers to the control panel of a B-52 bomber; and the 72 little loudspeakers that had been tacked around the studio certainly didn't enable them to make 72-track recordings. In fact, as Alex hadn't drilled holes between the control room and the recording area (for the cables to connect the console to the microphones and amplifiers), it wasn't possible to make *any* recordings. After holes were drilled, The Beatles did try to record, but all that came out was a load of noise, resulting in the costly yet cheap-looking console being junked and George Martin calling EMI to borrow a pair of four-track mixers.

Alex was never given the chance to try out his force shields.

The Apple studio was in the basement of a plush building at 3 Savile Row in central London. The Beatles' company HQ had relocated there from nearby Wigmore Street in July 1968, and what a money pit it turned out to be. While the executives bought cars on expense accounts, the staff managed to run up exorbitant food and liquor bills, and office furniture literally went out the front door. The Beatles were being robbed blind.

The Apple Corps headquarters at 3 Savile Row, a street normally associated with bespoke gentlemen's tailoring in the heart of London's West End that witnessed The Beatles' final live performance, atop the building, on January 30, 1969.

John and Paul took turns going into the office to direct operations, but this was about as successful as their efforts at editing *Magical Mystery Tour*. The group members had launched the company with a £1 million ($2.4 million) investment, but within months this was all gone and they were racing into the red. Outside help was desperately needed.

At the start of 1969, Paul turned to the New York law firm of Eastman & Eastman, whose partners, Lee and John, were the father and brother of Paul's girlfriend, Linda. For their part, John and Yoko met with strong-arm New York businessman, Allen Klein, and were so impressed by his cutthroat strategy that they subsequently convinced George and Ringo he should "sort out" Apple. Normally, The Beatles only did things that were agreed upon unanimously. This time, however, John, George, and Ringo didn't want to align themselves with the Eastmans, who they considered to be looking out for Paul's best interests, and so Paul was outvoted three-to-one.

Klein immediately fired many of Apple's top personnel while others handed in their resignations. Still, the books had to be balanced, and so, in May 1969, John, George, and Ringo appointed Klein's company, ABKCO, to manage The Beatles' various business interests. It was at this point that the band suffered an irreversible fracture. Paul, disliking and distrusting Allen Klein, refused to sign any such agreement. He did, however, put his signature to a Klein deal that secured the group a vastly improved royalty rate on record sales.

In 1969, due to miscalculations on their own part and betrayals on the part of certain trusted business associates, The Beatles lost their controlling interest in Brian's old NEMS organization, and the same applied to Northern Songs, the company that published the priceless catalogue of Lennon-McCartney compositions. By year's end, they had completely sold their interests in both, meaning others would now make decisions and earn the publishing royalties relating to most of the songs that John and Paul had written.

Somehow, while everything was falling down around their heads, Paul still felt that the band could survive if it put business to one side and got back to making music. In September 1969, during a meeting at Apple, he suggested that maybe The Beatles should turn up unannounced at some small clubs and perform just like they used to in the old days...

The Split: Sue You Blues

On September 13, 1969, during a flight from London to Toronto—where the hastily assembled Plastic Ono Band were due to play in the previously-mentioned rock festival—John informed Allen Klein that he intended to leave The Beatles. Klein responded that, with the group's business dealings in such a fragile state, and with a new royalty deal with EMI and Capitol in the works, it would be wise to delay announcing this to the other members. John initially agreed. However, having decided on his future, he wasn't able to keep this a secret for very long.

Back at Apple several days later, Paul made his pitch to the other three Beatles about undertaking some live performances. Ringo reportedly supported the idea while George, though not enthusiastic, didn't reject it outright. John, however, told Paul he was "daft." When Paul tentatively asked, "What do you mean?" he received a swift answer: "I'm leaving The Beatles. I want a divorce."

Stunned by this announcement, Paul nevertheless agreed that it would be best to delay making it public. It's possible that he hoped John would change his mind. But then a situation arose that pushed even this keenest member of The Beatles beyond his limits of endurance.

George had been the first of the Fab Four to branch out on his own musically, composing and producing the soundtrack to the 1968 movie *Wonderwall*. John had started collaborating with Yoko and various other musicians shortly afterwards, and now, at the end of 1969, Paul decided to follow suit, recording tracks for his first solo album, *McCartney*. When, around February of 1970, Paul phoned John to informed him that he, too, was leaving The Beatles, John replied, "Good. That makes two of us who have accepted it mentally." However, things took a definite turn for the worse when Paul learned that Allen Klein, supported by the other three soon-to-be-ex-Beatles, was trying to impede the release of *McCartney* so that it wouldn't clash with UA's scheduled release of the *Let It Be* film.

Once again, Paul felt the others were ganging up on him, and when Ringo, the band's diplomat, turned up at his house one night in order to explain the situation, Paul went ballistic. Threatening to finish Ringo off then and there, he ordered him to put on his coat and leave. Things were at an all-time low, yet the public didn't have a clue… until Friday, April 10, 1970, when a self-penned question-and-answer "interview" with Paul was distributed with media-review copies of the *McCartney* album.

In it, Paul made it perfectly clear that there was no future for The Beatles and that he didn't miss the assistance of John, George, or Ringo when recording his album. "Paul is Quitting The Beatles" screamed the front page headline of that morning's *Daily Mirror* newspaper in Britain. John was furious. Having kept his own mouth shut on the subject for more than six months, he'd now been beaten to the punch. "I was cursing because I hadn't done it," he later said. "I wanted to do it, I should have done it."

On April 17, *McCartney* was released in the U.K. It was issued in the U.S. on the 20th. Then, on May 8 (10 days before the U.S.), *Let It Be* appeared in U.K. record stores, and on May 13 the movie of the same name had its world premiere in New York. None of The Beatles attended, and neither did any of them turn up for the simultaneous London and Liverpool premieres a week later. The dream was truly over.

Paul was now left with a tough decision. If he didn't want Allen Klein to manage his business affairs, he would have to try to dissolve the legal partnership that bound him together with John, George, and Ringo. On December 31, 1970, he therefore filed a lawsuit in the London High Court seeking the dissolution of The Beatles & Co while requesting the appointment of a receiver to handle the band's dealings. It was the start of a messy battle that would drag on for years.

Hey Jude

"This was one of my earlier Beatles paintings. Back then, I didn't set the bar too high by trying to make them photo-real. Pieces like John '64 *were looser, showing a bit more brush stroke and spontaneity, but* Hey Jude *was different. Having small images of all four guys forced me to get in there tight to capture their facial features, and this resulted in a high-detail, photo-real look that people liked and which set the tone for much of my other work. As an artist, I enjoy the challenge of trying to match that standard.*

"The painting is a combination of multiple screen-grabs from the 'Hey Jude' video. Watching it, I loved the composition of the guys sitting in a circle— something we never normally see—and, when I paused the film, Paul was looking up at John. Being that, in this case, Paul was the lead singer, I painted him looking straight ahead, his eyebrows rising along with the pitch of his voice. At the same time, I liked John's positioning but he was too blurry in the screen-grab, so I had to find another image of him. As for George, his body was visible but his face was cut off, and in the images that I had of him singing backing vocals during the shoot his face was slightly distorted due to the movement of his top lip. Eventually, I found one where he looked a little less animated, while for Ringo I had to find another image because in the initial screen-grab the cymbal was blocking his face.

"In terms of the background, the orchestra and audience made the visuals too heavy. So, I just painted it very subtle and dark, and that in turn brought out all of the colors: the plum and green jackets of Paul and Ringo, the lavender and brown shirts of John and George. I was really happy with the end result."

– Eric Cash

Chapter 25

Free as a Bird—Life After The Beatles

Having spent 24 chapters telling you all about The Beatles' backgrounds, their influences, their pre-Fab adventures, their worldwide success, and so on, I'm going to compress their solo careers—three of which spanned far longer than that of The Beatles—into just a few pages.

John: Soldier of Love

John kicked off the 1970s much the same way as he ended the 1960s, indulging in offbeat adventures with Yoko and gaining plenty of attention in the process. These ranged from having eight erotic lithographs—in which John graphically depicted bedroom scenes from their honeymoon—confiscated by police during an exhibition at the London Arts Gallery, to issuing a hoax press release on April Fool's Day 1970 stating that the Ono-Lennons had entered the London Clinic for a dual sex-change operation.

During the same year, the couple spent four months in Los Angeles undergoing a course of "primal therapy" under Dr. Arthur Janov. In a nutshell, this encourages the patient to relive his or her most painful life experiences and then exorcise them by way of "primal screaming," letting out all of the anger and frustration that has been bottled up since childhood. In John's case, this gave rise to his landmark album, *John Lennon/Plastic Ono Band*, a harrowing collection of songs in which he vented his feelings against society, his parents, his fans, and his former colleagues. The gripping material, stark instrumentation, and direct expression of emotions spoke to artistic integrity of the highest order—it was as if John was having a private conversation with the listener.

The *Imagine* album, released the following year, managed to express many of the same themes in a far more lush and melodic way. The title song has since become a classic, summing up John's hopes for a united world full of peace and love, but these sentiments flew in the face of another of the album's standout tracks, "How Do You Sleep?" This featured, John—supported by George on lead guitar—delivering a full-scale verbal attack on Paul, accusing his former friend of everything from making vacuous muzak to being responsible for The Beatles' break-up. The song not only hit its target where it hurt, but also served to demonstrate that its author was a man of sharp contradictions.

On September 3, 1971, John and Yoko flew to New York for what was ostensibly intended as just a short visit but evolved into a permanent stay. Having managed to garner little more than ridicule in the British press, the couple felt much more comfortable in the Big Apple where they soon fell in with a crowd of left-wing political radicals and activists. Having preached all about peace and love, John was soon clenching his fist and advocating "Power to the People."

In 1972, he and Yoko issued the collaborative album, *Some Time in New York City*, that managed to espouse a whole range of then-fashionable political causes. Most of these dealt with feminism and American issues, but two songs, "Sunday Bloody Sunday" and "The Luck of the Irish," also took the British to task for their brutal involvement in the affairs of the Emerald Isle. Whether or not it was justified, this stance angered many of John's former countrymen and women who didn't like to be condemned by someone who they'd enabled to live very comfortably on the other side of the Atlantic.

Overall, *Some Time In New York City* was a bad career move as people opined that the artist's deeply held beliefs couldn't possibly be stretched across such a wide range of topics. John's response to the poor sales was to drop the sharp-tongued activism and return to the more tried and trusted themes of peace and love on his 1973 *Mind Games* album, even though by then his personal life was coming apart at the seams. For one thing, President Nixon's corrupt regime had taken note of the "politically subversive" former Beatle's left wing activities and was now using his 1968 drug rap as a means to deport him. John was fighting to stay, suing the U.S. Government while asserting—correctly, as it turned out—that he was being subjected to FBI surveillance and phone tapping. Meanwhile, this struggle was compounded by domestic problems—including his flagrant unfaithfulness on November 7, 1972, the night of Nixon's re-election—that put a strain on John's marriage to Yoko and resulted in their eventual separation.

In October 1973, John embarked on an affair with secretary May Pang at Yoko's instigation. After all, the Ono-Lennon relationship had hit the skids, Yoko decided they needed time apart to give it a chance to heal, and if her husband was going to have an affair then it should be with someone who she knew, trusted, and could hopefully control. Going along with this, John quickly relocated to L.A. with May Pang and the intended brief split turned into what he'd later describe as his 15-month "lost weekend." During that time he went completely off the rails, consuming large quantities of drugs and alcohol during crazed sessions for an aborted Phil Spector-produced album of rock 'n' roll oldies, before pulling himself together to record the well-received *Walls and Bridges* back in New York. While there, he also produced the subtly titled *Pussy Cats* album of friend and fellow imbiber, Harry Nilsson, and completed his own, acclaimed *Rock 'n' Roll* collection before returning to Yoko in January 1975.

Soon afterwards, Yoko became pregnant. Then, on October 7, the New York State Supreme Court voted to reverse the deportation order against John, and two days later, on his 35th birthday, Yoko gave birth to their first and only child, Sean Taro Ono Lennon. John was ecstatic, and after he finally obtained a Green Card in June 1976, entitling him to reside full-time in the U.S., the former hellraiser decided to hang up his guitar—figuratively speaking, because he never stopped writing songs—and become a househusband, attending to the needs of his new son while Yoko took care of business.

The only statue of John created during his lifetime was sculpted by Australian artist Brett-Livingstone Strong between 1979 and 1980 and unveiled by Mayor Tom Bradley outside L.A.'s City Hall on October 9, 1981. Subsequently unveiled in New York by Andy Warhol, the 10-foot-high bronze image also appeared on-stage in front of 300,000 people at a U2 concert and was exhibited worldwide throughout the 1980s.

That's pretty much how things remained until the summer of 1980 when, having kept to his five-year commitment to care for his youngest child, John joined Yoko at New York's Hit Factory studio to start recording songs for their comeback album, *Double Fantasy*. Released in November 1980, this record revealed a couple apparently living in a state of domestic bliss. True or not, the reviews were mainly positive, and John, at age 40, seemed energized and full of life in a number of interviews. He was also up to his old tricks, posing naked for the cover of *Rolling Stone* magazine.

Then the unimaginable happened. At around 10:50 on the night of December 8, John Lennon was shot five times at close range by a deranged fan, Mark David Chapman, who had been waiting in the shadows of the Dakota entrance as the Lennons returned from a recording session for Yoko's song, "Walking on Thin Ice." A police car rushed John to the nearby Roosevelt Hospital, but he'd already lost too much blood, and after frantic attempts to revive him he was pronounced dead at around 11:15. Ironically, only the year before, John and Yoko had contributed $1,000 to a fund providing New York City police with bullet-proof vests.

The entrance to The Dakota at 1 West 72nd Street in New York where John Lennon met his violent end.

The global outpouring of grief was immediate and on an unparalleled scale. A man who preached peace had suffered a violent death, and on Sunday, December 14, 1980, at 2:00 p.m. EST and 7:00 p.m. in the U.K., people around the world observed 10 minutes of silence in memory of John Lennon, the founder of The Beatles and one of the most beloved artists of all time.

During the ensuing years an entire industry has grown up around John's name, work, and image. Books have been written, films have been made, plays have been staged, tribute songs have been recorded, and many of his own unreleased recordings have been issued or broadcast. However, nothing can compensate for the loss to family, friends, and fans, or make up for what might have been—between 1962 and 1980, there were only 13 years when John actively produced music. So, how many more might we have experienced if he hadn't been so senselessly wiped out at age 40 by an assailant with a gun?

Strawberry Fields, the 2.5-acre landscaped section of New York's Central Park, across the street from The Dakota, that was dedicated to John's memory on October 9, 1985.

Paul: Knight of the Realm

In August 1971, having already released the solo albums *McCartney* and *Ram*, Paul plunged himself back into a band setup when he announced the formation of Wings with Linda on keyboards, American drummer

Denny Seiwell, and ex-Moody Blues singer-guitarist Denny Laine. Almost immediately, however, Paul had to deal with critical barbs regarding the inclusion of his wife—a noted photographer, not a musician—in the group's lineup.

Next, having been verbally attacked on record and in the press by John, Paul was further embarrassed when Wing's first album, *Wild Life*, was vilified by critics for its insipid pop content. Still, things could only get better, and they did. Henry McCullough was added to the band's lineup on lead guitar, and in early 1972 Wings did what Paul had long wanted The Beatles to do; turning up unannounced at assorted British universities and performing to the students for a basic admission price. Later that year, buoyed by the success of this venture, Wings undertook an indoor tour of Europe and this was followed by a more upscale British one in 1973.

Also during that time, Paul's compositional skills, which had seemed to desert him, started to make a comeback on a series of singles as well as the album *Red Rose Speedway*. Evidently, he could come up with the goods when his back was to the wall, and this was confirmed when, on August 9, 1973, just before flying to Nigeria's capital city, Lagos, to record Wings' next album, Henry McCullough and Denny Seiwell both quit. Paul, Linda, and Denny Laine carried on regardless, with Denny taking over on lead guitar and Paul filling in on drums, and the result was *Band on the Run*; by far Paul's most accomplished post-Beatles work up to that time and, some may say, to this day.

In one fell swoop, Macca had projected himself back to the top of the pop tree and, with a constantly evolving band lineup, he would consolidate this position with a steady stream of hit singles, bestselling albums, and a mammoth, sold-out world tour in 1975 and 1976 in support of the hit albums *Venus and Mars* and *Wings at the Speed of Sound*. For the former Beatle it was like a second coming. However, instead of setting trends as he once did with The Beatles, he was now following them, and never again would he recapture the heights that he scaled during the mid-seventies.

After a 1979 Wings tour of Britain following the previous year's *Back to the Egg* album, the band was scheduled to play 11 concerts in Japan between January 21 and February 2, 1980. Due to the McCartneys' previous busts for cannabis possession, the Japanese authorities had twice refused them permission to tour there. Now they had relented and the long-awaited tour was sold out. Yet, on January 16, when customs men at Tokyo's Narita Airport made a routine search of Paul's suitcase, they were astonished to discovered a large stash of cannabis inside his toiletries bag. Arrogance, stupidity, or both—it was baffling that one of the world's most famous rock stars hadn't done what others like him usually do and have one of his roadies carry the stash.

The Japanese tour was off, but that was the least of Paul's immediate problems. Thrown behind bars, he was informed by the local British consul that the Japanese authorities might make an example of him and slap him with a seven-year prison sentence. This was no joke, and Paul realized that, for once, his celebrity might actually work against him. Fortunately, after sitting in a bare cell for eight days, he was released and deported back to England while vowing to reporters that he would never smoke pot again…

Paul and Linda during the video shoot for his 'Take it Away' single at EMI's Elstree Film Studios, June 23, 1982.

John's death at the end of 1980 put the cap on what had been a bad year for Paul, save for the success of his solo album *McCartney II* that had spawned the U.S. chart-topping single "Coming Up." Dispirited, Wings broke up shortly afterwards and Paul resumed a solo career, releasing a succession of solid, if unspectacular, albums: *Tug of War* (1982), *Pipes of Peace* (1983), *Press to Play* (1986), *CHOBA B CCCP* ("Back in the U.S.S.R.," 1988), and *Flowers in the Dirt* (1989). There were also several commercially—yet not always critically—successful collaborations with artists such as Stevie Wonder, Michael Jackson, and Elvis Costello.

However, during that same decade Paul's career took a nosedive when, against the advice of colleagues and his own wife, he decided to take another stab at moviemaking; writing the script and composing the songs for his own starring vehicle, *Give My Regards to Broad Street*. It was like *Magical Mystery Tour* all over again. Clearly, Paul hadn't learned his lesson from that debacle, resulting in a box office disaster that was savaged by critics for its non-existent storyline.

To date, that has been Paul's last full-scale cinematic venture, yet it hasn't deterred him from writing and producing short animated films such as that focusing on the work of French artist Honoré Daumier (1992) and *Tropical Island Hum* (2004), while also dabbling in other fields outside his comfort zone. These have included poetry (the 2001 book *Blackbird Singing*); novel-writing (the 2005 children's adventure *High in the Clouds*, co-authored with Geoff Dunbar and Philip Ardagh); exhibitions of his own paintings at galleries in Germany and the U.K.; orchestral music (1991's *Liverpool Oratorio*, 1997's *Standing Stone*, 1999's *Working Classical*, 2006's *Ecce Cor Meum*, and 2011's *Ocean's Kingdom*); and electronica (1993's *Strawberries Oceans Ships Forest*, 1998's *Rushes*, and 2008's *Electric Arguments* as a duo named The Firemen with Youth of Killing Joke; 2000's *Liverpool Sound Collage*, credited to Youth, Super Furry Animals, and The Beatles; and 2005's *Twin Freaks* with DJ/producer Roy "Freelance Hellraiser" Kerr).

In 1993, Paul released his ninth solo studio album, the lackluster *Off the Ground*, and three years later, intent on reopening his old school, the Liverpool Institute, he collaborated with educator and entrepreneur

Mark Featherstone-Witty on having the once-derelict, now-renovated building reopened as the Liverpool Institute for the Performing Arts (LIPA). In 1997, in recognition of all that Paul had achieved during the preceding 35 years, Queen Elizabeth II bestowed a knighthood upon him, and that same year he released the impressive *Flaming Pie*. Then, in March 1999, 11 months after the death of Linda and seven before the release of *Run Devil Run*, Sir James Paul McCartney was inducted into the Rock and Roll Hall of Fame as a solo artist.

Since then, through the recording of albums *Driving Rain* (2001), *Chaos and Creation in the Backyard* (2005), *Memory Almost Full* (2007), *Kisses on the Bottom* (2012), and *New* (2013), as well as his marriages to Heather Mills and Nancy Shevell, the Beatle Knight of the Realm has continued to record and tour while serving as a spokesperson for charities related to environmental issues, animal rights, vegetarianism, landmines, poverty, and music education. Now in his seventies and as active as ever, he is, according to *Guinness World Records*, the "most successful composer and recording artist of all time," having accrued sales of more than 100 million singles and 100 million albums.

Paul rehearsing at London's Playhouse Theatre for his upcoming world tour, July 26, 1989.

George: Dark Horse

The breakup of The Beatles came as a welcome relief to George. For one thing, he had fallen out of love some time ago with being a member of the world's most famous supergroup, and for another, he was sick of playing third fiddle to John and Paul. Now he was free to record all of his own songs, which he did on the very successful 1970 triple-album *All Things Must Pass*. However, during the early 1970s, little else went right for The Beatles' former lead guitarist.

For starters, his worldwide smash hit single, "My Sweet Lord," immersed George in hot water when Bright Tunes, the copyright owners to the old Chiffons record, "He's So Fine," sued him for plagiarism. The case dragged on for years, until the courts finally ruled that George had subconsciously plagiarized "He's So Fine," meaning he had to make a deal with Bright Tunes... which in 1978 was purchased by Allen Klein.

Back in July 1971, Klein sat happily next to George at a New York press conference announcing the staging of two all-star concerts to aid the famine in Bangladesh. These took place at Madison Square Garden on August 1 and, in addition to George, others who performed for free included Ringo, Ravi Shankar, Bob Dylan, Eric Clapton, Leon Russell, and Billy Preston. There had been rumors of a Beatles reunion, yet John had pulled out when it became clear that Yoko wasn't invited. Reportedly, Paul also declined.

It was all for a good cause, but while there were problems releasing the revenue from the shows and the resulting live album, the American and British tax authorities also had their say. The concert and album proceeds had only ever been intended to help feed starving people in Africa, yet in 1974 George ended up having to pay £1 million ($2.4 million) in taxes to the British government.

It wasn't a good time for George. Although his 1973 album *Living in the Material World* and single "Give Me Love (Give Me Peace on Earth)" both topped the U.S. charts, he was disappointed by the LP's mixed reviews. At around the same time, his marriage to Pattie hit the rocks and she went to live with his best friend, Eric Clapton. Then, after forming his own label, Dark Horse Records, George issued the *Dark*

Horse album and undertook a full-scale North American concert tour. The problem was, a severe throat infection had badly affected his singing voice, prompting critics to dub the album "Dark Hoarse" while some fans at the sold-out concerts openly booed and jeered

George nevertheless continued to make records: 1975's soul-laced *Extra Texture (Read All About It)*, 1976's widely acclaimed *Thirty Three and 1/3*, and 1979's *George Harrison*. Thereafter, following the 1978 death of his father, Harold, and birth of his son, Dhani, George began dedicating more time to his home life than to his career, with John's murder further encouraging his withdrawal from the music business. In 1981, George was back on the singles charts with a musical tribute to John, "All Those Years Ago," which included contributions from Paul and Ringo, but he did nothing to promote the accompanying *Somewhere in England* album or its 1982 successor *Gone Troppo*. Instead, he was more interested in watching motor racing, collaborating with Ravi Shankar, and gardening in the enormous grounds of his Friar Park estate in Henley-on-Thames. (During the early 1970s, he'd also purchased a huge property in Letchmore Heath, just north of London, for fellow disciples of the Hindu faith.)

Indeed, from the late-seventies through the mid-eighties, George garnered most attention via his success as co-owner of HandMade Films, a production company he'd initially formed in 1978 to bail out Monty Python's *Life of Brian* when the production ran into financial difficulties. Investing £4 million of his own money, George ensured that the film was completed and released, and thereafter he and partner Denis O'Brien involved themselves in the production of numerous British motion pictures. These included *The Long Good Friday* (1980), *Time Bandits* (1981), *Monty Python Live at the Hollywood Bowl* (1982), *The Missionary* (1982), *Privates on Parade* (1982), *Bullshot* (1983), *A Private Function* (1984), *Water* (1985), and *Mona Lisa* (1986).

Sad to say, box office failures such as the 1986 Madonna/Sean Penn fiasco *Shanghai Surprise* eventually put a strain on HandMade, while a major falling-out also occurred between the two partners, with George alleging that Denis O'Brien had been living the high life on company money. After suing O'Brien, George was awarded extensive damages.

In 1987, George released his last solo album under his deal with Warner Brothers. Titled *Cloud Nine*, it was an unexpected international bestseller, while the album's first single, "Got My Mind Set on You," topped the U.S. charts. Shortly afterwards, he formed supergroup The Traveling Wilburys and enjoyed chart success alongside Roy Orbison, Tom Petty, Jeff Lynne, and Bob Dylan, while in 1991 George also undertook a short tour of Japan backed by Eric Clapton and his band. The following year, George headlined a concert for the final—and, in his native country, only—time when, during the U.K.'s prime ministerial election campaign, he was again backed by Clapton's musicians for a show at London's Royal Albert Hall in support of the Transcendental Meditation-based Natural Law Party.

George preferred life at home to that on the road, yet any feelings of being secure within the grounds of his Friar Park estate were shattered when, on December 30, 1999, he was attacked there by a 36-year-old intruder named Michael Abram. Managing to enter the bedroom that George shared with his wife Olivia, Abram used a kitchen knife to inflict more than 40 stab wounds on the ex-Beatle, who sustained a punctured lung and head injuries before Olivia managed to stop the attacker by repeatedly hitting him with a poker and a lamp. After being hospitalized, George issued a statement in which he asserted Abram "wasn't a burglar, and he certainly wasn't auditioning for the Traveling Wilburys," yet the damage had been done in terms of another battle that George had been waging.

A heavy smoker since his early teens, George had been treated for throat cancer in 1997. The knife attack now weakened him and in early 2001 he was diagnosed with lung cancer. Surgery to remove a tumor was considered a success, but unfortunately the cancer metastasized to the brain. After undergoing a course of radiotherapy at a hospital in Switzerland that July and some last-ditch treatments in New York just three months later, George died in L.A., with Olivia and Dhani at his bedside, on November 29, 2001. He was 58-years-old.

Ringo: All-Starr Jet-Setter

In a surprising turnabout, following The Beatles' break up it was actually Ringo who appeared to best find his own niche and establish himself as an all-round showbiz operator. By the end of 1973, he'd managed to direct a movie about glam-rock star Marc Bolan and T. Rex titled *Born to Boogie*; he'd received terrific reviews for his realistic performance in the 1950s nostalgia film *That'll Be the Day*; his self-titled album was riding high in the charts; and he'd also had a string of hit singles in the form of the Starkey-penned, Harrison-produced "It Don't Come Easy" and "Back Off Boogaloo," as well as U.S. chart-toppers "Photograph" (co-written by Ringo and George) and "You're Sixteen."

The above-mentioned *Ringo* album featured the Starr man performing catchy pop songs with the help of John, Paul, and George, as well performances by a multi-talented cast that included Marc Bolan, Harry Nilsson, Martha Reeves, Steve Cropper, Billy Preston, and The Band. The fact that John, George, and Ringo played together on the Lennon song "I'm the Greatest" quickly fueled reunion rumors among many Beatle People. For others, the fact that Paul at no point collaborated with John or George confirmed the exact opposite. Still, "I'm The Greatest" was the closest that the world would get to a Beatles reunion during the 1970s, and *Ringo* would also prove to be an all-time high in the recording career of the ex-Fab drummer.

Thereafter, he attempted to repeat the formula on *Goodnight Vienna* (1974) and *Ringo's Rotogravure* (1976), but the novelty soon wore thin, as did the material suited to Ringo's voice on the commercially disastrous, disco-oriented *Ringo the 4th* (1977) and *Bad Boy* (1978). Not even the musical, compositional, and production contributions of Paul McCartney, George Harrison, Harry Nilsson, Stephen Stills, and Ronnie Wood could save 1981's *Stop and Smell the Roses* from becoming yet another flop, and, after RCA canceled his contract, Ringo failed to get either U.S. or U.K. distribution for his 1983 album *Old Wave*. Still, he wasn't without friends or things to do.

Shortly after splitting up from Maureen in 1973, Ringo immersed himself in the jet-set life, partying all over the world and enjoying his own version of the "lost weekend" in Los Angeles with musical cronies John Lennon, Harry Nilsson, and Keith Moon. However, while Hollywood was fun for a while, where do the top glitterati often like to hang out? That's right, Monte Carlo, which is where Ringo decided to set up home and become a tax exile. He has since divided his time between there, America, and Britain—where he at one time lived in the Tittenhurst Park property he'd acquired from John—with second wife Barbara Bach.

In the meantime, while Ringo continued to drum for other artists, his distinctive voice was used for radio broadcasts, records, television ads, and narration of the hugely successful children's TV show, *Thomas the Tank Engine and Friends*. Furthermore, following his well-publicized and successful battle with alcoholism, he returned to touring the U.S. and Europe, headlining successful shows with his own "All-Starr" bands in support of studio albums such as *Time Takes Time* (1992), *Vertical Man* (1998), *Ringo Rama* (2003), *Choose Love* (2005), *Liverpool 8* (2008), *Y Not* (2010), and *Ringo 2012* (2012).

The featured players in these lineups have ranged from Joe Walsh, Jack Bruce, Billy Preston, Todd Rundgren, Dr. John, and Nils Lofgren, to Levon Helm, Rick Danko, John Entwistle, Clarence Clemons, Jim Keltner, and Zak Starkey. Some have taken a turn performing their own hit songs, yet inevitably the main man, with his unique brand of charm, draws the crowds, proving once and for all that he is more than capable of getting by... with a little help.

In 2004, Genesis Publications issued Ringo's book *Postcards from the Boys*, featuring facsimiles of 53 personal communications from John, Paul, and George, and this was followed nine years later by *Photograph*, comprising Ringo's equally fascinating snapshots of his life as a Beatle.

Chapter 26

Can I Have a Little More?—The Beatles Anthology

Throughout the 1970s, there were incessant rumors about The Beatles getting back together. These began with the individual participation of all four ex-members on the 1973 *Ringo* album and they were subsequently fueled by John and Paul both making comments that didn't confirm an imminent reunion, but also didn't rule out the possibility.

In 1976, American promoters Sid Bernstein (who had been responsible for the landmark 1965 Shea Stadium show) and Bill Sargent each tried to lure The Beatles into reuniting for just one show, offering them sums reportedly ranging from $20 million to $100 million. The former band members didn't take the bait, with George wryly commenting, "Since that man was also to have promoted that match with the shark, my suggestion about that was if Sargent would fight the shark in the tank, the winner could promote the Beatles concert."

Conversely and typically, on April 24, 1976, the former Beatles were tempted to accept the humorous on-air offer by *Saturday Night Live* producer Lorne Michaels for them to get together on his show in return for a $3,000 payday. "Divide [the money] up any way you want," Michaels said. "If you want to give less to Ringo, that's up to you."

"Paul and I were watching that show," John told *Playboy* magazine's David Sheff just over four years later. "He was visiting us at our place in the Dakota… He and Linda walked in, and he and I were just sitting there, watching the show, and we went, 'Ha-ha, wouldn't it be funny if we went down?' We nearly got into a cab, but we were actually too tired."

"That was a period when Paul just kept turning up at our door with a guitar," John also told Sheff. "I would let him in, but finally I said to him, 'Please call before you come over. It's not 1956 and turning up at the door isn't the same anymore. You know, just give me a ring.' He was upset by that, but I didn't mean it badly. I just meant that I was taking care of a baby all day and some guy turns up at the door."

A Beatles reunion was never destined to happen. Nevertheless, as Apple Corps CEO Neil Aspinall told *Mojo* magazine, "In '69, in all the chaos, the traumas—things were falling apart but they were still making *Abbey Road*—Paul called me saying, 'You should collect as much of the material that's out there, get it together before it disappears.' So I started to do that, got in touch with all the TV stations around the world, checked what we had in our own library, like *Let It Be*, *Magical Mystery Tour*, the promo clips, what have you. Got newsreel footage in, lots and lots of stuff."

Aspinall subsequently utilized this material to produce—without the Fab Four's involvement—a 90-minute documentary recounting The Beatles' story in their own words. Tentatively titled *The Long and Winding Road*, the project nevertheless suffered the same fate as many of the group's other dealings following the breakup: John, Paul, George, and Ringo could never seem to agree on what, why, and how things needed to be done. There were outstanding lawsuits and royalty deals to settle, as well as numerous solo projects that they each attached more importance to. As a result, *The Long and Winding Road* remained on the shelf while other documentary makers did their thing—only to be criticized by The Beatles for failing to tell "the *real* story."

Then, on November 28, 1980, in a legal deposition given to Apple Corps' New York lawyers for their planned litigation against the producers of the Broadway musical, *Beatlemania*, John stated: "I and the other three former Beatles have plans to stage a reunion concert, to be recorded, filmed, and marketed around the world." Purportedly, this would have been used as the grand finale to *The Long and Winding Road*, yet in all likelihood it probably had as much chance of happening as the concert that was proposed to conclude the doomed *Get Back* film. The fact is, in interviews that John did during the final months of 1980, he made it perfectly clear that he had no interest in The Beatles getting back together. So, the reason for his affidavit was almost certainly to just reinforce the legal claim that *Beatlemania*'s Fab Four impersonators were interfering with the real group's interests.

Still, the same week that John gave his deposition, a request was submitted to the New York Parks Department by an unnamed organization, asking for a feasibility study relating to the staging of a Beatles reunion concert in Central Park. Furthermore, in Keith Badman's book, *The Beatles Diary, Volume 2: After the Break-Up*, Yoko was quoted as saying: "Just days before his brutal death, John was making plans to go to England for a triumphant Beatles reunion. His greatest dream was to recreate the musical magic of the early years with Paul, George and Ringo... (He) felt that they had travelled different paths for long enough. He felt they had grown up and were mature enough to try writing and recording new songs."

If true, John's death certainly kiboshed that eventuality.

It wasn't until 1992 that Paul, George, and Ringo finally decided the time was at last right for their own enterprise to go into production. Besides, all the signs indicated that it would be a cash bonanza. Eventually retitled The *Beatles Anthology*, this evolved from a straightforward, tell-all documentary into a clear-the-decks project that also involved the simultaneous release of many of The Beatles' outtakes and previously unissued tracks. A number of these had already been bootlegged, others had never seen the light of day, and, in conjunction with Yoko, the three surviving Fabs also formulated an idea that turned out to be the mammoth undertaking's *coup de grâce*.

Back in the Studio

It was quite a concept: instead of just Paul, George, and Ringo reuniting to make a few new recordings to tie in with *The Beatles Anthology*, they would do so in conjunction with John. Not easy, given that he was no longer around. However, aware that John had continued to write and record demos of new compositions throughout his five-year retirement in the late-1970s, George asked Yoko whether she would loan some of them to The Threetles. The intention was to utilize John's lead vocals and overdub proper bass, drums, guitars, keyboards, and backing vocals to produce, in effect, new Beatles recordings. After all, numerous tracks on the "White Album" and *Abbey Road* hadn't involved the Fab Four's joint participation.

The germ of this idea had actually formulated inside George's head shortly after Roy Orbison's death in 1988. Since The Traveling Wilburys were about to record a second album, George, Bob Dylan, Tom Petty, and Jeff Lynne started to search for a replacement... and came up with Elvis Presley. That's right, they'd utilize his voice (under the guise of "Aaron Wilbury") in conjunction with a new recording. The Presley estate approved wholeheartedly of Elvis's new venture and provided the band with the rights to one of his songs, but there was a change of heart when George said that perhaps the idea was too gimmicky. Still, he happened to talk about it to Yoko and she was quite taken by the notion of perhaps resurrecting John for a Beatles reunion. Shortly afterwards, she provided several of his demo tapes.

George Martin, meanwhile, didn't share Yoko's enthusiasm. Even though he was producing and directing the compilation of the three *Anthology* double-albums, he made it clear that he didn't want to be involved with the new recordings. Jeff Lynne therefore got the call to produce them, with engineers Geoff Emerick and Jon Jacobs sitting behind the mixing console at Paul's home studio in Rye, Sussex, when the first session took place in February 1994. The initial song to be worked on was John's 1977 composition, "Free as a Bird."

In a 1995 interview in his own fan magazine, *Club Sandwich*, Paul talked about the attitude that he, George, and Ringo decided to adopt: "We got this scenario going of 'He's asked us to finish a tape.' And the key words for me were, I imagined him saying, 'I trust you. Just do your thing. I trust you.' And the trust was what I needed to know. So I made up a fiction and believed it and it was fine. I went in there—I think we all did—fully believing that this is something John would have wanted us to do."

In the same interview, Paul also stated that newspaper articles questioning the wisdom of such an enterprise only served as a challenge for him to prove the doubters wrong. However, achieving that wasn't totally straightforward. John's recording, made on a mono cassette, featured him singing and playing a piano. Even with modern computer technology, there was no way to separate the voice from the keyboard, and so Paul played another piano on top of John's, and he and George then added acoustic guitars. That brought them to the next problem: since John only recorded a home demo as a means of working out the song's structure, he hadn't concentrated much on the tempo. He therefore tended to speed up and slow down, and Paul and George had difficulty playing along to the recording. At this point the computers did come in handy, enabling John's voice and piano to be transferred to multitrack tape in perfect time.

Still, the song's bridge section had never been completed by John, so Paul wrote some new words for it. George didn't like them and neither did Jeff Lynne. However, just when a spot of *Let It Be*-type tension was threatening to rear its ugly head, adjustments were made and a compromise was agreed upon. (Paul may well have been tempted to say, "I'll write whatever words you want me to write, and I won't write at all if you don't want me to...")

After that, Paul's piano, his and George's acoustic guitars, Paul's bass, Ringo's drums, the Paul and George harmony vocals, and George's rhythm guitar and slide solo were overdubbed, in that order. Again, there was a disagreement, this time Paul asserting George's slide solo sounded better suited to "My Sweet Lord" than to a Beatles record. Eventually, he revised this opinion and, once the harmony vocals had been added, Ringo exclaimed, "It sounds like a Beatles record!" Finally, just to top things off, George played a small ukulele part and, in true *Sgt. Pepper* fashion, a snippet of John speaking was played backwards and mixed in right near the end. John's quote was "Turned out nice again," the catchphrase of George's hero, English music hall comedian/ukulele player George Formby. However, when reversed, it sounded uncannily like "made by John Lennon…"

A year later, in February 1995, The Threetles reunited to work on "Real Love," a song that John had demo'd at home in 1979. (An alternate version was also featured in the 1988 documentary film, *Imagine: John Lennon*, and on the accompanying soundtrack album.) Once again, the hiss, hum, clicks, and static on the original cassette were removed before overdubbing took place. This included Paul playing two different basses: an electric one and the upright double-bass that had once belonged to Elvis Presley's original bassist, Bill Black; a gift from Linda to Paul back in the late-seventies.

So, these would be the new Beatles singles: "Free as a Bird," credited to Lennon, McCartney, Harrison, and Starkey, and released December 4, 1995 in the U.K., December 12 in the U.S.; and "Real Love," written by John Lennon and released on March 4, 1996.

Meanwhile, the three *Anthology* albums amounted to six CDs of material, ranging from some of the band's earliest amateur recordings, a few Hamburg tracks, and part of their Decca audition to alternate takes of well-known songs, false starts, TV and radio appearances, concert performances, demo recordings, and certain songs that had never previously been released. Only *Anthology 1* had been compiled at the time of its November 20, 1995 release, as Paul, George, and Ringo wanted to monitor public and critical reaction before embarking on the other two albums. Still, one thing was for sure: they didn't need to worry about there being enough hype to plug the first installment.

Back on Film

During the 1970s, Apple CEO Neil Aspinall oversaw the production of the *Long and Winding Road* documentary, but this was rejected because, according to Ringo, "it was mainly airplanes landing and taking off."

Then, when the project was resurrected around 1989, Chips Chipperfield was brought in as the producer and he, in turn, enlisted the services of Geoff Wonfor as director and Bob Smeaton as the writer.

Between 1993 and 1995, Paul, George, and Ringo went before the cameras and recounted The Beatles' story as they each perceived it in a series of interviews with Jools Holland. The only others invited to voice their recollections were George Martin, Neil Aspinall, and press officer Derek Taylor; John's contributions came from interviews that he had done during his years as both a Beatle and a solo artist.

This small lineup led to obvious drawbacks. First, with no one but The Beatles and three of their intimates telling the story, the overall result was extremely subjective. Secondly, whereas Paul, George, and Ringo provided insights into their legend from the mature perspective of men in their fifties, John's mostly originated from when he was in his twenties and thirties.

Furthermore, when the surviving Fabs viewed the separate interviews, it was clear that they didn't always recall events the same way. Ultimately, compromises had to be reached so that sensibilities weren't offended, especially with regard to still-touchy subjects such as the events leading up to the band's breakup. Diplomacy won the day, so what viewers end up with is not the definitive, warts-and-all story of the meteoric rise and acrimonious split of the world's greatest supergroup. Rather, it is a celebration, with some trademark Lennon and Harrison cynicism thrown in to at least provide some sense of balance.

On November 19, 22, and 23 of 1995, *The Beatles Anthology* aired in three two-hour episodes in America before being split into six one-hour episodes for its transmission in the U.K. Since the U.S. broadcasts contained more advertising breaks, the U.K. version of the series actually had more footage. Still, when the documentary was released on video and laser disc in 1996, it extended to just under 10 hours wherever it was purchased, featuring extra interviews, concert footage, home movies, TV broadcasts, and so on. Curiously, however, while the promo video for "Free as a Bird" was also included, the one for "Real Love" wasn't.

Both videos received their world premieres on ABC TV in America in November 1995. "Free as a Bird," a stunning computerized collage that melded old footage of the band into brand new surroundings while referencing numerous Beatles songs, was broadcast at the end of the first episode; "Real Love," a more straightforward compendium of old clips interspersed with some very welcome 1995 footage of Paul, George, and Ringo at work in the studio, aired at the end of the second episode.

So much for all the details. Suffice it to say that, thanks to the massive publicity campaign surrounding the entire *Anthology* project, public expectations regarding the TV documentary ran much higher than they did for *Magical Mystery Tour*. Fortunately, this time around the masses weren't disappointed.

Back in the Spotlight and Back on the Charts

It was just like 1964 and 1965 all over again. Well, not quite. However, in the build-up to the transmission of the documentary, the first airing of the new single, and the release of the *Anthology 1* double CD set, The Beatles' names, images, and music were all over TV screens, radio airwaves, newspapers, and magazines around the world. Without a doubt, more than a quarter of a century after the band's demise, John, Paul, George, and Ringo were still massive news.

Major newspapers published special editions, with whole pages devoted to the Fab Four, both past and present. There were also magazines, with titles such as *Life*'s "Reunion Special—The Beatles from Yesterday to Today" and "Beatlemania is Back!" on sale everywhere. Even *TV Guide* published a "Special Collectors' Edition" for the week commencing November 18, 1995, featuring an updated version of the *Sgt. Pepper* album photo on the front cover and interviews with Paul, George, and Ringo inside.

As it turned out, although Dave Marsh interviewed Paul and Ringo in person for *TV Guide*, George simply responded to his questions by fax. Even after so many years, GH was adamant that, aside from posing for a set of official "reunion" photos taken by Linda McCartney and being interviewed for *Anthology*'s electronic press kit (as well as Dave Marsh's fax), he wouldn't do one iota of promotion relating to The Beatles. Not wishing to go it alone, Paul and Ringo generally felt obliged to follow the same course, except for just a few solo interviews.

Still, they managed to get by. Billboards and record store posters bore reproductions of the *Anthology* artwork, conceived by Klaus Voormann, the Hamburg friend and former Plastic Ono Band bassist who had designed the *Revolver* album cover. The top of the Capitol Records building in Hollywood was adorned with enormous reproductions of the four famous faces. TV news shows were continually drumming up items with some sort of link (however tenuous) to the Fabs. And ABC, the network transmitting the *Anthology* documentary in America, dubbed itself "ABeatlesC." (Back in February 1964, New York radio station WABC-AM had christened itself with that same name.)

The only missing elements were the hysterical fans, the more ludicrous merchandise, and The Beatles themselves. Three of them set the ball rolling; everyone else picked it up and ran like mad.

"Free as a Bird" peaked at #6 on the *Billboard* "Hot 100" chart in the U.S. and #2 in the U.K., while "Real Love" went to #11 in the U.S. and #4 in the U.K. Meanwhile, *Anthology 1* clocked the biggest ever first-week sales of a double album, shifting 855,473 copies during November 21-28, 1995, in the U.S. alone. What's more, with three consecutive albums topping the charts within a 12-month period, as well as an estimated 33 million copies of those *Anthology* sets being purchased in addition to their vastly popular back catalog, The Beatles were setting records and attaining sales figures in 1996 that they hadn't even achieved during their 1960s heyday.

"You can't reheat a soufflé," Paul had once asserted when asked about the viability of a Beatles reunion. Oh yeah?

Get Back

"For years, I'd wanted to paint an image of The Beatles performing on the rooftop of their Apple building at the end of the Let It Be *movie. However, a lot of the photos taken of them up there were fish-eyed and distorted, and it doesn't look good when you paint distortion. A close-up of Paul singing 'Get Back' didn't present me with that same problem, so I used an image of him in front of the mic for the body as well as for the background sky—which I made a little more dramatic for the painting—while adapting his head from a photo in the book that originally came with the album."*

– Eric Cash

PART 6

THE BEATLES' STUDIO CREW INTERVIEWS

This section, drawn from my interviews down the years with most of The Beatles'
major aides in the recording studio, allows them to tell their stories in their own
words—without being interrupted by me. While producer Sir George Martin
provides an overview of the band's entire recording career from 1962 through 1970,
the other interviewees provide us with a look into the specific periods when they were
involved, and what emerges is a unique, sometimes-conflicting description of the band
members' personalities, attitudes, and musical ingenuity.

Sir George Martin

When I interviewed the celebrated record producer in 1987, it was just prior to the twentieth anniversary of the release of The Beatles' landmark Sgt. Pepper album, and he had recently been involved in the transfer of the band's catalog to compact disc. Reacquainting himself with the original master tapes had helped to stir George's memory, and he proceeded to recall how his own role had evolved along with The Beatles' musical artistry.

"As far as the music was concerned, John Lennon was always looking for the impossible, the unattainable. He was never satisfied. He once said to me, in one of our evenings together when we were reminiscing, 'You know, George, I've never really liked anything we've ever done.' I said, 'Really, John? But you made some fantastic records!' He said, 'Well, if I could do them all over again, I would.'

"Looking back, some of the plopping sounds that we got on the mics were pretty awful, but I was out to get performance—the excitement of the actual live action—and technical things like that didn't worry me too much. Sometimes the engineers would express disdain that I wasn't worried, but it was important to get the feeling rather than anything else. The small vocal and instrumental mistakes that you might hear on The Beatles' records were never intended, but they did it that way. It was live and things such as that sometimes slipped my attention. Once something went through and I saw it was there, I didn't think it was worthwhile calling them in again to replace a line; life's too short!

"We didn't set out to specifically give an album a different sound from the last one, but there was this eternal curiosity that the boys had to try something new. They were growing up and they were like plants in a hothouse. When I first met them, George and Paul were 19 and 20 years old—kids. In just over a year they became world stars, and so their normal kind of growing-up period was taken away from them by the pressures of fame. They therefore grew up in the studio with me, and up to the point of *Pepper* they were expanding their ideas. Consequently, they were thirsty for knowledge, curious to find out what else they could have, and with their fame came the opportunity to experiment. So, George heard of a Rickenbacker 12-string, wanted to have one, and he got one. Then everybody wanted one.

"Once you started something, for a while it almost became the fashion. For example, once I'd turned John's voice around on 'Rain,' played his voice backwards to him and put it on the track, it was 'Great! Let's try everything backwards!' So, George started doing backwards guitar solos and there was backwards cymbal on 'Strawberry Fields,' until that was exhausted and it was on to the next gimmick. It was a healthy curiosity to find new sounds and new ways of expressing themselves.

"In order to record the backwards guitar on a track like 'I'm Only Sleeping,' you work out what your chord sequence is and write down the reverse order of the chords—as they are going to come up—so you can recognize them. You then learn to boogie around on that chord sequence, but you don't really know what it's going to sound like until it comes out again. It's hit or miss, no doubt about it, but you do it a few times and, when you like what you hear, you keep it.

"Aside from Paul's bass playing, none of the Beatles were the world's greatest musicians, but the sound that they produced was absolute magic. Ringo, for instance, gets a sound out of his drums which is all Ringo. His time-keeping isn't rigid, clinical, and of quartz-controlled accuracy, but he's got tremendous feel. He always helped us to hit the right tempo for a song and gave it that support—that rock-solid backbeat—that made the recording of all The Beatles' songs that much easier. His tempos used to go up and down, but up and down in the right way to help the song. His use of toms was also very inventive. The 'A Day in the Life' timpani sound on the toms was very characteristic.

"Obviously, in those days we never had the studio effects that there are now, but we used to try different things. That was always fun and it made life a little bit more interesting. The most notable case was 'Yellow Submarine,' of course, where you can hear the noise of bubbles being blown into tanks, chains rattling, and that kind of thing. We actually did that in the studio. John got one of those little hand mics which he put into his Vox amp and was able to talk through. So, all of that 'Full steam ahead...' you hear was done live while the main vocal was going on, and we all had a giggle.

"We weren't averse to putting recorded effects in, too. There were all sorts of sound effects that you could get on record, so in the case of 'Good Morning, Good Morning,' for instance, there was a whole farmyard of animals dubbed in from a disc.

"For his part, John Lennon never liked his own voice, and I could never understand this because I thought his voice was terrific. He always wanted it to be mixed down, and on 'Tomorrow Never Knows'—which borrowed lyrics and inspiration from the *Tibetan Book of the Dead*—he wanted me to make him sound like 'a Dalai Lama singing from the highest mountaintop,' while still being able to hear what he was singing. Of course, it was an impossible task, except that he obviously wanted a kooky effect, and artificial double tracking was the only thing we could think of. Needless to say, in those days we didn't have machines like harmonizers or anything like that, so what I did was to put his voice through the Leslie rotating speaker of the Hammond organ. That gave it the effect you can hear, and to my knowledge that was the first time anyone ever did that.

"Before The Beatles came along, I ran [EMI's] Parlophone Records label, and I was responsible for all of the financing and all of the contracts. Then, once The Beatles came along, 1962 went into 1963, Brian [Epstein] and I became firm friends and talked in terms of me producing his stable of artists, and I got on a golden treadmill—which actually turned out to be a copper treadmill for me, being that EMI was making all of the money—where I was in the studio all of the time. In 1963, I just recorded and recorded and recorded, every day, every weekend, and the administrative side of my job was falling away because I had so much work to do. That was the year that I had 37 weeks out of 52 at number one, and I never wanted to work that hard again. Consequently, that was the beginning of me not being involved in The Beatles' financial affairs.

"Their original contract that I signed them to was a miserly one. It secured them to EMI for five years, and after the first year I went to the Managing Director of EMI and said, 'Look, you should double their royalty.' He said, 'Why?' and I said, 'Well, because we've got them for another four years, they're giving us so much, and they're not getting enough in return.' He said, 'Okay, I'll double their royalty if you get another five-year option out of them.' I refused and said, 'No, if you want to do that, you do it yourself. I'll give The Beatles the money, but

I won't ask for any more from them.' They only had an old penny per single between the five of them, including Brian. So, when the contract was renegotiated at the end of the five years, Brian went directly to Sir Joe Lockwood, the head of EMI, and did a better deal.

"I was always very much my own boss at Parlophone and always a bit of a maverick, and I although I never had much money I did have my own way—and I will say that EMI let me have my own way. So, when it came to planning anything for the label, I had the final word. If I wanted to spend five months on doing an album, that was up to me. My neck was on the chopping block if I didn't make it, so there was no problem. I'm sure there was panic in the offices of EMI when we took four months to record *Pepper*, but nobody could say anything to me or threaten me because it was in my charge. They couldn't do anything about it.

"I must say that I never seriously lost my nerve at any point during the *Sgt. Pepper* project, but I did harbor very slight reservations about the orchestral sequences on 'A Day in the Life.' One part of me said, 'We're being a little bit self-indulgent; we're going a little bit over the top,' and the other part of me said, 'It's bloody marvelous! I think it's fantastic.' I was then thoroughly reassured before I put the thing together when I actually let an American visitor hear a bit of 'A Day in the Life.' When that happened, he did a handstand and I then knew my worries were over.

"After the project was finished, I felt we could extend that. I thought we could make another album that would be a little bit more controlled, in fact, while still allowing for The Beatles' originality and ingenuity. I tried to get the boys to accept that there had to be a definite form in the records, and Paul would listen to me but John wouldn't.

"Things began to get difficult during the making of the 'White Album.' The boys came back from India and they had 32 songs that they wanted to record. I listened to every one of them, and a lot of them I didn't think were great, and I told them so. I said, 'Look, recording 32 songs is silly. Let's get down to 14 or 16 songs, eliminate the dubious ones, and concentrate on making really great tracks.' They wouldn't have that, however. They said, 'Well, let's do them all and then you can turn them down if you want to.' They then proceeded to record all at the same time—George would be in one studio, John would be in another, and Paul in another—and so [engineer] Chris Thomas and I had to run between them to try to get the right recordings. It wasn't until long afterwards that I discovered that the reason for them wanting to have 32 tracks recorded wasn't entirely artistic. Their contract, which had been renegotiated by Brian, stipulated that it would expire within a certain period of time or within a certain number of titles recorded. Therefore, the more titles that they recorded, the quicker they got out of the contract. Meanwhile, I was naïve enough to think that their decision was just artistic.

"Personally, my favorites among all of their albums are—working backwards—*Abbey Road*, *Sgt. Pepper*, *Revolver*, and *Rubber Soul*, and I also have a sneaking affection for the first two [*Please Please Me* and *With the Beatles*]. I think we all knew that *Abbey Road* would be their swan song, but I look back on it as a happy time. We had been very unhappy during *Let It Be*—that was a miserable experience—and I never thought we would get back together again. So, I was quite surprised when Paul rang me up and asked me to produce another record for them. He said, 'Will you really produce it?' and I said, 'If I'm really allowed to produce it, I'll really produce it. If I have to go back and accept a lot of instructions which I don't like, then I won't do it.' But Paul said they wanted me to produce it as I used to, and once we got back in the studio it really was nice.

"The boys tended to record their own items, and sometimes we would work in different studios simultaneously. There again, for the tracks where more forces were needed, the other boys would come in. 'Because,' for example, was very much a John song, but it needed the combined singing of the three men [excluding Ringo], so obviously it became a joint effort. Between us we also created a backing with John playing a riff on guitar, me duplicating every note on an electronic harpsichord, and Paul playing bass. Each note between the guitar and harpsichord had to be exactly together, and as I'm not the world's greatest player in terms of timing, I would make more mistakes than John did. So, we had Ringo playing a regular beat on hi-hat to us through our headphones. We had no drum machines in those days, so Ringo was our drum machine. After that, the three boys sang the whole song together in harmony, and then we overlaid another three voices and then another three voices, so we had a nine-part harmony all the way through.

"*Abbey Road* was kind of '*Sgt. Pepper Mk. II*,' and I thought this time around we could make an album that was a little more controlled and boast a definite form; a continuously moving piece of music. However, while Paul went along with the idea, John didn't. So, it became a compromise, with one side of the album very much the way John wanted things—'Let it all hang out; let's rock a little'—and the other being what Paul had accepted from me: to try to think in symphonic terms, and think in terms of having a first and second subject, put them in different keys, bring back themes, and even have some contrapuntal work. Paul dug that, and that's why the second side sounds as it does. It still wasn't quite what I was looking for, but it was going towards it.

"They each learned a great deal in the decade we were together and all of them became excellent musicians. Still, when you get as rich and famous as The Beatles, everyone thinks you're fantastic—and you are, of course—and everybody tells you so. A lot of people don't mean to be sycophants, but they are, and they wouldn't dream of saying anything untoward. There aren't very many people who are able to say to the emperor, 'You aren't wearing any clothes, Jim,' but that's one thing I've always been able to do."

Norman Smith

Originally a composer and musician, Norman engineered The Beatles' first five albums. Yet, in line with convention up until the late-sixties, their records never credited him for his work. Later on, he'd produce the initial recordings of a fledgling band named The Pink Floyd before securing chart-topping success in his own right as that gravel-voiced pop star, Hurricane Smith. In our 1998 interview, Norman began by recalling how, after struggling to support his family as a 34-year-old jazz musician, he fooled the EMI Studios hierarchy into believing he was below the 28-year-old age limit when they hired him as a trainee engineer.

"I had to start right at the bottom as a gofer, but I kept my eyes and ears open, I learned very quickly, and it wasn't long before I got onto the mixing desk. In those days every prospective artist that came in had to have a recording test, and that's what we started doing as engineers, because we couldn't really cock anything up. Normally, each of the producers at EMI had their own assistants and they would be the ones to keep an eye on the potential talent, and that's what I was doing when one day, of course, this group with funny haircuts came in…

"At their recording test, The Beatles didn't make a very good impression, apart from visually. I mean, we heard nothing of John's and Paul's songwriting ability. They had tiny little Vox amplifiers and speakers which didn't create much of a sound at source. Of course, every sound engineer wants some kind of sound at source which he can then embellish and improve, but I got nothing out of The Beatles' equipment except for a load of noise, hum, and goodness-knows-what. Paul's was about the worst – in those days we had echo chambers to add onto the reverberation, and I had to raid the Studio 2 echo chamber in order to fix him up with a sound so that we could get something down on tape.

"Afterwards we brought them all up into the Studio 2 control room, and for about half an hour we laid into them about their equipment and the fact that we needed to get some decent sounds. They didn't respond at all, and so George Martin then asked them if they had anything to say to us. Perhaps there was something they didn't like. Well, George Harrison looked George Martin up and down and said, 'Yeah, I don't like your tie.' With that I just creased up. I'd always admired the Liverpudlian accent; it sounded very humorous, and that just about confirmed it for me. Afterwards the rest of them joined in with the wisecracks, and that was far more impressive than the musical side of things. When they left, George Martin said to me, 'Well, what do you think of that lot?' and I said that I'd never seen anything like them. They were so different.

"At that time there was an enormous number of groups coming in for tests, and none of them really showed any potential or anything visually different, but of course these guys did. I said, 'For that alone we should sign them. Just because of their humor and the way they present themselves.' So, George said, 'Well, I'll think about it,' and of course shortly afterwards he did sign them.

"When they returned to record 'Love Me Do,' we did, in fact, have a very hard time. George [Martin] didn't even come in for the first part of the session. It was his assistant, Ron Richards, and myself who attempted to get the damned thing done, but it took a few weeks to finish it. Now, two sessions may not sound like a long time, but it does when you consider we did The Beatles' very first album [*Please Please Me*] in one day.

"George Martin specialized more in producing comedy material, and so he often left the pop records to Ron Richards, but in the case of The Beatles I think he got involved largely because of Brian Epstein's influence. They had a pretty good rapport—as I did with Eppy; he was a very nice man—and Brian really wanted George to come in and give his okay to 'Love Me Do.' Then, once the single got into the charts and sold well, here was confirmation that we did have a hit act on our hands, and therefore the boss of Parlophone had to take over from hereon in.

"At the recording test we had heard Pete Best's drumming, and frankly I thought it was okay. I therefore think—and this is just speculation on my part—that there must have been something else involved in the group's decision to get rid of him. For some reason they really wanted Pete out and Ringo in; whether that was political or due to friendships, I don't know. Ringo himself was never a great drummer, even at the height of their fame, and he himself knew that, but he was adequate for The Beatles, and of course the main thing about Ringo was his personality. On the other hand, I personally didn't see any reason why [session man] Andy White was brought in for 'Love Me Do,' because a little boy could have played the drum part on that song.

"The truth of the matter is that, to the best of my memory, Paul had a great hand in practically all of the songs that we did, and Ringo would generally ask him what he should do. After all, Paul was no mean drummer himself and he did play drums on a couple of things. Ringo, for his part, came up with the odd thing and he did have an off-the-cuff ability.

"To be honest, it was only because 'Love Me Do' did better than we expected that The Beatles got the chance to do an album, and thank God they did, because that enabled their writing ability to come out, and after that they had many, many number one hits. Still, although saying that they recorded their first album in one day sounds impressive – and I suppose it was – you also have to remember that they had a whole day booked in the studio, and at that time that was pretty rare for a pop group. Normally, an artist would only have a few hours booked, and so perhaps an album might be recorded in about ten hours or so, but over the course of a few days.

"Having said that, I really don't know how The Beatles' voices held out for that entire session. In fact, John's very nearly didn't for the last number, 'Twist and Shout.' Paul found it pretty easy to sing, but John was always under a bit of strain, given the timbre of his voice. I remember they did have a large jar of cough sweets, as well as a carton of cigarettes, and he just went for it. Due to the state of his voice we knew we had to get 'Twist and Shout' in one take, and fortunately we did. There again, if you listen to it, perhaps the sore throat and the hoarseness improved the performance. It's a terrific performance.

"EMI always gave us—the engineers—the chance to experiment on our own in the control room if we had a certain kind of sound that we were after. We could go in and try different ideas, and out of that did come certain things, such as tape delays, ADT [artificial double tracking], and other things of a semi-technical nature. Actually, back then the sound engineers were judged—quite unfairly, in my view—by the number of hits that they'd worked on. Consequently, once The Beatles broke through I was walking on water at Abbey Road and I could do no wrong, so I could more or less do exactly as I wanted. Before then, Ron Richards and myself had been struggling to get hits with people like Shane Fenton, who later became Alvin Stardust, and Paul Raven, who would become Gary Glitter, and so The Beatles made it for me, and from then on I was the number one engineer.

"Up until the time when I became a sound engineer, the other engineers would always use screens. Everything was screened off so that the separation was good on each mic, but I didn't like that idea for The Beatles once it had been decided that I was going to record them. I wanted to set them up the way that they looked, in line with their attitude and how they approached things, and it seemed to me that they would be far happier if they were set up in the studio as though they were playing a live gig. I therefore threw all of the screens away, and the Abbey Road management warned me that I was taking a little bit of a chance, but The Beatles performed as they did onstage and although the separation on each mic wasn't terribly good, it did contribute to the overall sound. We also got a bit of splashback from the walls and the ambience of the actual studio, and in my view that helped create what the press dubbed the 'Mersey Sound.' I'd receive phone calls and letters from America asking how I managed to get all of that sound on tape.

"You see, as far as my side of it was concerned—and all of the other engineers, for that matter—we were sort of restricted. The material had to be transferred from tape onto acetate, and therefore certain frequencies were very difficult for the cutter to get onto disc. I mean, if we did, for instance, slam on a lot of bass, it would only be a problem when it got up to the cutting room, but at the same time we were all a little bit frustrated that we couldn't get certain kinds of sounds that we would have liked. Instruments like the sitar were terribly, terribly difficult to record due to the range of sound frequencies – the meter would be bashing over into the red, and so you didn't get any value for money.

"During those years we were limited as to how much bass we could put on a record without causing too much difficulty for the disc cutter. Well, Paul McCartney would often ask me for more bass frequencies, and I'd say, 'All I can give you is 2 dBs.' After that they would call me '2 dBs Smith,' as well as 'Normal.' Of course, there was more equipment becoming available as time went on, and then there was the contribution of all six of us – or five of us, not counting Ringo – so all of that contributed to the progression of sounds, as did the kinds of songs that were coming across. Don't forget that their writing was changing, too, and this demanded a different sort of approach.

"Believe it or not, I once very nearly had one of my own compositions recorded by The Beatles—I had always been interested in songwriting, ever since I was 10-years-old. Anyway, it was a Friday evening; I shall never forget it as long as I live. They'd recorded 13 songs for the *Help!* album, but we always aimed for 14, and so they said, 'Well, what are we going to do now for this last one?' They were running through different ideas and discarding them, and I was sitting up in the control room with George Martin and [music publisher] Dick James, so I turned to George and said, 'I happen to have written a song for John and it's in my inside pocket.' He said, 'Well, tell them over the talkback.' I said, 'No! I can't do that! You tell them. But don't get them all to come up. Only Paul.'

"So, George Martin asked Paul to come up and he told him that I'd written a song. Paul said, 'Really, Norm?' I said, 'Yeah, I have actually.' 'Well, let's hear it then! Come down…' I said, 'No, no, no. I'm so nervous about it. Let's go across to Studio 3 and I'll play it to you.' So that's what I did and he really did think it was good. He said, 'That's terrific, Norm! It sounds good for John.' I said, 'Well, no offense, Paul, but I've written it for John.' 'Oh, right. Let's get John in.' So John came into Number 3, I performed it again, and he said the same. 'Yeah, smashing. We'll do that.' I couldn't believe it!

"When we returned to the control room both Paul and John asked me to record a little demo over the weekend in time for the session on Monday, and that's what I did, but in the meantime Dick James immediately offered me £15,000 to buy the song outright. Well, of course, back in the mid-sixties that was a terrific amount of money, and to me it was staggering, being that I had about fourpence in the bank! I was about to say, 'I'll take it,' but George Martin was sitting behind Dick James and he was shaking his head as if to say I should ask for more, so I went, 'Well, I'll tell you what, Dick; I'll think about it and I'll let you know on Monday.'

"When Monday came I was sitting with my demo at the mixer a couple of hours early, but when the guys came in they said 'Hello' and walked straight down into the studio. I thought, 'That doesn't look too good,' and then Paul spoke over an open mic and asked me to come down. I went down and Paul said, 'Look, Norm, don't be upset about this, but do you realize that on this album we haven't done a song for Ringo?' Ringo always had a song, so they now had one [Buck Owens' "Act Naturally"] for him to record, and Paul said, 'We promise you that we'll do your one first on the next album.' Well, the next album was *Rubber Soul*, by then their attitudes had changed, and so that was the closest I ever got to having one of my songs recorded by The Beatles. As for what it was called, that produces another ache in my heart, because not only could I never ever find that damned manuscript or the little demo that I gave them, but I can't even remember the blasted title either! It was a good song with a solid beat, almost like the solid beat of 'Twist and Shout,' but with a bit of romance, too... I try not to think about it too much.

"By the time of *Rubber Soul* we were dealing with completely different types of songs and, to be honest with you, the attitude towards not only the recording but also each other was beginning to show not too nicely. Up to that time we'd had a kind of family setup between the four guys, George, and myself. It was superb, and you can probably imagine what a great time it was to be part of all that. Also—and I don't want to take anything away from anyone—production of The Beatles was very simple, because it was ready-made. Paul was a very great influence in terms of the production, especially in terms of George Harrison's guitar solos and Ringo's drumming. It was almost like we had one producer up in the control room and another producer down in the studio, and of course John Lennon also knew what sounds he wanted.

"When *Rubber Soul* came around it was taking a lot longer to record each title. I could see the friction building up and I didn't like it at all. I thought, 'To hell with this,' and I told George Martin, 'I don't like what I see and I want to get off this train.' He said, 'They're going to be very upset about this,' but I said, 'Well, that's the way it is.' Anyway, a few days later what should appear by special delivery but a solid gold travel clock from [London jeweler] Aspreys, inscribed with thanks from The

Beatles. That was a sweetener to stay on, and initially I agreed, but it was nevertheless very difficult and I still didn't like what I could see coming up, particularly between Paul and John who were the main force really. I could see them drifting apart and I did not like that one little bit.

"Fortunately, EMI had offered me a job as an in-house producer, and so I was able to go anyway. Meanwhile, Geoffrey Emerick had started as a button pusher, and the boss at Abbey Road asked me to coach him and get him ready to take over as engineer for The Beatles, which I did. I told him that if he ever got into trouble he could call me, and a few times he did ask for my advice. However, I left engineering completely behind and I moved full-time into production…"

Geoff Emerick

Geoff was only 20 when he took over from Norman Smith as The Beatles' main recording engineer in 1966. His tenure started out by conjuring up the hallucinatory sounds on Revolver*'s "Tomorrow Never Knows." It was an auspicious debut, and his contribution the following year to the band's groundbreaking* Sgt. Pepper *album earned him a Grammy Award. Full of fresh ideas, devoid of preconceptions, and ably assisted by his colleagues at Abbey Road, Geoff was a true innovator in his field and was also the first person to earn an engineering credit on a Beatles record— even though his name on the* "White Album*" was misspelled as "Jeff." In 1996, I spoke with him about the unforgettable start to his outstanding career and the manner in which it came full circle.*

"George Martin and I worked so closely together over the years that we knew exactly what the other was thinking and wanted. It was a great working combination, just incredible. In fact, everybody used to think it was a little bit odd sometimes, because we'd virtually go through a session and not say two words to each other. We didn't need to. We just got on with our own jobs and it worked out fine.

"From the time that I started working with The Beatles on the *Revolver* album, there were hardly any vocals or instruments that weren't doctored in some way, and I have to say that a lot of this was pretty innovative. You see, up until that time the technical approach had roughly been that, if something didn't look right on paper, then you couldn't do it. Without any disrespect, that was like the BBC approach, because if something was being broadcast and the vocal happened to be sibilant, the offending engineer would be hauled onto the carpet and told off. These were the guidelines according to technical people who weren't really doing the job in practice—'You can't do that, because you're going to overload that stage in that amplifier,' and so on.

"The things that we were doing in the mid-sixties were considered horrendous and would never have been allowed by EMI 18 months earlier. We were basically driving the equipment to its limit. On the *Sgt. Pepper* album, for instance, 'A Day in the Life' was a milestone recording. We put a lot of tape echo on the vocal and that sound always suited John's voice. He could hear it in his headphones and he used that echo for rhythmic feel on a lot of the songs that he performed. He had a cutting voice that used to trigger the echo so well.

"There was a great feel about 'A Day in the Life.' It was very exciting, especially when the day came to dub on the orchestra. Everything had been building up to that. At the end of the track, by careful fader manipulation, I gradually built the orchestra up to its climactic peak, and my technique for something like that back then was a little bit psychological. I brought the sound up to a point and then, about halfway through the crescendo, slightly faded it back in level without the listener being able to discern this. That gave me more room for maneuver, so that I could push the level up to its maximum over a longer period of time instead of shoving it straight up there to start with. It was a case of having a feel for the music rather than just concentrating on the technical side. People couldn't understand how, after a certain point, the sound got louder and louder but the meters hardly moved. For that famous final piano chord I had to fade up and up and up as the chord decayed in order to get every last drop of sound. That's why the hiss and amplifier noise increase right at the end.

"George Harrison's Indian track, 'Within You Without You,' presented problems in the recording technique because hearing very quiet instruments being amplified almost like electric guitars caused concern to the musicians who had never heard them that way. The tablas, especially, sounded so different being close-miked and compressed. That was a great track. There again, another thing that I recall about the *Pepper* album is the sound of the rhythm parts on the 'Sgt. Pepper' theme at the beginning and during the 'Reprise'; the way that the bass drum and snare sort of thundered out. No one had heard the bass drum sounding that way before, and that was largely achieved by padding it with chunky woolen sweaters to give a really hard and solid effect. Later on, we would take the skin off the bass drum, but this was before that idea came about. Stuffing the drum with cushions and rags to deaden the sound has now become a normal practice, but in those days it was novel.

"*Pepper* was a very personal project and everyone had become very close to it, but we never realized the impact that it was going to have. We knew it was different, but that could have gone one way or the other.

You know, it could have been stamped as awful. Thankfully, it wasn't. For me that album is still the thing that I'm most proud of and get the most excitement from. A lot of people think that *Abbey Road* is a better album, but *Pepper* is better to me. Still, it's amazing that *Abbey Road* was put on a pedestal of its own, considering what it had to live up to. Most people said that The Beatles would never be able to follow *Sgt. Pepper*, but they did with *Abbey Road*. On the other hand, the 'White Album' meant nothing to me, nothing at all. I hated it. Because of all the personal tensions, I walked out halfway through, but that record just never meant a thing—and it shouldn't have been a double album either.

"By the time of the 'White Album,' all four Beatles rarely recorded in the same room at the same time, and so it didn't seem all that odd when Paul, George, and Ringo got together at the start of '94 to do the overdubs for 'Free as a Bird.' They did a couple of run-throughs in order to work out who was going to play what, and then, when it came to the actual recording, everything was done one at a time. It was much the same when they did 'Real Love' the following year, and, all in all, each of the songs took about two-and-a-half weeks to complete. We didn't work long hours—usually, it was from midday to, like, seven at night, five days a week—and I have to say that a lot of the session time was actually taken up with good conversations about the past. In fact, I think that [producer] Jeff Lynne was quoted as saying that the conversation was more interesting than the actual sessions! They were just reminiscing about the old days and it was great.

"I tried to clean up the actual sound as best I could, but in terms of employing effects I really didn't dare attempt to try anything. Basically, the sound that you hear on there is the sound that was on John's cassette—which was really Lennonish—albeit a hundred percent cleaner after I faded stuff up and down. There were no clever tricks added to that. Jeff just tried to space out the gaps between the words in order to make the whole thing fit together more rhythmically, but that was it. We originally tried to overdub straight to the vocal tape, but there were too many variants, so we just spun in a few words and lines. This applied more to 'Free as a Bird,' as we had to open it up in order to put Paul and George's new verses in.

"We didn't want to add any sort of modern devices to the mixes, and the same applied to the entire *Beatles Anthology* project. Originally, I had been Norman Smith's second engineer and he had really taught me my job. So, knowing how he had worked, I sort of bore that in mind when I was mixing the first two *Anthology* sets. It's hard to put a finger on how his sound varied from mine—maybe it was just a bit softer, more mellow—but on *Anthology 1* and *2* I tried to mix as I thought Norman would have done.

"Personally, I'm anti-computers. They've got this de-noising system at Abbey Road to remove all of the hiss and crackles, but first of all there was no noise on the original tapes, and secondly it screws the sound up in my opinion. That's why I made sure they didn't use the de-noiser on the second and third *Anthology* sets. It was more useful on *Anthology 1* because that made use of a load of old tapes. But even then it was like listening to the first Edison recording on a cylinder where some surface noise tells you it's dated, and then removing this and leaving a terrible phasey swish across it. I think they went a bit too far in that respect. They should have left a bit of surface noise on it. If that was the way it was recorded, then that's the way it is and that's the way it should be."

Eddie Kramer

Famous for his association with Jimi Hendrix, as well as his work with, among others, Led Zeppelin, Kiss, The Small Faces, Traffic, and David Bowie, Eddie also helped record a couple of tracks by The Beatles when they ventured outside Abbey Road to use the famed independent Olympic Studios facility in Barnes, South London. After assisting studio manager Keith Grant on the May 11, 1967 recording and mix of "Baby, You're a Rich Man," Eddie then took charge of engineering the backing track and some of the vocals for "All You Need is Love" alongside George Martin on June 11, as the band prepared to perform the song live in front of a worldwide TV audience just 11 days later. In 1997, he recalled those sessions.

"With 'Baby, You're a Rich Man' we had a point to prove. You know, they'd booked us because they couldn't get into their studio, and Keith and I just had to prove to the world that we were as good as EMI or better. We recorded and overdubbed and mixed that entire song in one night, starting at nine o'clock and finishing at three in the morning. Not bad!

"John Lennon was a fantastic vocalist and he was to the fore on both of the songs that we worked on. The guy was at the top of his game, it was his song, he'd know how he was going to sing it, he had complete command of the material and the direction, and he'd open his voice and it would be there. I didn't have to do anything. It's like recording any great artist—like Hendrix's guitar or John Bonham's drums: stick a bloody mic up and away you go! It's not rocket science.

"During the 'All You Need is Love' session, John sat next to me, we rigged up this talkback mic on the console, and he sang into that, so he sang into the bloody headphones. The four of them came into the control room and said [in a thick Liverpudlian accent], 'Oh yeah, well, we need to do this song, y'know, for a TV show,' and it was incredible, because they filtered out into the studio and Paul picked up Keith Grant's string bass, George played lead guitar, George Martin played harpsichord, and Ringo sat at the drums. And then once they got going, they didn't stop. They'd go to the end of the song and then John would count, 'One-two-three,' and they'd be off again. No stopping for half an hour. Then they came into the control room, picked the take they liked, said, 'Okay, that's the one. Do us a rough mix,' and 'See you later.' Pretty amazing. I have to tell you, it was the only time in my life that I was ever really nervous on a session, and I didn't dare ask if I could take photographs. Because, you know, I used to keep my camera with me all the time, but I just didn't have the balls to ask them to take a picture.

"You have to imagine the scene outside Olympic Studios in those days. The Beatles would hang out on a Stones session, and that was heavy enough, but outside there'd be John Lennon's painted Rolls and Jagger's Bentley, and as buses passed by you'd see them slow down and the drivers would comment to each other about what was going on…"

Ken Scott

When, in mid-July 1968, during the recording of "Cry Baby Cry," Geoff Emerick walked out on the "White Album" sessions due to The Beatles' in-fighting and increasingly churlish attitude toward him and George Martin, Ken Scott was the first person to take Geoff's place behind the Abbey Road Studio 2 console. Ken subsequently engineered not only "Cry Baby Cry," but 20 of the 30 "White Album" tracks, and while the picture that's normally painted of that project is a gloomy one—highlighting the discord that would boil over during the disastrous and destructive January '69 Get Back/Let It Be *sessions, Ken's 2012 recollections of the sessions with which he was involved were altogether more upbeat.*

"My first session as a second engineer for The Beatles [during the June 1964 recording of the *A Hard Day's Night* album] had been scary, but my first session as an engineer with them [during the September '67 recording of the *Magical Mystery Tour* EP] was absolutely terrifying. Up until then, not allowed to touch mics or anything, I'd learned recording techniques by mostly sitting and watching. There were three pop engineers at Abbey Road during the time I was assisting—Norman Smith, Malcolm Addey, and Peter Bown—and then the great thing was I got to see how three incredible classical engineers worked as well: Chris Parker, Bob Gooch, and Neville Boyling. Still, once I got the call to engineer, it was as if I'd been dropped in the fire, especially since I was now on my own to record the biggest band in the world. It was a case of sink or swim, and luckily I swam.

"The *Magical Mystery Tour* project came just after the death of Brian Epstein and the whole thing was un-together. I hate to use the word 'floundering', but that's almost what was going on, whereas for the 'White Album' their heads were a little straighter. Considering the drugs that were being taken, this may seem hard to believe, but I think by then they'd come to terms with Brian's death and they appeared to have a much better idea as to what they should be doing. A perfect example of this was 'Birthday,' which was written and recorded the same day,

"Paul was the first to arrive in the studio. He began playing the riff on the piano and he'd basically composed the song by the time the other guys arrived, at which point he taught it to them while I worked on the sound. This was at a time when George Martin was on holiday. Chris

Thomas was his assistant, and when Chris came back from his own holiday [at the end of the first week of September '68], there was a note from George [Martin] saying he had also gone on vacation and that Chris should go along to the studio and help out.

"Suddenly, having never produced anything in his entire life, Chris was The Beatles' producer, and thanks to him mentioning that the classic rock 'n' roll movie *The Girl Can't Help It* was going to be on TV the same night they were recording 'Birthday,' it was decided that we'd all take a break and go around the corner to watch it at Paul's house. They'd already laid down the backing track, and when we returned to the studio—perhaps because the movie inspired everyone—the pace really picked up and we overdubbed the piano, handclaps, tambourine and lead vocals, as well as the backing vocals by Yoko and [George's wife] Pattie.

"We had a four-track Studer tape machine in the Studio 2 control room when the 'White Album' sessions began, but EMI had acquired a couple of 3M eight-tracks from America that were being tested and modified by our technical experts at around the same time as The Beatles were recording 'Hey Jude' and 'Dear Prudence' at [Central London's] Trident Studios. One day, George Harrison saw one of those 3M machines sitting in a corridor at EMI and he immediately told me we should have it in Studio 2. So, without asking anyone's permission, I told our technical engineer Dave Harries to nab the machine and the next day Dave and I were reamed new rear ends.

"Again, this was while George Martin was away, and it wasn't until much later that I found out he not only knew EMI had acquired the eight-track machines, but that he'd actually been asked if he wanted to use them on the 'White Album' sessions and had said no. This was because George knew The Beatles would hit the roof when they discovered that, without the 3M being modified, they couldn't do many of the things that they'd been used to doing on four-track... and they did.

"The first eight-track recordings that The Beatles did at EMI were some overdubs for 'While My Guitar Gently Weeps.' The basic track, with George playing electric guitar, Paul playing bass, John playing the organ, and Ringo on drums, had been recorded on the four-track. But then, during the time when Ringo had quit the group, we transferred it to the eight-track and George attempted to overdub a backwards solo. The next day, Ringo returned and, when he walked into the studio, the whole place, including his drum kit, had been decorated with flowers by George. He was the only one who would think of doing something like that.

"George didn't like the solo he'd done the previous day, so he recorded a new version but didn't like that either, and at that point he decided to scrap the entire song and start all over again. He sang and played acoustic guitar while John played electric guitar, Ringo drummed, and Paul played the piano. John then overdubbed the organ and Paul overdubbed his bass.

"At EMI, those of us who had just become engineers always started off using the same miking techniques as those who had come before us. So, during the *Magical Mystery Tour* project I would have been copying Geoff Emerick precisely, but then I would have started experimenting. After all, working with The Beatles meant you had time to experiment and to learn things like what mics to choose because they were all up for experimenting. So, for the 'White Album' I may have copied what Geoff did, but it also may have varied slightly.

"I remember Paul and I would go into the mic storage room and he would find a mic that he thought would look good and we'd have to use it. 'Oh, I like the look of that one. Let's try it.' It was a case of putting different mics in different places. Like on the piano, we'd do everything from putting the mic above it to underneath it and probably try placing it up the pianist's arse at some point.

"Anyway, we did a lot of band takes of 'While My Guitar Gently Weeps,' but George still wasn't happy. So, the next day he suddenly showed up with Eric Clapton, and Eric attempted the solo. All I remember is that Eric didn't want his guitar to sound like an Eric guitar; he wanted it to sound like a Beatles guitar. So, the way we dealt with that was to ADT and flange it during the mix. It's not as if we always did that with George's guitar, but we did do it with everything and everyone at some point or another.

"The flanging achieved a phasing-type effect, but because the 3M eight-track machine still hadn't been modified to do ADT or flanging, Eric's solo had to be recorded on the four-track while Chris Thomas spent several hours wiggling an oscillator back and forth to vary the speed of the tape to flange Eric's guitar and John's organ part before we bounced the four-track across to the eight-track.

"Recording The Beatles was a wonderful experience, but while there were times when their creative juices were flowing and it was incredibly exciting, there were others when it was as boring as hell. For instance, I remember it took three days just to get the basic track of 'Sexy Sadie'. Primarily, they were down in the studio, figuring out the different parts, and all we had to do was make sure the tape was constantly running. What got me through those times was the firm belief that, in the end, it would turn into something amazing, and generally that was the case. But then, I didn't have to work on 'Revolution 9.'

"An awful lot has been written about The Beatles being at odds with each other the entire time they were recording the 'White Album,' but that to me is completely false. Most certainly they acted as backing musicians for each other up to a point, but there were also times when they were closer than they'd been in ages. After Ringo quit the band and then returned, suddenly they were a band again. They were so close, it was amazing, and we got more work done during that period than they'd previously done in months.

"You've got to take into consideration, they were working on that album for close to six months, and there isn't a project I have worked on—even a two-week project—where at some point someone hasn't lost their temper. So, spread that over six months and it's going to happen a few times. But I repeat, it wasn't that bad. And there were also outside influences that people don't take into consideration. We were working on 'Hey Jude', and the first night, when everyone was up and The Beatles were still sorting out the arrangement, a couple of guys came by the studio because the next night there was going to be a film crew coming in for a documentary [*Music!*] being made by the National Music Council of Great Britain. 'Don't worry,' they told us. 'We'll be in tomorrow but you won't know we're here.' Yeah, right.

"The next night, the film crew came in and of course they were in everyone's faces. Well, there ended up being a huge row between George and Paul—George was playing a guitar phrase that responded to each of Paul's vocal lines and Paul vetoed it. However, this wasn't because the band members weren't getting along; it was because the outside sources were putting everyone on edge, someone was going to blow his top, and it just happened to be those two.

"For my book, I did an interview with Chris Thomas, and when I ended our interview with the standard 'Is there anything else you would like to say?' Chris's immediate comment was, 'Yeah, please let everyone know it was fun. It was nowhere near as bad as has been stated. We loved it.' So, there are several of us who don't see it the same way as other people. We had a blast. It was great.

"Here I was, at the age of 21, working with the greatest band in the world. How could it not be exciting for me? To my mind, one of the most brilliant things about The Beatles was their ability to make decisions on the fly. There could be a mistake somewhere along the line and instantaneously we'd hear, 'Hang on, I like that, let's keep it.' I witnessed that several times and their instincts were flawless. They didn't have any rules because they weren't technically trained. They just did what sounded good to them and what felt right to them and they came up with absolutely incredible things, even when a lot of it was by accident. Many of their musical ideas and technical demands caused difficulties for us in the control room, but they'd push us to sort those things out and I'm so glad they did."

Glyn Johns

From The Beatles to The Rolling Stones, Led Zeppelin to The Who, The Kinks to Eric Clapton, Glyn's career was about the best working with the best. Nevertheless, his 1969 assignment for the Fab Four was a tough one, being asked to engineer and largely produce them at what turned out to be a low-point of their career: the troubled Get Back *movie sessions at Twickenham film studios (where he could work as a member of the filmmakers union) and then at the group's own Apple facility. Thereafter, he compiled and mixed the soundtrack album with an unvarnished, overdub-free sound, only for this to be discarded in favor of Phil Spector applying some heavy-handed overdubs. Still, "Glynis"—as John Lennon nicknamed him—bore no grudges when recalling the experience some 20 years later.*

"I'm fairly strong-willed as a person and in the way that I work, but I never seek to overrule artists out of hand unless I think they are making an enormous boo-boo, in which case I have to stand up and put my foot down. In the main, my job is to represent the artists to the best of my ability and to show them in their best light. The fact that we are working together means we have a mutual respect, so if they feel really strongly about something I'm not going to argue about it. You can't make artists do something that they don't want to do, and there's little point in it anyway.

"With The Beatles' *Get Back* project it wasn't specified as to what capacity I was being retained in. I was just asked to work with them, and it became fairly clear as I walked in the door that they wanted me to produce, but that was never really stated. George Martin wasn't there and I was. Anyway, one night I took the tapes with me to Olympic and I ran off some mixes of what they had been doing in the rehearsals. I then had an acetate cut the next day and I said, 'Look, this is just an idea, but I think the album could be like this because I think it's wonderful.' I gave each of them a copy, and when they came back in the next day they all pooh-poohed it and said, 'No, that's totally ridiculous.' So, I said, 'Okay, forget it.' End of project.

"We started *Abbey Road* almost immediately afterwards and a few

335

days later I went off to America to do something else [record the Steve Miller Band]. Then, when I came back home to England, I got a call, and Paul and John met me at EMI and said, 'Okay, we think that we should go with the idea that you had all those weeks ago,' and they gave me the tapes and let me loose on my own to go and make an album. So, I went and put an album together, had acetates cut, and gave them one each, and they all came back and said that they loved it. This was while we were working on *Abbey Road*. Then [manager] Allen Klein said, 'We can't release the album, we've got to make the film first. The album should be the soundtrack to the film.' Well, the film was a year in the editing—which was a complete disaster area—and, by the time it was delivered, The Beatles had broken up and John Lennon hated my version of *Let It Be*. Without the consent of anyone else in the band, he gave the master tapes to Phil Spector, who he'd recently befriended, and he told him to go and make an album. So, Spector took the tapes and overdubbed these schlocky strings and choirs.

"My idea had been that, as The Beatles had proven themselves to be the masters of the 'produced' record, it would be wonderful to release all of this completely live stuff without an overdub on it. It was very, very raw and yet it was still great. It showed their humor and, although it was like a bootleg album, it was good, and I thought it would be a pretty neat idea to release something that was completely the opposite of what everybody had come to expect from the band. That is why they thought I was off my tree when I first gave them my rough version, because it was too much for them to deal with, but I thought that Spector's record was embarrassing. Still, I didn't lose too much sleep over it. I was working my arse off 24 hours a day, seven days a week, so I didn't pay a lot of attention to what was going on.

"There had been a lot of bad publicity about in-fighting between the members of the band, and my version of the record basically took that and chucked it out of the window. It really showed them getting on well. I mean, at the start of the project they'd had some problems among themselves, but they didn't stretch beyond that. Even when it was unpleasant between two of them, it certainly never extended to anybody else. They were always excellent with everyone, from the tea lady to whoever, and they were fantastic to work with. I had a great time."

John Kurlander

An Abbey Road in-house engineer for just under 30 years, John started out recording rock, pop, and "easy-listening" orchestral sessions before carving out a niche with show recordings and then becoming the studio's chief classical engineer. As such, he worked with many of the world's top conductors and opera performers, which was a long way from the early days when he assisted on some Beatles sessions. After relocating to L.A. in 1996, John talked with me about those initial, unforgettable studio experiences.

"When just one of The Beatles was on a session it would be absolutely great, with two of them it would be okay, with three of them the atmosphere would get a bit tense, and when the four of them were together it would occasionally be unbearable.

"Towards the end, because of all the tension and the kind of hours that The Beatles liked to work, the assistants weren't exactly lining up to be on their sessions. Just before I started at Abbey Road, Richard Lush had been the second engineer on *Sgt. Pepper*, and then for the 'White Album' John Smith and Mike Sheady did the job, followed by Alan Parsons on *Let It Be*. Well, when it came to *Abbey Road*, I was given the assignment, and I remember asking Richard Lush incredulously, 'Why isn't anyone else doing this one?' to which he said, 'We've done our stints, now it's your turn…'

"There were times when the *Abbey Road* album degenerated into solo projects with, say, Paul recording in Studio 2 and John in 3, and so Geoff Emerick and Phil McDonald would be called upon to do the engineering, and Alan Parsons and I would assist them. It was interesting. If there were only two Beatles in the studio at one time along with George Martin, Geoff Emerick, and myself, then it would be a case of the five of us just working together. However, when John, Paul, George, and Ringo were all together, something would happen and they would become 'The Beatles.' They would close ranks as The Beatles, and so George Martin, Geoff Emerick, and I would then close ranks as 'The Production Team.' That didn't mean we were taking sides and arguing; it was more like there being these two cliques, and as a youngster it kind of surprised me that George Martin was in our camp rather than theirs. The Beatles were incredible as a self-contained musical unit, but the chemistry worked in a negative way insofar as the atmosphere was concerned...

"When The Beatles were in the studio, there would be this incredible parade of really famous people from the world of entertainment coming in almost every day to hang out for a few hours. In fact, there weren't many times when they were alone. It was as if life carried on and we would do bits of recording in between them going about their daily routine and bits of business. I remember after John and Yoko had a car crash in Scotland, a bed was set up for Yoko in a corner of the studio and again she would be there with a group of visitors. So, they would be recording with open mics, and Yoko and her visitors would have to be asked to stop talking while the red light was on.

"When we were compiling the *Abbey Road* album, that short track which ends it—'Her Majesty—was originally cross-faded between 'Sun King' and 'Polythene Pam.' So, the last note of 'Sun King' was the first note of 'Her Majesty' and the last note of 'Her Majesty' was the first note of 'Polythene Pam.' We put it together in the middle of the night, and when he heard it Paul said, 'No, it doesn't work there, I don't like it, chuck it out.' Well, being that the track was already cross-faded and this was only a demo assembly of the album, I wasn't going to undo the cross-fade and restore the original. So, I just cut 'Her Majesty' out, leaving the last note of that song over the first note of 'Polythene Pam,' and instead of throwing 'Her Majesty' away I put 20 seconds of red leader tape at the beginning of it and wrote, 'Unwanted version of "Her Majesty" after red leader.'

"The next morning, while we were all asleep, [engineer] Malcolm Davies cut a reference of the record, and again he had the same attitude as I had—don't throw anything away. So, he just stuck on 'Her Majesty' as a separate track 20 seconds after the end of all of the other songs. The band therefore listened to the album and, just when they thought it was all over, this track suddenly came in at the end, still missing the final note. This appealed to them, especially as it would leave the album sounding totally unfinished, and so they used that same rough mix with the last note missing. A lot of things would happen by accident that way and they would say, 'Yeah, I like it,' and then later on everyone would write about how brilliant it was.

"After The Beatles broke up, I worked with John, Paul, and George on some of their solo albums. I worked on *McCartney*, and when Paul would describe how he wanted something to sound, if Geoff [Emerick] or Phil [McDonald] asked him to be more specific he would usually say, 'Just make it sound good!' That was his most common reply. I also did the odd session on George's *All Things Must Pass*, and one day, while he and Phil Spector were doing something in Studio Three, they needed a rough mix of 'My Sweet Lord.' I therefore went into Room Four— which was a little remix suite—with Spector, and although I'd done virtually nothing up to that point engineering-wise, over the course of 20 minutes he dictated to me how to achieve his famous 'Wall of Sound.' It was like, 'Put on the tape. Lift that fader. Run that tape echo. Spin the echo around... A bit more, bit more, bit more... That's it. Now let's bring in this track...' I did everything, but I was like a puppet as he dictated the whole process step by step. In terms of the kind of delays and the kind of reverbs that he was using, I think there was a formula, but in all other respects he did it by ear. It was amazing. Within 20 minutes he had dictated how to turn a very dry eight-track recording into his trademark sound."

Alan Parsons

The engineer of Pink Floyd's Dark Side of the Moon *who subsequently became a producer before indulging his songwriting abilities via his own Alan Parson Project, this multi-talented man began his career at EMI Studios, cutting his musical teeth as an assistant on The Beatles'* Get Back/Let It Be *and* Abbey Road *projects. In 1993, he recalled that auspicious start.*

"If you look at The Beatles, half of the strength in their music was the experimentation, and had they not spent days and nights literally just getting a vocal sound, then maybe it would have turned out completely different. There again, the first two albums [*Please Please Me* and *With The Beatles*] were recorded in a day and a week respectively, so how can you knock that kind of output even without the technology?

"Back in the late-sixties, you never got through three hours without some piece of equipment packing up. You know, power packs went down, mic amps in the desk used to spring out so we'd push them back in or kick them, and the early condenser mics were always packing up. That's why, when they were putting together their own studio, The Beatles thought they would overcome all of these problems. However, Magic Alex's console lasted approximately half an afternoon. All I can remember about it were all of these pretty colors, and from a distance you thought, 'Oh, that looks good!' But then you went up close and got a look at the workmanship, and you saw that nothing was quite straight and all of the holes had been cut wrong. It had clearly been carved by hand and you could almost see the bits of metal hanging off. It was quite funny, and within a few minutes it was very clear that no music was going to be forthcoming from this machine.

"Still, to be involved in the creative aspects of making a Beatles record far outweighed any of the drawbacks and it was very exciting for me. It's hard to be associated with the greatest rock 'n' roll band of all time without there being some kind of influence, but essentially I've felt influenced by everybody whom I've worked with. I consider that to be a healthy part of my upbringing in music."

Take Two

"Like Summer Tour '66, this is a combination of two photos. The Abbey Road sessions took place at a time when George really resented Paul, and yet here they are, brothers in the recording studio. They truly worked together, each respecting the other's talents, and while we've heard numerous stories about the arguments between all four members of The Beatles, we'll never fully know the intricacies of their relationships. Sure, toward the end there was plenty of friction—especially between Paul and the other three—but there are also many photos of them sharing some lighter moments. There's enough footage from the Let It Be movie for it to have been edited to show them totally getting along, and as the Abbey Road album proves, when it came to the music they bonded incredibly as a group until the very end. Take Two pays tribute to that partnership."

— Eric Cash

APPENDIX A

BEATLES CHRONOLOGY

Below you'll find a selective listing of events that, in one way or another, had a significant impact on The Beatles and/or their careers together and separately. Only a few items relating specifically to the group are listed after 1969.

May 20, 1930:

Harold Harrison and Louise French, parents of George, are married.

September 19, 1934:

Brian Samuel Epstein, The Beatles' future manager, is born.

1936:

Richard Starkey and Elsie Gleave, parents of Richard Starkey (Ringo Starr), are married.

December 3, 1938:

Alfred Lennon and Julia Stanley, parents of John, are married.

June 23, 1940:

Stuart Fergusson Victor Sutcliffe is born in Edinburgh, Scotland.

July 7, 1940:

Richard Starkey (Ringo Starr) is born at the Royal Liverpool Children's Hospital.

October 9, 1940:

John Winston Lennon is born at Oxford Street Maternity Hospital, Liverpool.

November 24, 1941:

Randolph Peter Best (Pete Best) is born in Madras, India.

Spring 1941:

John is left in the care of his aunt, Mary Smith (Aunt Mimi), and Uncle George.

1941:

James McCartney and Mary Patricia Mohin, parents of Paul, are married.

April 1942:

Alfred Lennon, having been away at sea for long periods, leaves Julia for good, while she moves in with her new man, John Dykins.

June 18, 1942:

James Paul McCartney (Paul McCartney) is born at Walton Hospital, Liverpool.

February 25, 1943:

George Harrison is born at 12 Arnold Grove, Wavertree, Liverpool.

1943:

Ringo's parents divorce.

July 1946:

After failing to repair his marriage to Julia, Alf Lennon takes John on a holiday to Blackpool where it is agreed that the boy will remain in Julia's custody. Thereafter, she places him back with her sister, Mimi.

April 17, 1953:

Ringo's mother, Elsie, marries Harry Graves.

June 5, 1955:

John's uncle, George Smith, dies suddenly.

October 31, 1956:

Paul's mother, Mary Patricia McCartney, dies suddenly.

May 1956:

John's world is turned around when he hears Elvis Presley's recording of "Heartbreak Hotel" for the first time.

March 1957:

John forms The Black Jacks skiffle group with sidekick Pete Shotton, before renaming it The Quarry Men after a week and recruiting other schoolmates.

June 9, 1957:

First official Quarry Men engagement, auditioning in Carol Levis' "TV Star Search" at Liverpool's Empire Theatre.

July 6, 1957:

Paul attends a Quarry Men performance at the St. Peter's Church Garden Fete in Woolton, Liverpool, where he meets John for the first time.

July 20, 1957:

Paul is invited to join The Quarry Men. He accepts but doesn't make his debut for several weeks.

August 7, 1957:

The Quarry Men perform at Liverpool jazz venue, The Cavern Club.

October 18, 1957:

Paul makes his Quarry Men debut at the New Clubmoor Hall in Liverpool, but flunks his lead guitar solo. Hereafter he plays rhythm.

February 6, 1958:

The probable date of George Harrison's first encounter with The Quarry Men, at Wilson Hall in Garston, Liverpool.

July 15, 1958:

While she is crossing Menlove Avenue after visiting Mimi, John's mother, Julia, is killed when she is struck by a car being driven by an off-duty policeman.

Mid-1958:

The Quarry Men, comprising John, Paul, George, and pianist John "Duff" Lowe, but without a drummer, tape amateur recordings of Buddy Holly's "That'll Be the Day" and the Harrison-McCartney composition "In Spite of All the Danger" at a home studio owned by Percy Phillips.

November 1958:

The band changes its name to Johnny and the Moondogs and then Japage 3.

August 29, 1959:

Now renamed The Quarrymen and comprising John, Paul, and George with Ken Brown on bass, the band plays without a drummer at the opening night of the Casbah Coffee Club, owned by Mona Best, mother of Pete.

January 1960:

After a furious row, Ken Brown quits The Quarry Men, leaving the hardcore trio of John, Paul, and George. Soon thereafter, John's Art College friend Stuart Sutcliffe becomes the band's bassman.

March 1960:

The Quarrymen become The Beatals.

May 10, 1960:

The Beatals become The Silver Beetles and audition to back Billy Fury, but Fury's manager, Larry Parnes, books them to tour Scotland behind another of his singers, Johnny Gentle.

May 20–28, 1960:

The Silver Beetles, featuring "Long John" Lennon, Paul "Ramon" (McCartney), "Carl" Harrison, Stu de Stael (Sutcliffe), and Tommy Moore on drums, tour Scotland with Johnny Gentle.

Early/mid-June, 1960:

The Silver Beetles become The Beatles before reverting back to The Silver Beetles.

Early July, 1960:

The Silver Beetles become The Silver Beatles.

July 1960:

The Silver Beatles back a stripper named Janice at the New Cabaret Artistes club, owned by booking agent/manager Allan Williams. For a short time afterwards the band is joined by Norman Chapman on drums.

August 12, 1960:

After a quick audition Pete Best joins The Silver Beatles in time for their first trip to Hamburg.

August 16, 1960:

The band changes its name permanently to The Beatles and sets off for Hamburg.

August 17-October 3, 1960:

The Beatles play at the Indra Club on Hamburg's Grosse Freiheit.

October 4-November 30, 1960:

The Beatles play at the nearby but larger Kaiserkeller Club.

October 15, 1960:

John, Paul, George, and Ringo record together for the first time, along with bassist Walter Eymond of Rory Storm and the Hurricanes, in the tiny Akustic Studio located behind Hamburg's train station.

November 21, 1960:

George is deported from West Germany for being underage and therefore ineligible for nightclub work after midnight.

November 29, 1960:

Paul and Pete are thrown in jail for supposedly "setting fire" to their living quarters at the Bambi Kino.

November 30, 1960:

Paul and Pete are released from jail but then deported from West Germany. John leaves voluntarily on November 10, but Stu remains in Hamburg to be with his new love, Astrid Kirchherr.

December 27, 1960:

A performance at the Litherland Town Hall in Liverpool incites the first scenes of Beatlemania.

February 9, 1961:

The Beatles perform the first of nearly 300 gigs at The Cavern Club. The Quarry Men also appeared here more than three years earlier.

April 1-July 1, 1961:

The Beatles make their second trip to Hamburg and perform at the Top Ten Club on the Reeperbahn.

June 22–23, 1961:

The Beatles play in a professional recording studio for the first time, backing singer Tony Sheridan and performing a couple of numbers without him for producer Bert Kaempfert.

October 28, 1961:

According to Brian Epstein's later recollections, a Liverpool youth named Raymond Jones walks into the Epstein family record store, NEMS, and asks for a copy of "My Bonnie," as recorded by Tony Sheridan and The Beatles.

November 9, 1961:

Accompanied by his assistant, Alistair Taylor, Brian Epstein visits the Cavern during a lunchtime session and sees The Beatles for the first time.

December 3, 1961:

The Beatles and Brian Epstein hold their first business meeting.

December 6, 1961:

The Beatles agree in principle to Brian Epstein becoming their manager. They meet again on December 10 to discuss the terms.

January 1, 1962:

The Beatles audition for Decca Records A&R man Mike Smith, recording 15 songs.

January 4, 1962:

The Beatles top a popularity poll in the local music paper *Mersey Beat.*

January 24, 1962:

The Beatles sign a management contract with Brian Epstein. Brian himself doesn't add his signature until October of 1962.

Early February, 1962:

Decca Records turn down The Beatles.

February 13, 1962:

Brian Epstein meets George Martin, EMI Records' head of A&R, and plays him the recording of The Beatles' failed Decca audition.

March 7, 1962:

The Beatles make their radio debut, performing at Manchester's Playhouse Theatre, where they appear in suits for the first time.

April 10, 1962:

Stuart Sutcliffe dies of a brain hemorrhage at the age of 21.

April 13-May 31, 1962:

The Beatles make their third trip to Hamburg, performing at the newly opened Star-Club on the Grosse Freiheit.

May 9, 1962:

George Martin meets Brian Epstein for a second time and offers The Beatles a recording contract while scheduling their first recording session for June 6.

June 6, 1962:

The Beatles visit the EMI Studios on Abbey Road for the first time and embark on their initial recording session.

August 15, 1962:

Ringo Starr is approached to join The Beatles. He accepts.

August 16, 1962:

Pete Best is sacked as The Beatles' drummer.

August 18, 1962:

Ringo Starr makes his debut as a Beatle, at Hulme Hall in Port Sunlight, Birkenhead.

August 22, 1962:

The Beatles perform before TV cameras for the first time when they are filmed at The Cavern by Granada Television. Deemed unsuitable, the footage is shelved until the group becomes famous the following year.

August 23, 1962:

John marries Cynthia Powell at Liverpool's Mount Pleasant Registry Office.

September 4, 1962:

The Beatles return to Abbey Road for their first formal recording session with Ringo Starr.

October 5, 1962:

The Beatles' first single, "Love Me Do"/"P.S. I Love You," is released in the UK. It eventually peaks at #17.

October 17, 1962:

The Beatles make their TV debut with a live appearance on Granada Television's *People and Places.*

November 1–14, 1962:

The Beatles make their fourth trip to Hamburg, playing at the Star-Club.

December 18–31, 1962:

The Beatles make their fifth and final trip to Hamburg, playing at the Star-Club.

January 2–6, 1963:

The Beatles tour Scotland.

February 2, 1963:

The Beatles undertake their first proper package tour of Britain.

February 11, 1963:

The Beatles record 10 new tracks for their first album, *Please Please Me,* in just under 10 hours.

Late February, 1963:

The "Please Please Me" single tops the *New Musical Express* and *Disc* magazine charts, even though it peaks at #2 on the BBC chart.

March 9, 1963:

The Beatles embark on their second British concert tour.

March 22, 1963:

The Beatles' first album, *Please Please Me,* is released in the UK. It will be the first of 11 Beatles albums to top the British charts during the next seven years.

April 8, 1963:

A son, John Charles Julian, is born to John and Cynthia Lennon.

April 12, 1963:

The Beatles' third single, "From Me to You," is released in the UK. This will commence a cycle of eleven consecutive singles by the band to top the British charts through 1966.

May 18, 1963:

The Beatles embark on their third British tour.

August 3, 1963:

The Beatles play for the last time at The Cavern Club.

October 13, 1963:

The Beatles' live appearance on the network TV show, *Val Parnell's Sunday Night at the London Palladium,* causes a sensation across Britain.

October 23, 1963:

The Beatles fly to Sweden for their first ever foreign concert tour.

October 31, 1963:

Thousands of fans gather at London Airport to greet The Beatles on their return from Sweden. On hand to witness the pandemonium is Ed Sullivan.

November 1, 1963:

First night of *The Beatles' Autumn Tour* of Britain.

November 4, 1963:

The Beatles appear at the *Royal Command Performance,* where John asks the glitterati to rattle their jewelry.

January 3, 1964:

A clip of The Beatles performing is shown on *The Jack Paar Show* in the U.S.

January 15, 1964:

The Beatles perform in Versailles, France prior to commencing a two week season at the Olympia Theater in Paris.

January 16, 1964:

The Beatles learn that, in the January 25 edition of America's *Cashbox* magazine, "I Want to Hold Your Hand" has jumped 43 places to top the singles chart.

February 7, 1964:

The Beatles arrive at Kennedy Airport in New York.

February 9, 1964:

The Beatles make their landmark television appearance on *The Ed Sullivan Show.*

March 2, 1964:

The Beatles commence shooting their first feature film, *A Hard Day's Night.*

April 3, 1964:

The Beatles hold the top six positions in a local singles chart in Sydney, Australia.

April 4, 1964:

The Beatles have the top five positions in America's *Billboard* singles chart.

June 3, 1964:

Ringo collapses with tonsillitis and pharyngitis just prior to The Beatles' first "World Tour." He is replaced in Denmark, the Netherlands, Hong Kong, and Australia by 24-year-old session drummer, Jimmy Nicol.

June 15, 1964:

Ringo rejoins The Beatles in Australia, and performs with them there and in New Zealand.

July 6, 1964:

A Hard Day's Night receives its royal world charity premiere at the London Pavilion cinema.

August 18, 1964:

The Beatles leave London Airport for their first North American concert tour.

February 11, 1965:

Ringo marries Mary (Maureen) Cox.

February 22, 1965:

The Beatles fly to the Bahamas to begin shooting their second film, later to be titled *Help!*

May 20, 1965:

The Beatles record their last ever music session for BBC Radio.

June 11, 1965:

At midnight it is announced that The Beatles are to be awarded with MBEs.

July 29, 1965:

Help! receives its royal world charity premiere at the London Pavilion.

August 15, 1965:

The Beatles open their second U.S. tour with a landmark concert at New York's Shea Stadium, witnessed by a then-record audience of 55,600.

August 27, 1965:

The Beatles meet Elvis Presley at his Beverly Hills home on Perugia Way.

September 13, 1965:

A son named Zak is born to Ringo and Maureen Starkey.

October 26, 1965:

The Beatles receive their MBEs from the Queen inside the Great Throne Room at Buckingham Palace.

December 3, 1965:

The Beatles embark on what turns out to be their last ever UK tour.

January 21, 1966:

George marries Patricia (Pattie) Ann Boyd.

March 4, 1966:

London's *Evening Standard* newspaper publishes an interview with John in which he states that The Beatles are "more popular than Jesus now..."

May 1, 1966:

The Beatles give their last ever British concert performance.

July 5, 1966:

The Beatles run into major problems in the Philippines after being accused of "snubbing" the First Lady, Imelda Marcos.

July 29, 1966:

American teen magazine *Datebook* publishes John's *Evening Standard* interview, asserting that he said The Beatles are "bigger" than Jesus. Uproar ensues, especially in the country's "Bible Belt" region.

August 29, 1966:

The Beatles give their last ever concert performance at San Francisco's Candlestick Park.

November 9, 1966:

John attends a private preview of Yoko Ono's art exhibition, *Unfinished Paintings and Objects,* at London's Indica Gallery.

March 30, 1967:

The famous cover photo for the *Sgt. Pepper's Lonely Hearts Club Band* album is shot by Michael Cooper.

April 19, 1967:

A legal business partnership, The Beatles & Co, is formed to bind the group together until 1977.

May 20, 1967:

The BBC imposes a radio and TV ban on "A Day in the Life" due to the song's overt drug references.

May 26, 1967:

First release, in the UK, of the landmark *Sgt. Pepper* album.

June 25, 1967:

The Beatles perform "All You Need is Love" before a worldwide television audience.

August 19, 1967:

A second son, Jason, is born to Ringo and Maureen Starkey.

August 24, 1967:

The Beatles, wives, and friends, attend a lecture by the Maharishi Mahesh Yogi at London's Hilton Hotel.

August 25, 1967:

The Beatles and their entourage travel to Bangor, North Wales, to attend a weekend seminar by the Maharishi.

August 27, 1967:

Brian Epstein is found dead in the bed of his London home.

August 29, 1967:

Brian Epstein's funeral is held in Liverpool. Strictly a family affair, it is not attended by The Beatles.

September 11, 1967:

The Beatles start shooting their own TV movie, *Magical Mystery Tour*.

December 5, 1967:

John and George attend a party heralding the opening of The Beatles' Apple Boutique two days later.

December 25, 1967:

Paul and Jane Asher end more than four years of speculation by announcing their engagement.

December 26, 1967:

BBC1 Television transmits the world premiere of *Magical Mystery Tour.*

Mid-February, 1968:

The Beatles and their entourage fly to Rishikesh, India, to study Transcendental Meditation under the Maharishi Mahesh Yogi.

May 11, 1968:

John and Paul fly to New York for five days, during which time they announce the setting up of their Apple business venture, and John also takes the opportunity to denounce the Maharishi.

May 22, 1968:

John and Yoko Ono appear in public for the first time, attending a launch party and press conference for another Apple boutique.

July 17, 1968:

The Beatles' animated feature film, *Yellow Submarine*, receives its world premiere at the London Pavilion.

July 20, 1968:

Jane Asher announces that her relationship with Paul is over.

July 31, 1968:

The Beatles' Apple Boutique on Baker Street closes down, while they also relinquish control of their second clothing store.

August 22, 1968:

Cynthia Lennon sues John for divorce on the grounds of his adultery with Yoko Ono.

August 23, 1968:

Ringo quits The Beatles during recording sessions for the "White Album".

September 3, 1968:

Ringo rejoins The Beatles.

September 30, 1968:

Hunter Davies' authorized biography, *The Beatles*, is published in the UK.

October 18, 1968:

John and Yoko are charged with possession of cannabis and obstructing the police.

November 29, 1968:

John and Yoko's controversial *Two Virgins* album is released in the UK.

January 2, 1969:

The Beatles begin filming their troubled *Get Back* project (eventually retitled *Let It Be*).

January 30, 1969:

The Beatles' give their last ever live performance, atop the roof of their Apple office building in Central London.

February 3, 1969:

Allen Klein becomes The Beatles' business manager.

February 4, 1969:

The New York firm of Eastman is appointed as general counsel to Apple Corps.

March 12, 1969:

Paul marries Linda Louise Eastman, and George and Pattie are busted for cannabis possession.

March 20, 1969:

John marries Yoko Ono in Gibraltar.

March 25, 1969:

John and Yoko commence their seven-day "Bed-In" for peace at the Hilton Hotel in Amsterdam, Holland.

April 22, 1969:

John formally changes his middle name to Ono during a ceremony on the roof of the Apple building.

May 8, 1969:

Paul refuses to sign his name to a contract appointing Allen Klein's company, ABKCO, as business manager of several of The Beatles' own companies.

May 26, 1969:

John and Yoko commence their second "Bed-In" for peace, at the Queen Elizabeth Hotel in Montreal, Canada.

August 8, 1969:

The Beatles are photographed walking along the zebra-crossing outside the EMI Studios in North London, for the cover of *Abbey Road*.

August 20, 1969:

All four Beatles are together for the last time inside a recording studio, when they attend a mix and album running-order session at Abbey Road.

August 22, 1969:

The Beatles are photographed together for the last time, in the Tittenhurst Park grounds of John's home in Sunningdale, Ascot.

August 28, 1969:

A daughter, Mary, is born to Linda and Paul McCartney.

Mid-September, 1969:

John decides to quit The Beatles. He tells the group of his decision shortly after returning from Toronto, Canada, where he has performed a concert with The Plastic Ono Band.

November 25, 1969:

John returns his MBE to the Queen.

January 4, 1970:

The Beatles, minus John, participate in their last ever recording session... during John's lifetime.

April 10, 1970:

Newspapers around the world carry Paul's statement that The Beatles will never work together again.

May 13, 1970:

The Beatles' film, *Let It Be*, receives its world premiere in New York. None of the group members attend.

July 7, 1970:

George's mother, Louise, dies.

November 11, 1970:

A daughter, Lee Parkin, is born to Ringo and Maureen Starkey.

December 31, 1970:

Paul files a lawsuit in the London High Court seeking dissolution of the partnership, The Beatles & Co, as well as the appointment of a receiver to handle the group's affairs.

February 19, 1971:

The hearing for the dissolution of the Beatles & Co partnership commences in the London High Court.

September 13, 1971:

A second daughter, Stella Nina, is born to Paul and Linda McCartney.

March 31, 1973:

Allen Klein and ABKCO reach the end of their term as business managers of Apple and other Beatles companies.

August 14, 1974:

The first Beatles-related stage show, *John, Paul, George, Ringo...and Bert*, opens in London.

January 9, 1975:

The Beatles & Co partnership is formally dissolved in the London High Court.

July 17, 1975:

Ringo and Maureen Starkey are divorced.

October 9, 1975:

A son, Sean Taro Ono, is born to John and Yoko.

January 5, 1976:

The Beatles' former assistant, Mal Evans, is shot and killed by Los Angeles police.

January 26, 1976:

The Beatles' recording contract with EMI expires.

March 18, 1976:

Paul's Father, James, dies.

April 1, 1976:

John's father, Alf, dies.

January 10, 1977:

All outstanding litigation between Allen Klein and The Beatles is settled.

May 4, 1977:

A live album, *The Beatles at the Hollywood Bowl*, is released in the U.S. (May 6 in the UK.)

May 25, 1977:

The Beatles Live! At the Star-Club in Hamburg, Germany, 1962 is released in the UK. (June 13 in the U.S.)

May 1978:

George's father, Harold, dies.

June 9, 1977:

George and Pattie Harrison are divorced.

September 12, 1977:

A son, James Louis, is born to Paul and Linda McCartney.

August 1, 1978:

A son, Dhani, is born to George and his girlfriend, Olivia Arias.

September 2, 1978:

George and Olivia marry.

May 19, 1979:

Paul, George, and Ringo reunite for a jam session at a garden party celebrating the marriage of Eric Clapton to the former Pattie Harrison.

December 8, 1980:

John Lennon is shot dead at the age of 40.

December 14, 1980:

At 2:00 p.m. EST, 7:00 p.m. GMT, 10 minutes of silence is observed around the world in memory of John Lennon.

May 15, 1981:

George's tribute to John, "All Those Years Ago," featuring backing by Paul and Ringo, is released as a single in the UK.

April 9, 1984:

Liverpool opens its first permanent tribute to the Fab Four, the Beatle City exhibition center.

March 29, 1986:

Beatles recordings are officially released in the Soviet Union for the first time.

February 26, 1987:

The first four official Beatles compact discs—*Please Please Me, With The Beatles, A Hard Day's Night,* and *Beatles for Sale*—are released by EMI.

June 1, 1987:

On the 20th anniversary of the official release date of *Sgt. Pepper's Lonely Hearts Club Band,* Granada Television in the U.K. screens a two-hour documentary entitled *It Was Twenty Years Ago Today,* featuring interviews with Paul and George.

December 5, 1991:

John's aunt, Mimi Smith, dies.

November 30, 1994:

The Beatles album, *Live at the BBC,* is released in the U.K. (December 6 in the U.S.)

November 19, 1995:

The three-part, six-hour documentary, *The Beatles Anthology,* starts airing on ABC-TV in the U.S. (It airs in six parts in the U.K. during December.)

November 21, 1995:

The double album, *The Beatles Anthology 1,* is released worldwide.

December 4, 1995:

The new Beatles single, "Free as a Bird," is released in the U.K. (December 12 in the U.S.)

March 4, 1996:

The second new Beatles single, "Real Love," is released in the U.K. (March 12 in the U.S.)

March 18, 1996:

The double album, *The Beatles Anthology 2,* is released in the U.K. (March 19 in the U.S.)

September 5, 1996:

The extended eight-part, ten-hour version of the *Beatles Anthology* documentary is released on video and laser disc in the U.S.

October 28, 1996:

The double album, *The Beatles Anthology 3,* is released in the UK. (October 29 in the U.S.)

March 11, 1997:

Paul McCartney is knighted by Her Majesty Queen Elizabeth II.

April 17, 1998:

Sir Paul's wife, Linda, dies from cancer.

November 13, 2000:

U.S. and U.K. release of *1,* a compilation of The Beatles' chart-topping singles that will itself top the trans-Atlantic charts en route to selling more than 30 million copies worldwide.

November 29, 2001:

George Harrison dies of cancer.

June 11, 2002:

Paul marries Heather Mils.

October 28, 2003:

A daughter, Beatrice Milly, is born to Paul and Heather.

June 30, 2006:

Cirque du Soleil's Beatles-related show, *Love,* premieres at The Mirage in Las Vegas.

November 20, 2006:

The *Love* soundtrack album of remixed Beatles music is released in the U.S. and U.K.

May 12, 2008:

Paul's divorce from Heather is finalized.

October 9, 2011:

Paul marries Nancy Shevell on what would have been John Lennon's 71st birthday.

November 11, 2013:

U.S. and U.K. release of *On Air—Live at the BBC Volume 2*.

APPENDIX B

THE BEATLES ON THE CHARTS

Single Releases and Chart Positions

Following are the singles that were released by EMI in the UK between 1962 and 1970, and the two *Anthology* singles, as well as the chart positions published by the widely recognized *Record Retailer* and, after February 13, 1969, British Market Research Bureau.

Single	Release Date	Position
Love Me Do/P.S. I Love You	Oct. 5, 1962	17
Please Please Me/Ask Me Why	Jan. 11, 1963	2
From Me to You/Thank You Girl	April 11, 1963	1
She Loves You/I'll Get You	Aug. 23, 1963	1
I Want to Hold Your Hand/This Boy	Nov. 29, 1963	1
Can't Buy Me Love/You Can't Do That	Mar. 20, 1964	1
A Hard Day's Night/Things We Said Today	Jul. 10, 1964	1
I Feel Fine/She's a Woman	Nov. 27, 1964	1
Ticket to Ride/Yes It Is	Apr. 9, 1965	1
Help!/I'm Down	Jul. 23, 1965	1
We Can Work it Out/Day Tripper	Dec. 3, 1965	1
Paperback Writer/Rain	Jun. 10, 1966	1
Eleanor Rigby/Yellow Submarine	Aug. 5, 1966	1
Strawberry Fields Forever/Penny Lane	Feb. 17, 1967	2
All You Need is Love/Baby, You're a Rich Man	Jul. 7, 1967	1
Hello, Goodbye/I Am the Walrus	Nov. 24, 1967	1
Lady Madonna/The Inner Light	Mar. 15, 1968	1
Hey Jude/Revolution	Aug. 30, 1968	1
Get Back /Don't Let Me Down	Apr. 11, 1969	1
The Ballad of John and Yoko/Old Brown Shoe	May 30, 1969	1
Something/Come Together	Oct. 31, 1969	4
Let It Be/You Know My Name (Look Up the Number)	Mar. 6, 1970	2
Free as a Bird	Dec. 4, 1995	2
Real Love	Mar. 4, 1996	4

Following are the singles that were released by Vee Jay, Swan, Tollie, and Capitol in the U.S. between 1963 and 1970, and the two *Anthology* singles, as well as the chart positions published by the widely recognized *Billboard* magazine.

Single	Release Date	Position
Please Please Me/Ask Me Why	Feb. 25, 1963	-
From Me to You/Thank You Girl	May 27, 1963	116
She Loves You/I'll Get You	Sep. 16, 1963	1
I Want to Hold Your Hand/I Saw Her Standing There	Dec. 26, 1963	1
Please Please Me/From Me to You	Jan. 30, 1964	3
Twist and Shout/There's a Place	Mar. 2, 1964	2
Can't Buy Me Love/You Can't Do That	Mar. 16, 1964	1
Do You Want to Know a Secret/Thank You Girl	Mar. 23, 1964	2
Love Me Do/P.S. I Love You	Apr. 27, 1964	1
Sie Liebt Dich/I'll Get You	May 21, 1964	97
A Hard Day's Night/I Should Have Known Better	Jul. 13, 1964	1
I'll Cry Instead/I'm Happy Just to Dance with You	Jul. 20, 1964	25
And I Love Her/If I Fell	Jul. 20, 1964	12
Matchbox/Slow Down	Aug. 24, 1964	17
I Feel Fine/She's a Woman	Nov. 23, 1964	1
Eight Days a Week/I Don't Want to Spoil the Party	Feb. 15, 1965	1
Ticket to Ride/Yes It Is	Apr. 19, 1965	1
Help!/I'm Down	July 19, 1965	1
Yesterday/Act Naturally	Sep. 13, 1965	1
We Can Work it Out/Day Tripper	Dec. 6, 1965	1
Nowhere Man/What Goes On	Feb. 21, 1966	3
Paperback Writer/Rain	May 30, 1966	1
Eleanor Rigby/Yellow Submarine	Aug. 8, 1966	2
Strawberry Fields Forever/Penny Lane	Feb. 13, 1967	1
All You Need is Love/Baby, You're a Rich Man	July 17, 1967	1
Hello, Goodbye/I Am the Walrus	Nov. 27, 1967	1
Lady Madonna/The Inner Light	March 18, 1968	4

Hey Jude/Revolution	Aug. 26, 1968	1
Get Back /Don't Let Me Down	May 5, 1969	1
The Ballad Of John And Yoko/Old Brown Shoe	June 4, 1969	8
Something/Come Together	Oct. 6, 1969	1
Let It Be/You Know My Name (Look Up The Number)	March 11, 1970	1
The Long and Winding Road/For You Blue	May 11, 1970	1
Free as a Bird	Dec. 12, 1995	6
Real Love	March 12, 1996	11

EP Releases and Chart Positions

Following are the four-song extended-play records that were released only in the UK, as well as the chart positions published by *Record Retailer*. (Note: *Magical Mystery Tour* had six songs.)

EP	Release Date	Position
Twist and Shout	Jul. 12, 1963	1
The Beatles' Hits	Sep. 6, 1963	1
The Beatles (No. 1)	Nov. 1, 1963	2
All My Loving	Feb. 7, 1964	1
Long Tall Sally	Jun. 19, 1964	1
Extracts from the Film A Hard Day's Night	Nov. 6, 1964	1
Extracts from the Album A Hard Day's Night	Nov. 6, 1964	8
Beatles for Sale	Apr. 6, 1965	1
Beatles for Sale (No. 2)	Jun. 4, 1965	5
The Beatles' Million Sellers	Dec. 6, 1965	1
Yesterday	Mar. 4, 1966	1
Nowhere Man	Jul. 8, 1966	4
Magical Mystery Tour	Dec. 8, 1967	1

Album Releases and Chart Positions

Following are the albums that were released by EMI in the UK between 1962 and 1970—the only versions that The Beatles took an active interest in—a live album in 1977, and the three *Anthology* sets, as well as the chart positions published by *Record Retailer*. (No post-1970 compilations of previously released material are included.)

Album	Release Date	Position
Please Please Me	Mar. 22, 1963	1
With the Beatles	Nov. 22, 1963	1
A Hard Day's Night	Jul. 10, 1964	1
Beatles for Sale	Dec. 4, 1964	1
Help!	Aug. 6, 1965	1
Rubber Soul	Dec. 3, 1965	1
Revolver	Aug. 5, 1966	1
A Collection of Beatles Oldies	Dec. 9, 1966	7
Sgt. Pepper's Lonely Hearts Club Band	Jun. 1, 1967	1
The Beatles	Nov. 22, 1968	1
Yellow Submarine	Jan. 17, 1969	3
Abbey Road	Sep. 26, 1969	1
Let It Be	May 8, 1970	1
The Beatles at the Hollywood Bowl	May 6, 1977	1
Live at the BBC	Nov. 30, 1994	1
Anthology 1	Nov. 21, 1995	1
Anthology 2	Mar. 18, 1996	1
Anthology 3	Oct. 28, 1996	1
On Air—Live at the BBC Volume 2	Nov. 11, 2013	12

Following are the albums that were released by Capitol, UA, and Vee Jay in the U.S. between 1963 and 1970. Prior to the release of *Sgt. Pepper* in 1967, each of these consisted of tracks culled from various sources (including albums with identical names to those in the UK), and The Beatles took little or no interest in how they were compiled. Thereafter, with the exception of the *Magical Mystery Tour* and *Hey Jude* albums, the U.S. and UK releases were identical. There's also the live album released in 1977, and the three *Anthology* sets, as well as the chart positions published by *Billboard* magazine. (No post-1970 compilations of previously released material are included.)

Album	Release Date	Position
Introducing the Beatles	Jul. 22, 1963 &	
	Jan. 27, 1964	2
Meet the Beatles	Jan. 20, 1964	1
The Beatles' Second Album	Apr. 10, 1964	1
A Hard Day's Night	Jun. 26, 1964	1
Something New	Jul. 20, 1964	2
The Beatles' Story	Nov. 23, 1964	7
Beatles '65	Dec. 15, 1964	1
The Early Beatles	Mar. 22, 1965	43
Beatles VI	Jun. 14, 1965	1
Help!	Aug. 13, 1965	1
Rubber Soul	Dec. 6, 1965	1
"Yesterday"... and Today	Jun. 20, 1966	1
Revolver	Aug. 8, 1966	1
Sgt. Pepper's Lonely Hearts Club Band	Jun. 2, 1967	1
Magical Mystery Tour	Nov. 25, 1967	1
The Beatles	Nov. 25, 1968	1
Yellow Submarine	Jan. 13, 1969	2
Abbey Road	Oct. 1, 1969	1
Hey Jude	Feb. 26, 1970	2
Let It Be	May 18, 1970	1
The Beatles at the Hollywood Bowl	May 4, 1977	2
Live at the BBC	Dec. 6, 1994	3

APPENDIX C

FILMS, VIDEOS, DOCUMENTARIES, AND BIOPICS

The Beatles' Films

A Hard Days Night (1964)

Help! (1965)

Magical Mystery Tour (1967)

Yellow Submarine (1968)

Let It Be (1970)

The Beatles' Official Promo Videos 1965–1970 and 1995

1965 "We Can Work it Out" (three versions)

    "Day Tripper" (three versions)

    "Help!"

    "Ticket to Ride"

    "I Feel Fine" (two versions, one unreleased)

1966 "Paperback Writer" (four versions)

    "Rain" (three versions)

1967 "Strawberry Fields Forever"

    "Penny Lane"

    "A Day in the Life"

    "Hello, Goodbye" (four versions, one unreleased)

1968   "Lady Madonna"

           "Hey Jude" (two versions)

           "Revolution" (two versions)

1969   "Get Back"

           "Don't Let Me Down"

           "The Ballad of John and Yoko" (two versions)

           "Something"

           "Let It Be"

Documentaries

The following is a selective list of Beatlesrelated documentaries available on blu-ray and/or DVD:

All Together Now: A Documentary Film—The story behind the partnership between The Beatles and Cirque du Soleil that resulted in the creation of *Love.*

The Beatles Anthology—The Beatles' official version of their own story.

Beatles Stories—More than 50 interviews with anyone from Sir George Martin, Graham Nash, and Art Garfunkel to Smokey Robinson, Brian Wilson, and Denny Laine, giving their personal recollections of meeting or associating with John, Paul, George, and Ringo.

Best of the Beatles: Pete Best—Mean, Moody and Magnificent—The story of the group's early years from the perspective of its former drummer, alongside interviews with the likes of Astrid Kircherr, Klaus Voorman, Cynthia Lennon, and Neil Aspinall.

The First U.S. Visit—Albert and David Maysles' classic 1964 fly-on-the-wall look behind the scenes of The Beatles February '64 visit to New York, Miami, and Washington D.C.

George Harrison: Living in the Material World—Martin Scorsese's authorized, fascinating, yet strangely incomplete biography of the youngest Beatle.

Going Underground: Paul McCartney, The Beatles and the U.K. Counter-Culture—A look at how Paul, more than his fellow Fabs, immersed himself in the counter-cultural London arts scene of the 1960s and helped bring the avant-garde into the mainstream.

Good Ol' Freda—The recollections of The Beatles' devoted friend and fan club secretary Freda Kelly.

Imagine: John Lennon—The 1988 Yoko-authorized documentary of John's life and career, both as a Beatle and as a solo artist.

Strange Fruit: The Beatles' Apple Records—A look at the group's troubled label and its roster of artists.

You Can't Do That: The Making of a Hard Day's Night—The 1994 authorized documentary about The Beatles' classic first movie, narrated by Phil Collins.

Biopics

Here's a selective list of the films featuring actors portraying—or spoofing—The Beatles during the band years:

The Rutles: All You Need is Cash (1978)—The most celebrated of all Beatles spoofs, conceived by—and starring—Eric Idle and Neil Innes, with a cameo appearance by George Harrison.

I Wanna Hold Your Hand (1978)—A feature film about fan frenzy surrounding The Beatles' first U.S. visit and their debut on *The Ed Sullivan Show*.

Birth of The Beatles (1979)—A TV dramatization of the band's early years, utilizing Pete Best as technical advisor.

Beatlemania (1981)—A film musical based on the stage show.

The Hours and Times (1991)—A fictional retelling of the Spanish vacation that John Lennon and Brian Epstein took in 1963.

Backbeat (1994)—A feature film dramatization of The Beatles' pre-fame years and their relationship with Stuart Sutclifffe.

Nowhere Boy (2009)—A big-screen biopic about John Lennon's adolescence, upbringing, and creation of The Quarry Men, as well as the band's evolution into The Beatles.

The Fifth Beatle (2014)—A biopic of Beatles manager Brian Epstein, from his discovery of the group to his death by accidental overdose.

APPENDIX D

RECOMMENDED READING

Here's a selective bibliography listing the Beatles-related books that were utilized while researching *Beatles 101*. (The titles and publishers listed are British, unless otherwise stated.)

Babiuk, Andy, *Beatles Gear: All the Fab Four's Instruments from Stage to Studio* (U.S.: Hal Leonard, 2002).

Badman, Keith, *The Beatles Diary, Volume 2: After the Break-Up, 1970-2001* (Omnibus Press, 2001).

Baker, Glenn A., *The Beatles Down Under: The 1964 Australia & New Zealand Tour* (Australia: Wild & Woolley, 1982).

Beatles, The, *The Beatles Anthology* (Chronicle, 2000).

Best, Pete and Patrick Doncaster, *Beatle! The Pete Best Story* (Plexus, 1985).

Braun, Michael, *Love Me Do: The Beatles' Progress* (Penguin, 1964).

Brown, Peter and Steven Gaines, *The Love You Make: An Insider's Story Of The Beatles* (Macmillan, 1983).

Buskin, Richard, *John Lennon: His Life and Legend* (U.S.: Publications International, 1991).

Buskin, Richard, *Beatle Crazy!—Memories and Memorabilia* (Salamander, 1994).

Carr, Roy, *Beatles at the Movies* (HarperPerennial, 1996).

Carr, Roy and Tony Tyler, *The Beatles: An Illustrated Record* (New English Library, 1975).

Castleman, Harry and Wally Podrazik, *All Together Now* (U.S.: Pierian Press, 1975).

Castleman, Harry and Wally Podrazik, *The Beatles Again?* (U.S.: Pierian Press, 1977).

Castleman, Harry and Wally Podrazik, *The End of The Beatles?* (U.S.: Pierian Press, 1985).

Coleman, Ray, *John Winston Lennon, Volume One 1940–1966* (Sidgwick & Jackson, 1984).

Coleman, Ray, *John Ono Lennon, Volume Two 1967–1980* (Sidgwick & Jackson, 1984).

Coleman, Ray, *Brain Epstein: The Man Who Made The Beatles* (Viking, 1989).

Coleman, Ray, *McCartney: Yesterday and Today* (Boxtree, 1995).

Davies, Hunter, *The Beatles* (Heinemann, 1968).

Di Franco, J. Philip, *A Hard Day's Night: A Complete Pictorial Record of the Movie* (U.S.: Chelsea House, 1977).

DiLello, Richard, *The Longest Cocktail Party* (Charisma, 1973).

Dowdling, William J., *Beatlesongs* (U.S.: Simon & Schuster, 1989).

Emerick, Geoff and Massey, Howard, *Here, There and Everywhere: My Life Recording the Music of The Beatles* (U.S.: Gotham, 2006).

Epstein, Brian, *A Cellarful of Noise* (Souvenir Press, 1964).

Evans, Mike, *The Art of The Beatles* (Anthony Blond, 1984).

Friede, Goldie / Titone, Robin / Weiner, Sue, *The Beatles A to Z* (Eyre Methuen, 1980). Harrison, George, *I Me Mine* (Genesis, 1980).

Harry, Bill, *Mersey Beat: The Beginnings of The Beatles* (Omnibus Press, 1977).

Hertsgaard, Mark, *A Day in the Life* (Macmillan/Delacorte, 1995).

Howlett, Kevin, *The Beatles at the Beeb: The Story Of Their Radio Career, 1962–1965* (BBC, 1982).

Howlett, Kevin and Lewisohn, Mark, *In My Life: John Lennon Remembered* (BBC, 1990).

Kozinn, Allan, *The Beatles* (U.S.: Phidon, 1995).

Kozinn, Allan, *Got That Something! How The Beatles' "I Want to Hold Your Hand" Changed Everything* (Byliner, 2013).

Leigh, Spencer, *The Best of Fellas: The Story of Bob Wooler, Liverpool's First DJ* (Drivegreen, 2002).

Lennon, Cynthia, *A Twist of Lennon* (Star, 1978).

Lewisohn, Mark, *The Beatles Live!* (Pavilion, 1985).

Lewisohn, Mark, *The Beatles: 25 Years in the Life* (Sidgwick & Jackson, 1987).

Lewisohn, Mark, *The Complete Beatles Recording Sessions: The Official Story of the Abbey Road Years* (Hamlyn, 1988).

Lewisohn, Mark, *The Complete Beatles Chronicle* (Pyramid, 1992).

Lewisohn, Mark, *The Beatles: All These Years, Volume One—Tune In* (Little Brown, 2013)

MacDonald, Ian, *Revolution in the Head* (4th Estate, 1994).

Martin, George, with Jeremy Hornsby, *All You Need Is Ears* (Macmillan, 1979).

Martin, George, with William Pearson, *Summer of Love—The Making of Sgt. Pepper* (Macmillan, 1994).

McCabe, Peter and Robert D. Schonfield, *Apple to the Core: The Unmaking of The Beatles* (Martin Brian & O'Keeffe, 1972).

Miles, *The Beatles in Their Own Words* (Omnibus, 1978). Norman, Philip, *Shout! The Beatles in Their Generation* (Elm Tree, 1981).

Norman, Philip, *Shout! The Beatles in Their Generation* (Elm Tree, 1981).

Pawlowski, Gareth L., *How They Became the Beatles,* (U.S.: E.P. Dutton, 1989).

Rodriguez, Robert, *Fab Four FAQ 2.0: The Beatles' Solo Years, 1970-1980* (U.S.: Backbeat, 2010).

Rodriguez, Robert, *Revolver: How The Beatles Reimagined Rock 'n' Roll* (U.S.: Hal Leonard, 2012).

Rodriguez, Robert, *Solo in the 70s: John, Paul, George, Ringo—1970-1980* (U.S.: Bemis, 2013).

Schreuders, Piet / Lewisohn, Mark / Smith, Adam, *The Beatles' London* (Hamlyn, 1994).

Scott, Ken and Owsinski, Bobby, *Abbey Road to Ziggy Stardust: Off-the-record with The Beatles, Bowie, Elton & so much more* (U.S.: Alfred Music, 2012).

Sheff, David and Golson, G. Barry, *The Playboy Interviews with John Lennon and Yoko Ono* (Playboy Press, 1981).

Shipper, Mark, *Paperback Writer*, Grosset and Dunlap, 1978).

Shea, Stuart and Rodriguez, Robert, *Fab Four FAQ: Everything Left to Know About The Beatles...and More!* (U.S.: Hal Leonard, 2007).

Shotton, Pete, and Schaffner, Nicholas, *John Lennon: In My Life* (Coronet, 1984).

Southall, Brian / Vince, Peter / Rouse, Allan, *Abbey Road* (Omnibus, 1997).

Spizer, Bruce, *The Beatles' Story on Capitol Records, Part One: Beatlemania & The Singles* (U.S.: Four Ninety-Eight, 2000).

Spizer, Bruce, *The Beatles' Story on Capitol Records, Part Two: The Albums* (U.S.: Four Ninety-Eight, 2000).

Stannard, Neville, *The Beatles: The Long & Winding Road—A History of The Beatles on Record* (Virgin, 1982).

Sulpy, Doug and Schweighardt, *Drugs, Divorce and a Slipping Image* (The 910, 1994).

Sussman, Al, *Changin' Times: 101 Days That Shaped a Generation* (U.S.: Bemis, 2013).

Taylor, Alistair, with Martin Roberts, *Yesterday: The Beatles Remembered* (Sidgwick & Jackson, 1988).

Taylor, Derek, *As Time Goes By* (DavisPoynter, 1973).

Taylor, Derek, *Fifty Years Adrift* (Genesis, 1984).

Turner, Steve, *A Hard Day's Write* (Carlton, 1994).

Wenner, Jann, *Lennon Remembers* (Penguin, 1973).

Wiener, Allen J., *The Beatles: The Ultimate Recording Guide* (Bob Adams, 1994).

Williams, Allan and Marshall, William, *The Man Who Gave The Beatles Away* (Elm Tree, 1975).

Acknowledgments

My heartfelt appreciation goes to my interviewees over the past three-plus decades whose words and/or insights appear within these pages: Peter Brown, Roy Cicala, Jack Douglas, Geoffrey Ellis, Geoff Emerick, Bill Harry, Keef Hartley, Glyn Johns, Jon Kelly, Eddie Kramer, John Kurlander, Tommy LiPuma, Sir George Martin, Jim Mawer, Dennis Muirhead, Hugh Padgham, Alan Parsons, Ken Scott, Norman Smith, Eric Stewart, Tony Visconti, Peter Vince, Len Wood, and Shelly Yakus.

That said, down the years the help of many people has contributed to the research for—and information—in this book. Among them, I wish to extend special thanks to Mark Lewisohn for much of that information (no surprise there, given his widely acclaimed body of unrivaled Beatles-related work), as well as for his constant, invaluable friendship; my publishing partner and fellow podcaster Robert Rodriguez for his help editing this book; Thomas White for the design and layout of its interior; Rick Wey for not only enabling it to come to fruition, but also for hooking me up with highly talented artist, Eric Cash; and Allan Kozinn for his friendship, frightening intellect, and musicological expertise.

Finally, a shout-out to all of the Beatle People who I've encountered and who continue to come my way. It's a vast, ever expanding family, and it's getting better all the time.

Richard Buskin—Chicago, 2014

Index

The author talking with **Paul** and **Linda McCartney** outside **Abbey Road** Studios, 1988.

INDEX

A

B

C

D

301

Owen, Alun 212-214, 217,

P

"Paperback Writer" 37, 193, 195-196, 251

Parnes, Larry 106, 107, 109, 160, 350

Parsons, Alan 340, 343

Perkins, Carl 34, 79, 84, 85, 97-98, 186

Plastic Ono Band 46, 272, 277, 280, 306, 364

Please Please Me (album) 39, 40-41, 168, 170, 176, 317, 320, 343, 355, 368

"Please Please Me" (song) 168, 176, 185, 192, 205, 355

Powell, Cynthia 48-49, 50, 54, 55, 100, 102, 234, 235, 237, 255, 257-258, 263, 266, 267, 354, 355, 362

Presley, Elvis 10, 12, 16, 61, 78, 79-80, 88, 91, 100, 105, 134, 154, 186, 191, 208, 301-302, 348, 358

R

"Real Love" 20, 174, 303, 305, 306, 328, 368

Revolver 19, 36, 40, 46, 225, 254, 306, 317, 326

Richard, Cliff 123, 164, 166, 226

Ringo (album) 297, 299

Rolling Stones 19-20, 51, 154-155, 205, 226, 238, 244, 255

Rubber Soul 36, 40, 168-169, 317, 324, 380

Rutles, The 19

S

Scott, Ken 174, 332-336

Sgt. Pepper's Lonely Heart's Club Band 13, 19, 20, 31, 36, 40, 163, 173-174, 216, 220, 254, 265, 306, 313, 316, 317, 326-328, 340, 360, 368

"She Loves You" 12, 35, 39, 82, 178, 180, 186, 192, 205

"She Said, She Said" 34, 254

Sheridan, Tony 118, 122-124, 132, 146, 352

Shevell, Nancy 53, 293, 370

Shotton, Pete 45, 69, 88-89, 91, 92, 99, 348

Smith, Mimi 25, 68, 71, 72, 73, 88, 91, 100, 101, 150-151, 250, 347, 368

Smith, Norman 38, 39, 158, 164, 165, 170-171, 319-325, 326, 329, 332

Some Time in New York City (album) 285

Stanley, Julia 53, 67, 71-72, 88, 89, 92, 346, 347, 349

Starkey, Elsie 62, 70, 346, 347

Starkey, Zak 53, 54, 55, 237, 298, 358

"Strawberry Fields Forever" 78, 196, 235, 265, 314

Sunday Night at the London Palladium 81, 177-179, 191, 193, 201, 203, 356

Sutcliffe, Stuart 45, 96-97, 98, 100, 101, 104-106, 107, 108, 111, 112, 116, 117, 118, 119, 120, 121, 123, 128, 146, 346, 349, 350, 351, 353, 381

T

"The End" 38

CPSIA information can be obtained at www.ICGtesting.com
Printed in the USA
BVOW06s1908200516

448899BV00006B/21/P